The Science of Parenting Adopted Children

by the same author

Welcoming a New Brother or Sister Through Adoption
Arleta James
ISBN 978 1 84905 903 9
eISBN 9780 8 5700 653 0

of related interest

Seven Core Issues in Adoption and Permanency
What They Are and Why They Matter
Sharon Kaplan Roszia and Allison Davis Maxon
ISBN 978 1 78592 823 9
eISBN 978 1 78450 930 9

The A-Z of Therapeutic Parenting
Strategies and Solutions
Sarah Naish
ISBN 978 1 78592 376 0
eISBN 978 1 78450 732 9

**Parenting Strategies to Help Adopted and Fostered
Children with Their Behaviour**
Trauma-Informed Guidance and Action Charts
Christine Gordon
Illustrated by Corinne Watt
ISBN 978 1 78592 386 9
eISBN 978 1 78450 738 1

The Unofficial Guide to Adoptive Parenting
The Small Stuff, The Big Stuff and The Stuff In Between
Sally Donovan
ISBN 978 1 84905 536 9
eISBN 978 0 85700 959 3

**A Therapeutic Treasure Box for Working with Children
and Adolescents with Developmental Trauma**
Creative Techniques and Activities
Dr. Karen Treisman
ISBN 978 1 78592 263 3
eISBN 978 1 78450 553 0

THE SCIENCE OF PARENTING ADOPTED CHILDREN

A Brain-Based, Trauma-Informed Approach
to Cultivating Your Child's Social, Emotional
and Moral Development

Arleta James, LPCC

Jessica Kingsley *Publishers*
London and Philadelphia

The concept and design of Table 5.1, Table 5.2, Table 8.2 and Table 13.1 is
credited to the California Department of Education—www.cde.ca.gov.
The author has revised and updated these tables.

First published in 2019
by Jessica Kingsley Publishers
73 Collier Street
London N1 9BE, UK
and
400 Market Street, Suite 400
Philadelphia, PA 19106, USA

www.jkp.com

Library of Congress Cataloging in Publication Data
A CIP catalog record for this book is available from the Library of Congress

British Library Cataloguing in Publication Data
A CIP catalogue record for this book is available from the British Library

ISBN 978 1 78592 753 9
eISBN 978 1 78450 572 1

Printed and bound in the United States

Certified Chain of Custody
Promoting Sustainable Forestry
www.sfiprogram.org
SFI-01268

SUSTAINABLE FORESTRY INITIATIVE

SFI label applies to the text stock

Contents

Acknowledgements

My first thanks go to the many adoptive parents and their children with whom I've had the privilege to work for 24 years now. I've shared joys and struggles as they've worked to achieve the healing needed to come together as families. A sample of their stories are woven throughout this book. Names and details have been changed to protect their confidentiality. Readers will see how their lives were temporarily uprooted by the arrival of the traumatized adoptee and the hard work it took to restore a balance in their families. Each has a unique journey to healing, but all arrived. Their examples show the benefit of reaching out for help, and of never giving up hope.

I thank my mentors, Sebern Fisher and David Kaiser. Sebern nudged me and my colleagues into the world of neurofeedback. It's been the most effective service we've ever added. David is a participant in the treatment of each child who receives neurofeedback. He is the driving force behind continually updating the protocols we use. Both, Sebern and David, have extensive knowledge. They both reviewed the neuroscience that is sprinkled throughout this book. They both willingly and gladly offer their time and perspectives whenever we need them. I appreciate them both immensely. I would like to thank Mike Cohen too. He taught us the ins and outs of our software and how to run a session correctly. Mike continually supports our office and encourages us to keep pushing the limits of the neurofeedback.

I thank Stephen Jones, at Jessica Kingsley Publishers, who made this book a reality. This is my second book with Stephen. He is so easy to work with! It is so much less daunting to write a book with Stephen guiding the process from proposal to publication.

Elaine Zusy and Kayla Boros are the administrative assistants at my office. They obtained and formatted the references utilized in this book. This was no small task! They are efficient and hardworking. I couldn't have made the publishing deadline without you! Thank you for everything you do!

Introduction

Today's adoptees—infants to adolescents—arrive in their forever family with much capacity to recover from the early trauma that, most often, put them on the path to adoption. This book offers parents a comprehensive approach, ready to tap into, to bring about the healing of their son or daughter, or in the case of relative placements, their niece, nephew, cousin or grandchild. The content is applicable to domestic and international adoptees. The focus of this book is cultivating the well-being of the child who has joined the family via adoption.

Parents want their children to know the joy of relationships and learning. The tips in this book are designed to advance the social, emotional, moral and cognitive skills that children need to be successful at home, in school and in the community. There is also an overlay of information coming from the field of neuroscience. Brain development is impacted by one's early environment. Yet the brain too can learn new ways to function.

Children proceed through stages of development within the context of nurturing relationships with parents. For example, learning to talk is a progression that starts with smiling, babbling and cooing. When the course of growth is interrupted by unfortunate experiences—like prenatal substance exposure, maternal depression or stress, abandonment, neglect, deprivation of an orphanage setting, sexual or physical abuse, moving from one foster home or orphanage to another—skills that should emerge are thwarted. The child with an early trauma history is kept "immature." So, moms and dads adopting a child must also adopt a new style of parenting. The approach must guide the child through trauma recovery.

The book is laid out in chapters alternating content with corresponding parenting tips. We'll start with a definition of *complex trauma* and we'll take a broad look at how various traumatic experiences weaken the child's developmental foundation. We'll move to chapters, each with an in-depth focus about a specific aspect of child development like creating attachments, being able to cope, having emotional well-being and learning to laugh and play. These slices of content explain how trauma has impacted the growth of skills in this area. The tips show the way to rebuild the skills. Combined, the strategies make a powerful tool box to developmentally renovate—to *grow up*—your adopted child.

The principal audience of this book is parents. I view parents as the primary healing resource. Moms and dads know their child best. The content is certainly suitable for professionals who have contact with children with early trauma—mental health professionals, child welfare workers, early-intervention therapists, occupational, speech and physical therapists, pediatricians, educators, court officers and CASA volunteers. Infants, toddlers, preschoolers, tweens and teens benefit when we use a trauma-informed lens to design their services and academic learning.

Along the way I have conveyed the need to seek help—quickly—even if that means making a drive or catching a flight. If a child has cancer, juvenile diabetes or cystic fibrosis you wouldn't "wait to see if they grow out of it." You wouldn't say, "love will be enough." These conditions are treated aggressively. The most informed physicians and the most advanced treatment regimens would be sought. I would like to see us react as assertively to treating trauma. Trauma, left to fester, robs children of living a life in which they can experience the simple day-to-day pleasures that come from interacting with others, and the self-worth that comes with recognizing ones' own growth and accomplishments. I have also worked to strike a balance between portraying trauma's unsympathetic wrath with that of optimism and hope. I parsed in the value of nurture and humor too. Our office has many, many success stories. I've highlighted several of these cases in the vignettes throughout the book. The names have been changed to protect confidentiality. In each of these cases, the adoptee, mom, dad, brothers and sisters invested time and effort. They accepted and applied the guidance offered at my office, Adoption & Attachment Therapy Partners. Today, their families are thriving! Your family can too!

I've also written *Welcoming a Brother or Sister through Adoption*. This book offers pre- and post-adoption strategies to smooth the integration of an adoptee with a history of trauma into a family whose composition includes children developing age-appropriately. The two books combined offer parents peace of mind that they're tending to the unique needs of all children living in a family built by adoption.

CHAPTER 1

Trauma Interrupts Development. So, Think "Younger!"

I approach daily life by getting up and completing all the chores I dislike most first! I approach therapy the same way. I say to the child clients, "Let's talk about what's hardest for you first—then we'll be on the downhill. Therapy and life will get easier!"

So, in writing this book, I decided to talk about what's hardest for all of us first—the trauma. The content is applicable to both domestic and international adoption. It's difficult for parents to think about the experiences the child had before their arrival in the forever family. Yet, it is critical to the healing of the child to acknowledge these events. Really, we can't expect children to grow and heal if we, ourselves, cannot look at their trauma and talk with them about their trauma. The more we can understand their experiences, the better we can parent and provide services to these kids. In turn, these youngsters, tweens and teens can forge connections to their families, and they can learn to function at school and in the community!

The most important thing to glean from this chapter is that trauma interrupts the child's development. The child joins the family and often lacks the skills associated with their age. The adoptee with an early history of trauma is "younger" than anticipated.

Trauma is Complex

Today's adoptee frequently joins their family after having endured multiple traumas. As examples:

Mary's birth parents abused an array of drugs. Mary needed to stay in the hospital 21 days after her birth to detox. Mary's birth mother left the hospital 3 days after Mary's birth. Mary left the hospital 18 days later with a foster family. Social services attempted to reunify Mary with her birth family to no avail. Fifteen months later Mary was legally free for adoption. The foster family opted not to adopt Mary due to their ages. Mary joined her adoptive family several months later. Overall, early in life, Mary experienced the insult of drug exposure, an extended hospital stay with no parent present, abandonment, a move to a foster placement and a move to an adoptive home. For Mary, these situations were multiple traumas. Her mom kept changing and so did her home!

Bobby was abandoned at birth. He was placed in an orphanage where he resided for 9 months. He met his adoptive family. He left the orphanage and stayed in a hotel for several days. Then, Bobby and his family began the process of airport to airplane to home—a place where nothing felt, sounded, tasted, looked or smelled the same! Again, this is a multiple trauma situation. There is an abandonment, a lack of psychological care giving, due to a poor ratio of staff to infants in the orphanage, and the move to a new country! Of course, Bobby needed to learn to live in a family now too!

Lisa shortly after her birth, accompanied her birth mom from one crack house to another. She was left to sit in a car seat while her birth mom got high. Bottles were provided sporadically. Bottle propping was the norm. Diaper changes were sporadic as well. Fights often erupted in these drug dens. The birth mom prostituted herself to support her drug habit. The birth mom was agreeable to prostituting Lisa as well. Daily, Lisa was exposed to violence, neglect, drugs and whatever sexual acts were preferred by her abusers. She finally entered foster care at age 6. She was adopted by her foster family.

Mary, Bobby and Lisa arrived in their homes with "complex trauma." Each experienced many traumas starting early in life—in the prenatal period and shortly after birth. The trauma occurred as a string of events or all at the same time. Complex trauma includes that the adults that were to care for the child did not. Maybe these care givers even threatened the very existence of the youngster. Parents or other caring adults should have been a source of safety and stability. They were not.[1] Instead the adults, inadvertently or outrightly, caused the child a persistent fear—terror—and put the child in situations in which they were helpless.

Complex trauma interrupts development. The child's social, emotional, cognitive and physical skills may be delayed. Many children will not just "catch up" once placed in a loving family. Many families will adopt an infant, toddler or older child who requires a variety of services and specialized parenting interventions to heal.

The Specific Types of Trauma

This segment breaks the larger, broader term—trauma—into pieces. As you read this, put yourself in the youngster's shoes: "What would it be like to experience these atrocities?" "How would I be affected?" "What would I need to recover?" "How long would it take me to recover?" "Would I recover just because I have a new family?"

Abandonment: "Why don't I live with my birth mother?"

When the people who were supposed to be your parents aren't your parents any more, it causes lots of emotional pain. Period. I often cringe when I browse social media and see statements made by adoptive parents that contradict this. Really, websites like Ancestry.com and 23andme.com flourish. People from all walks of life want to find family members, or they want to learn their cultural make-up. There is a strong desire to know one's self and one's roots—adoptees are included in this quest! I am always suspicious when a parent says, "She never talks about her birth mom" when this silence is taken to mean that the child is resolved about the abandonment. In my experience, it is a rare adoptee who lacks curiosity about their birth family. Many adopted children believe it would hurt the adoptive parents' feelings to talk about their birth parents. Many are so emotional about the abandonment, they strive to avoid these painful feelings. Others feel it is only a matter of time before they will be reunited with their birth parents, so there is no need to talk about them. There is also no need to attach to the current family. If the birth mom, the abuse, the drug use, etc. isn't popping up for conversation from time to time—ask! If it's hard for you to cope with sharing the love of your child—seek help for yourself. This isn't a rejection. Most parents love more than one child. Most couples love their family of origin and their in-laws. Most adopted kids love their birth family and their adoptive family. Some love a few foster parents or orphanage care givers too!

Fears of being abandoned again interfere with the development of trust. Kids tend to especially focus on the abandonment by the birth mother until they more fully comprehend sex. Then, they recognize that there was also a birth dad with whom they could have lived. Boys and girls are plagued by questions like, "Why did she leave me?" "Why didn't she want me?" "Why did she put me in the orphanage?" "What did I do to make her go away?" "Am I ever going to see her again?" "Is she okay?" "Why did she take so many drugs?" "Why weren't my birth parents married?" "Why didn't he stay with my birth mom?" "Will I ever know who my birth dad is?"

Carl, adopted from an orphanage, at age 3, is certain that his birthmother left him, as a newborn infant, at the hospital, due to his being born with Cerebral Palsy. He genuinely believed that if his legs were like those of "other kids," she would have "kept me." Carl's condition was diagnosed when he was age 2 by a team of American doctors who were visiting his orphanage. His birth mother had no idea he had Cerebral Palsy when she abandoned him.

Susan's birth mother became angry with her due to Susan's mishandling of a glass doll, a birthday gift from the birth grandmother. The doll shattered when Susan accidentally dropped it. The birth mother subsequently dragged Susan up a flight of stairs and dropped her over the railing. This resulted in Susan sustaining several broken ribs. Susan and her older siblings were quickly removed from their birth mother's care. The children never returned to their birth home despite a significant family reunification effort. Susan stated, "If I hadn't made her mad, we would still be with her."

Children don't always have the capacity to understand that they are "better off" with their adoptive family. They aren't always readily able to comprehend that a birth mother may choose a voluntary abandonment to provide the child with greater opportunity. They lack knowledge of the safety risks posed by neglect, abuse or a substance abusing lifestyle. They don't comprehend that they would have languished in orphanage care until adjudicated at an older age. Even those with memory of the trauma often believe that as they are currently older, they could keep themselves safe, and they could help their birth parents. These children think they could make life work with their birth family if only they could "get back to them."

Kids frequently believe that they were somehow "defective," "bad" or "dumb" and this contributed to the separation from the birth family. Some boys and girls will strive to be "perfect" to compensate. These youngsters go all-out to excel at everything they do—academics, sports, music, art, chores and so on. Other youngsters think they made their birth mom angry and so, she "went away." Still others think that the adoptive family is to blame. "If you hadn't adopted me, I could be with her."

Abandonment makes it hard to attach to parents—and to trust adults. Many adoptees fear being abandoned again. Trust is essential to learn and grow. If you can't trust your parents, you don't feel safe. You don't take their advice. You don't follow their rules, etc. You don't trust the teacher to manage the classroom or to discipline fairly or to teach accurately. Abandonment makes it hard to believe that you are a "good kid." It can be heartbreaking to listen to kids talk about themselves. I frequently hear, "I'm just a bad kid." One youngster I assessed kept telling me, "There is nothing in my brain. I'm just the stupidest kid." Or, they ask, "Why would this family want me when my own birth family didn't want me?"

Sexual Abuse

Certainly, sexual abuse is a difficult topic to think about. Speaking with kids about sexual matters is hard too. Child sexual abuse is any interaction between a child and an adult (or another child) in which the child is used for the sexual stimulation of the perpetrator or an observer. Sexual abuse can include inappropriate kissing; fondling of a child; the child fondling or masturbating an adult; exposing the child to pornography; sextortion;[2] having the child participate in oral sex, intercourse, pornography, voyeurism, exhibitionism, etc. Child sexual abuse affects both girls and boys—of all ages, races, ethnicities and economic backgrounds—in all kinds of neighborhoods and communities.[3]

Child sexual abuse is not rare. As many as one out of four girls and one out of six boys will experience some form of sexual abuse before the age of 18.[4] Approximately 10 percent of sexual abuse victims are between the ages of 0 and 3 years. Between ages 4 and 7 years, the percentage almost triples to 28.4 percent. Ages 8 to 11 account for a quarter (25.5%) of cases, with children 12 years and older accounting for the remaining 35.9 percent of cases.[5] Clinical experience with boys and girls adopted from institutional settings makes clear that such settings are not immune to sexual abuse either. Many sexually abused children will become part of adoptive families. Often this is a trauma that comes to light post-adoption. It's crucially important that new adoptive parents are alert and sensitive to a disclosure of sexual abuse when moving a child into their home.

Ava, sexually abused as a preschool and school-age child, wrote in her adolescent years:[6]

> "It's not fair. You weren't there. You didn't care. It's not fair you hated me so much when all I need was a mothers love touch. It's not fair you took my childhood. It's not fair all the things I never understood. It's not fair you let guys rape me. It's not fair. It wasn't the way it was sappost to be. It's all the pain you put on me. It's not fair. I have no family. It's not fair I couldn't be like other kids. It's not fair all the things I missed. That's not the way a father was sappost to kiss a daughter. It's not fair that you don't care that he hurt me as long as he was here for you. But were you here for me? I had to cry when he touched me. Or how I feel be the way he love me. It's not fair. I'm all alone. It's not fair the way he wanted me. This isn't how it sappost to be. I was so young. You were my mother. We sappost to help and love each other. I have to work through it. I thought it was my fault. I have to get over you."

I think Ava's poignant journal entry makes clear the emotional toll sexual abuse takes on children.

Overall, sexual abuse leads to less trust in those around you, self-perceptions as different from others and poor self-esteem. Victims see themselves as less able to succeed socially. These children have fewer friends during childhood, less satisfaction in relationships and report less closeness with their parents. Lower academic performance is common. Sexually abused children have higher rates of depression. They are 18 percent to 21 percent more likely to become substance abusing by adolescence. They have increased numbers of sexual partners and much higher rates of sexually transmitted diseases. Rates of physical symptoms like headaches, stomach pain, asthma, bladder infections, chronic pelvic pain, etc. are greater. They exhibit more suicidal behavior and suicidal ideation.[7] Sexual abuse can impair a "normal" family life, social life and academic life. Yet, quality relationships with emotional connection can be a key component to restoring basic trust for female survivors—especially with men.[8] So, dads, uncles, grandfathers can all play a healing role post-adoption.

If you are feeling overwhelmed right now, this is normal. I think this is also good. You are now relating to the fact that traumatized children carry around their trauma residue each day—this is overwhelming!

Neglect

Neglect means that parents are absent, physically and psychologically. The child is ignored, their cries unanswered. There is a failure to engage the infant through talk, play and affection. The neglected child may be left to their own devices. I can't even count the number of children I have provided therapy to that were found wandering the street or picking through a trash can—as toddlers! Neglect is also a lack of food, clothes, medical care and housing. Neglect can mean that the child lived in a chronic state of hunger, filth and loneliness.

> **Peter** was born six weeks premature. He tested positive for caffeine, nicotine, amphetamines and barbiturates. He was admitted to the hospital when 1 month old. He was placed on a ventilator for four days. He had severe bronchitis that had been left untreated. Later, it was

learned that Peter was often left alone while his birth mother searched for drugs to satisfy her addiction. Social workers opened a case and began a process of monitoring the birth home. The apartment was cleaned. Visiting nurses and early intervention services were initiated. He was again admitted to the ER at 5 months of age for pneumonia. The apartment was without heat. Social services provided a voucher to the gas company to restore the heat. A social worker arrived at the residence to check on Peter and found him "difficult to arouse." The paramedics were called. Peter had swallowed rubbing alcohol. He was 8 months old. The birth mother was nowhere to be found. Peter was finally brought into foster care. Can you imagine being an infant on a ventilator? Or, sick from rubbing alcohol poisoning? Or living in filth? Or, being alone? Delaying Peter's removal caused unnecessary neglect—trauma! Many professionals working to support this child in the community wasn't enough.

Neglect occurs domestically and in orphanages abroad. Folks often comment that their child came from a "good" orphanage that was "clean." Yet, the ratio of one orphanage staff to five or more infants or toddlers was "not good." This was a neglectful situation! This would be like having quintuplets—only your mother, mother-in-law, sisters, aunts, friends, etc. aren't available to help!

The outcome of neglect can include the experience of adults as unreliable. One time the child may cry and someone may come; however, at other times, the child's cries are dismissed or go unheard because no one is there. In fact, many children who are neglected are left alone for hours and in frequent instances for days. One of our clients was strapped in a car seat, for hours at a time, over a long period of time, while his birth mother partook in drugs. He arrived in his adoptive home with a curved spine. He had to wear a back brace for several years to correct the spinal damage. There was no one playing peek-a-boo, rocking him or just spending time gazing in his eyes telling him what a beautiful baby he was. Neglect, then, contributes to a lack of trust that adults can meet the child's needs. The neglected child believes, "I must take care of myself. You big people can't be counted on." These boys and girls are controlling. They prefer to do things on their own. They rarely ask for help.

The child of neglect has a poor or very limited positive sense of self. Accomplishments go unrecognized. A harried orphanage staff person or an absent birth parent isn't clapping and cheering when the infant rolls over, smiles, sits up or takes a first step. No one is filming the event for a Facebook post either! The infant learns to stop seeking validation. He feels unworthy of the adult's attention and love.

It takes abundant positive interactions with children to facilitate an attachment and flourishing cognitive, physical, social and emotional development. When this nurture and attention is not provided, basic brain pathways wither and die. We'll learn more about how the brain develops in a subsequent chapter. Now is a good time to say that the brain requires nurture and nutrition to develop. Brain development is thwarted when trauma occurs prenatally and in infancy. As one example, babies need to experience face-to-face talk, and they need to hear countless repetitions of sounds to build the brain circuitry that will enable them to start making sounds and eventually say words. Language delays may follow neglect.[9] In my experience with traumatized children with attachment challenges, speech and language delays abound. Later, poor reading comprehension becomes a source of much school frustration.

Failure to Thrive

Failure to thrive is a medical diagnosis given to children who don't gain weight or who are consistently underweight in comparison to children of the same age. Most diagnoses of failure to thrive are made in infants and toddlers. The neglectful parent isn't always feeding the child enough. Lonely babies become depressed and eat less. Propping a bottle only works if the child can manage to suck the contents on his own, and if the contents contain something healthy. Failure to thrive can be caused by any of the following factors:

- Neglect.
- Poverty.
- Parental depression, history of abuse as a child or substance abuse problems.
- Gastroesophageal reflux, chronic diarrhea, cystic fibrosis, chronic

liver disease and celiac disease (these conditions limit the body's ability to absorb nutrients).

- Cleft palate or premature birth (these conditions can prevent calorie intake).
- Parasites, urinary tract infections, tuberculosis (these conditions consume energy; nutrients are utilized rapidly).
- HIV/AIDS.
- Cerebral Palsy.
- Down Syndrome.[10]

Nutrition is necessary for brain development.[11] The child's brain grows more in the first year of life than at any other time. Poor nutrition, during this critical window, impacts subsequent development. Nutritional deficiencies during pregnancy and infancy are likely to affect cognitive skills, behavior and productivity throughout the school years.[12]

Failure to thrive usually occurs within the context of a high-risk environment. So, it is often one factor combining with many others to inhibit the child's health and well-being. It is a part of complex trauma.

Malnutrition

Malnutrition, a lack of proper nutrition, can occur when the birth family or orphanage can't provide enough food, or enough healthy food, or the child can't absorb the nutrients from the food provided. I see malnutrition mentioned in the histories of many boys and girls treated at our office. I think this is given little thought or attention. Yet malnutrition, both before birth and during the first few years after birth, is linked to social and cognitive deficits. A cognitive deficit can include problems with perception, memory, reasoning, problem-solving, concept development and abstract thought. For example, iron deficiency (the most common form of malnutrition in the United States) can result in cognitive and motor delays, anxiety, depression, social problems and problems with attention.[13] Protein deficiency can result in motor and cognitive delays and impulsive behavior.[14] The social and behavioral impairments may be more difficult to "repair" than the cognitive impairments, even after the nutritional problems are corrected.[15]

Neglect, malnutrition and failure to thrive can have serious consequences. Once the child is placed in a healthy family, is eating and gaining weight, we tend to think that the problem is solved. Unfortunately, this may not be the case. In fact, the child's future can be jeopardized. I have included this information to shed light on these very concerning factors that lie in many adopted children's backgrounds. These kids need copious nurturing interactions upon placement in a healthy family. Long-term, they often require help attaching and developing social and emotional skills.

Physical Abuse/Domestic Violence

As a child, I never considered hitting my mother. It didn't even occur to me that I had that option. Even during times when I was particularly angry with her, I accepted her decision with no violence. Yet, there are some adopted children who daily, hit, kick, bite, slap, push and shove their parents and siblings, or do damage to the walls or break household items! It is simply terrible to live with violence in your own home. It is totally contrary to the meaning of family!

> **Joseph**, age 9, adopted internationally, arrived for his first therapy appointment at our office. I asked him to sit in the waiting room for a few minutes while I became acquainted with his parents. He was agreeable only if he could have his mom's phone. She replied "no." As Joseph's mom and dad were making themselves comfortable in my office, loud thumping and banging began. Joseph was kicking the waiting room walls, damaging the dry wall. He emptied all the buckets of LEGO® toys and blocks out into the hallway. Joseph decided that aggression was the way to let us all know of his unhappiness about the phone. His parents reported that this could go on for "hours." Dad also said that, "It requires great stamina to tell Joseph 'no' and mean it." Joseph was aggressive with the family upon his arrival at age 3. His parents thought he would "grow out of it." It took much intervention to finally cease this behavior.

Youngsters reared in homes (or orphanages) replete with domestic violence and physical abuse, come to believe that aggression is a means to solving problems. These boys and girls think that it's the strongest member of the family who gets what he wants.[16] Children enter the adoptive family and attempt to use violence to obtain "wants" and meet "needs."

A child who has been a victim of unpredictable sexual or physical abuse learns that if this abuse is going to happen, it is far preferable to control it when it happens. As a result, children who have been physically assaulted will frequently engage in provocative, aggressive behavior to elicit a predictable response—anger—from their environment.[17] Children provoke adoptive parents to get an angry response. These children "expect" violence to occur in all families. They have no ability to discern between their "abusive" birth home or orphanage, and their "healthy" adoptive family. Indeed, in my clinical work with adoptive parents they report, "I never thought I could be so angry!" Brothers and sisters also report, "I get so angry with him that I hit him back." "She makes me so mad that I get in her face and scream at her. I just can't help myself!" "Once he made me so mad, I pushed him onto the couch!"

Overall, the child exposed to violence may exhibit an inability to adapt to a peaceful adoptive family setting. He continues to use the aggressive coping skills of his trauma-laden environment. Remorse, empathy and respect for authority are lacking.

Emotional Abuse

"Sticks and stones may break my bones, but words will never break me" is a rhyme we all know. The rhyme was designed to help kids ignore name calling. This is hard when the child is bombarded by emotional abuse day in and day out. Criticizing, blaming, isolating, belittling, rejecting, corrupting, harassing and terrorizing a child are all examples of emotional abuse. Verbal aggression is emotional abuse. Withdrawing affection or exposing a child to a violent or sexually inappropriate environment also constitutes emotional abuse. Poor self-concept, poorer social functioning, depression and relationship difficulties result.[18]

Morgan came to therapy when he was 11 years old. He spent 5 years in orphanage care. Morgan was small in stature. He was "picked" on in the orphanage. He said, "the bigger kids told me I was stupid. I heard it every day. Then, they'd push me down."

To date, Morgan acts less intelligent than IQ testing indicates. He feigns the need for help with everything. Homework is particularly challenging. Morgan gets agitated as soon as he opens a book. He looks at the assignment, pushes the book back and exclaims, "I can't do this!" He spirals downward from there.

Lisa, Kendra and Leslie, ages 5, 6 and 7½, resided with their birth mom and dad. A neighbor called 911 one evening to report the following. "I can hear an argument. I can hear a lot of swearing like 'f—lazy b—. Kids you need to say good-bye. Your mother can find you another father. I don't need to live with such a pathetic b—.'" When the police arrived, the birth father was waving a gun. He was threatening to "kill everyone" if the police tried to arrest him. He was arrested. Lisa, Kendra and Leslie entered foster care.

Lisa, Kendra and Leslie each have a lot of shame. The girls believe they should have done more to protect their birth mother. In therapy, they learned that the birth mother had choices. She had been offered services in the community numerous times. She wouldn't take the help. The girls' shame reduced as they shifted the responsibility for the abuse from themselves to their birth parents.

It is true that "words will not break me." It is also true that repairing the after effects of verbal assaults may take a long time.

Multiple Moves

The longer a child remains in care, the more placements they're likely to have.[19] Thirty-seven percent of foster children were reported to have three or more placements. This means that the child has lost at least three sets of parents, siblings, friends, school mates, pets, communities, etc. Each new family has a unique set of rules, values, beliefs, ways of celebrating and so on.

Joyce resided with her birth mother at her grandparent's home until she was 7 months old. The birth mother then opted to move to the home of her paramour. Substance abuse and violence were prevalent here. Unfortunately, the birth mother overdosed and died. Joyce, now 18 months old, moved to the home that eventually became her adoptive home. The adoptive mom had been employed at the same place as the birth mother. She and her husband knew Joyce as they had provided child care for her. Joyce continued to have contact with her birth grandparents.

The new child flying from abroad to America with their new parents is experiencing at least a third move—birth family to orphanage to adoptive family. The international adoptee experiences the loss of their birth family, orphanage care givers, siblings, culture and so on.

Ronnie, for example, feels he lost many "brothers and sisters" in his transition to his adoptive family. Ronnie resided in an orphanage in Ukraine for almost 7 years. He developed close ties to many of the children in this Ukrainian institution. Ronnie has ongoing guilt regarding the fact that he now has a rich life full of food, toys and family members while these "siblings" remain in residence in grim conditions. He has a profound sense of sadness over the loss of these brothers and sisters. He wonders every day, "How are they doing?" "Did they get adopted?" "Will I ever see them again?"

The losses for Joyce, Ronnie and boys and girls like them are overwhelming. Kids lose everything most important—time and time again. People and things begin to lack meaning. Toys can be removed for behavioral infractions and the child is not fazed. Things are often lost or broken. There will be more at the next house. Living is based on today because tomorrow could mean another move, on to new people and new experiences. There is no point getting settled and making plans. There is no point getting attached.

Donna, currently 18, was adopted at age 10 after three failed reunification efforts and 11 foster care placements, states, "It was hard for me to move from foster home to foster home and settle down to a family that cares. Trying to trust them and love them back is really hard because it got messed up somewhere in between all the homes I've been in. My adoptive family has bent over backwards to show their love for me, but it is still hard for me. I know in my head that they won't do the things to me that my birth family did but there is still that side of me that says, 'be careful someone might leave you or you might get hurt.'"

Children moving through a series of foster homes or orphanages suffer fractured attachments. The consistent nurture needed to create close connections is inconsistent. The parents or orphanage ladies keep changing! When I am invited to speak to parents or social workers, I ask, "How many of you would like to get divorced two or three or more times?" The immediate response is that no one in the audience wants to experience this. It's painful! It affects every aspect of life! If we think about dating, "It is always nicer to be the dumper than the dumped."

Boys or girls who have experienced more than one placement "test" the adoptive parents. They violate rules to see if you are going to "keep me." "Are you really going to be my forever family. Or, will you 'throw me back' too?" Parents must have stamina when a child with a history of multiple placements arrives.

Moving many times also leads to poor educational outcomes, behavioral problems, aggression and greater teen sexual activity.[20]

Drug and Alcohol Exposure

Prenatal drug and alcohol exposure is a concern in the US as well as in many sending countries. Among the drugs in question are alcohol, cocaine, tobacco, opiates and marijuana.

It can be difficult for the adoptive family to know whether, and if so, which, specific types of substances were utilized by the birth mother during her pregnancy. This is because obtaining such information is often via self-report rather than by toxicology screening upon the birth of the child. Birth parents feel shame about such use and have not been well enough counseled about the importance to their child's future health, growth and well-being of rising above that shame to pass along this information. Parenting styles, quality of care during early childhood, exposure to violence and continued parental drug use are strong environmental factors—complex trauma—influencing children's lives.[21]

Below are some of the outcomes believed to be associated with alcohol, cocaine, opiates, marijuana and tobacco.

Alcohol

In the United States, alcohol use during pregnancy is the leading preventable cause of birth defects, developmental disabilities, and learning disabilities.[22] Fetal Alcohol Spectrum Disorders (FASD) is an umbrella term describing the range of effects that can occur in an individual who is exposed to alcohol during the prenatal period.[23]

Under FASD there are several categories to describe alcohol-related effects:

- **Fetal Alcohol Syndrome (FAS):** FAS represents the most involved end of the FASD spectrum. People with FAS might have abnormal facial features and stunted physical growth. People with FAS can have problems with learning, memory, attention span, communication, vision, or hearing. They might have a mix of these problems. People with FAS often have a hard time in school and trouble getting along with others.
- **Alcohol-Related Neurodevelopmental Disorder (ARND):** Previously referred to as fetal alcohol effects (FAE), ARND is now the term utilized when alcohol leaves in its path intellectual disabilities and problems with behavior and learning in a person whose mother drank alcohol during pregnancy. These kids might do poorly in school and have difficulties with math, memory, attention, judgment, and poor impulse control.
- **Alcohol-Related Birth Defects (ARBD):** People with ARBD might have problems with the heart, kidneys or bones, or with hearing. They might have a mix of these.[24]

Neurobehavioral Disorder Associated with Prenatal Alcohol Exposure (ND-PAE)

ND-PAE was first included as a recognized condition in the Diagnostic and Statistical Manual 5 (DSM 5) of the American Psychiatric Association (APA) in 2013. A child or youth with ND-PAE will have problems in three areas: (1) thinking and memory, where the child may have trouble planning or may forget material they have already learned; (2) behavior problems, such as severe tantrums, mood issues (for example, irritability) and difficulty shifting attention from one task to another; and (3) trouble with day-to-day living, which can include problems with bathing, dressing for the weather, and playing with other children. In addition, to be diagnosed with ND-PAE, the mother of the child must have consumed more than minimal levels of alcohol before the child's birth, which the APA defines as more than 13 alcoholic drinks per month of pregnancy (that is, any 30-day period of pregnancy) or more than two alcoholic drinks in one sitting.[25]

The symptoms that fall out of FASD include:

- Abnormal facial features, such as a smooth ridge between the nose and upper lip (this ridge is called the philtrum).
- Small head size.
- Shorter-than-average height.
- Low body weight.
- Poor coordination.
- Hyperactive behavior.
- Difficulty with attention.
- Poor memory.
- Difficulty in school (especially with math).
- Learning disabilities.
- Speech and language delays.
- Intellectual disability or low IQ.

- Poor reasoning and judgment skills.
- Sleep and sucking problems as a baby.
- Vision or hearing problems.
- Problems with the heart, kidneys or bones.[26]

There is no cure for FASD. Yet early intervention can improve the child's development. There are also protective factors that can help reduce the effects of FASD. These factors include a diagnosis before age 6, a loving, nurturing and stable home environment during the school years, an absence of violence, and involvement in special education and social services.[27]

Opiates

As I write this book, the United States is experiencing an opiate epidemic of epic proportions. Opiate usage is now second to alcohol consumption. The opiates that have been researched—sparsely—include heroin and methadone. Currently, there is concern about the abuse of opiate-based prescription medication, Vicodin, Buprenorphine or OxyContin. No studies have yet been published on the effects of these drugs on the infant.[28]

Post-birth many infants exposed to opiates in utero undergo a Neo-natal Abstinence Syndrome (NAS.) This is characterized by such symptoms as excessive crying, irritability, poor sleep, increased muscle tone, tremors, excoriations of the skin from excessive movements (i.e. causing sores due to excessive picking of one's skin), hyperthermia (i.e. elevated body temperature), loose stools, yawning, sweating, nasal stuffiness and sneezing. Some infants experience seizures due to the treatment protocol for NAS.[29]

Long-term opioid exposed children may be more likely to have attention deficit disorders and disruptive behavior.[30]

Cocaine

Babies born to mothers who use cocaine during pregnancy are often prematurely delivered, have low birth weights and smaller head circumferences, and are shorter in length than babies born to mothers who do not use cocaine.[31] Parents may see shaking, arching of the back, clenching of the fists, curling of the toes, trouble feeding, sleep disturbances and frequent startle reactions.

> **Jody** arrived in her adoptive home at 3 days old. A toxicology screen at birth confirmed several drugs present in her system. Jody couldn't accept any nurture. She pushed away and shrieked! Jody's mom described that she was having to hold her—tightly—to get her to take any formula. The mom said, "I'm practically holding her down! I feel like I'm forcing her to eat. Yet, she needs to eat!" This struggle didn't match at all with this mom's image that feeding her baby would be a time of mutual gazing and love. As a new parent, she was sad to miss blissful moments with her newborn.

The issues that fall out of substance abuse may feel rejecting or create guilt in that the parent is unable to console and enjoy their long-awaited child. Jody and her family were referred to an Occupational Therapist for sensory integration therapy (see Chapter 4). Via a variety of techniques, Jody was able to settle. Various types of early intervention services exist in most communities. I recommend parents seek out these services when a baby or young child arrives with a history of complex trauma.

Prenatal cocaine/crack cocaine has been the subject of much debate sine the 1980s. Current information from the National Institute of Drug Abuse notes:

> Many recall that "crack babies," or babies born to mothers who used crack cocaine while pregnant, were at one time written off by many as a lost generation. They were predicted to suffer from severe, irreversible damage, including reduced intelligence and social skills. It was later found that this was an exaggeration. However, the fact that most of these children appear normal should not be overinterpreted as indicating that there is no cause for concern. Scientists are now finding that exposure to cocaine during fetal development may lead to subtle, yet significant, later deficits in some children, including deficits in behavior/self-regulation, cognitive performance, processing information, and attention to tasks—abilities that are important for success in school.[32]

Marijuana

Marijuana does not have a direct effect on the pregnancy, yet there is an impact on fetal brain development. Children whose mothers have used marijuana during pregnancy have a higher rate of learning and behavioral problems, especially related to planning and follow through with a task.

Tobacco

Tobacco is one of the most harmful substances a woman can use during pregnancy. It produces a very high rate of low birth weight, premature birth and health problems in the newborn and child. In addition, a woman who admits to using tobacco during pregnancy is more likely to have used alcohol or illegal drugs as well.[33]

I'll let Donna conclude this section:

> **Donna** was placed in foster care at age 7. In therapy, seven years later, she stated, "Everything was about the drugs. The free food was sold to buy drugs. Any presents my birth aunt gave me for Christmas were sold for drugs. The men she sold herself to were because of the drugs. When we had no heat, it was because of the drugs. The beatings were because she was high and so were her boyfriends. Everything that happened was because of the drugs. The social workers told me it was because of the hitting. Really, it was because of the drugs."

Long-term risks associated with tobacco include lower IQ, attention problems during early elementary school years, depression, anxiety, behavioral problems and a likelihood of tobacco use in the tween and teen years.[34]

"Growing Up": Healing the Adoptee with a History of Trauma

We have now learned many of the ways trauma interrupts the child's "normal" developmental processes. Attachment is fractured. Trust is shattered. Self-concept is negative. Moral development lags. Remorse and empathy inhibit appropriate displays of care and concern for others.

Playing and getting along with friends is hard. The development of hobbies or interests—industry and initiative—may not exist. This child appears "lazy." Chronic cries of "I'm bored" occur. School work is a struggle. Impulsivity and immediate gratification dictate actions. Generating new and positive solutions escapes the child with a history of trauma. Emotions swirl out-of-control—frequently, dominating the ability to have logic and reasoning. Reciprocity was never learned. Cause-and-effect thinking—the ability to learn from mistakes—is non-existent! The same behaviors are repeated over and over and over! New learning takes time, patience and repetition—lots of repetition!

Not all children will present with all these delays. These are the most common types of deficits that surface after a youngster experiences early childhood trauma. The child with a history of complex trauma arrives with some, many or most major foundational skills—skills that fall into place in the first few years of life—ruptured or cracked. Like a house with a faulty foundation, the structure falters. This is true for human development. New growth cannot occur at a "normal" pace when the foundation isn't solid and stable. A main goal as parents and professionals is to help advance the development of the infant, toddler, preschool age, school age, tween or teen!

Healing happens when we "grow up" the traumatized adoptee! Chapter by chapter, we'll look at ways to bolster a son's or daughter's development. Children whose development is more accord with their chronological age fair better in the family, at school and in the community!

Before we move on, let's get a visual picture of the delays. Let's "see" the impact of trauma on child development.

"Seeing" the Impact of Complex Trauma

One way we can "see" the delays is by conducting developmental testing. We prefer to perform a Vineland Adaptive Scale on each child client at our office. The Vineland is an interview with the parents about various activities the child engages in. The Vineland shows us the age at which the child is functioning in various areas of development, as shown in Table 1.1.

Table 1.1: Vineland areas of development

Communication Domain:	Daily Living Skills Domain:
Receptive How the individual listens and pays attention, and what they understand. **Expressive** What the individual says; how they use words in sentences to gather and provide information. **Written** What the individual understands about how letters make words, and what they read and write.	**Personal** How the individual eats, dresses and practices personal hygiene. **Domestic** What household tasks the individual performs. **Community** How the individual uses time, money, the telephone, the computer and job skills.
Socialization Domain:	**Motor Skills Domain:**
Interpersonal Relationships How the individual acts with others. **Play and Leisure Skills** How the individual plays and uses leisure time. **Coping Skills** How the individual demonstrates responsibility and sensitivity to others.	**Gross** How the individual uses arms and legs for movement and coordination. **Fine** How the individual uses hands and fingers to manipulate objects.

Adapted from: Vineland Adaptive Behavioral Scale, Second Edition (Vineland-II). Pearson Education, Inc. Authors: Sara S. Sparrow, Dominec V. Cicchetti, David A. Balla.

The Vineland scores of Alyssa and Neil follow. They are not unique or "worst case" scenarios. Alyssa entered services, at our office, when she was chronologically age 13 years, 11 months old—almost 14. Neil entered services when he was 6½ years old.

In short order, I think their scores clarify the impact of complex trauma:

Table 1.2: Alyssa Vineland scores

Alyssa, chronological age almost 14:	
Communication	**Daily Living Skills**
Receptive 1 year, 6 months	**Personal** 8 years, 6 months
Expressive 3 years, 2 months	**Domestic** 7 years, 5 months
Written 9 years, 2 months	**Community** 7 years, 6 months
Socialization	**Motor Skills**
Interpersonal Relationships 2 years, 0 months	**Gross** 5 years 11 months
Play and Leisure Skills 2 years, 11 months	**Fine** Age equivalent Maladaptive behaviors clinically significant
Coping Skills 3 years, 4 months	

Table 1.3: Neil Vineland scores

Neil, chronological age 6 years, 6 months:	
Communication	**Daily Living Skills**
Receptive 3 years, 11 months	**Personal** 5 years, 0 months
Expressive 5 years, 7 months	**Domestic** 3 years, 11 months
Written 7 years, 0 months	**Community** 4 years, 11 months
Socialization	**Motor Skills**
Interpersonal Relationships 1 years, 9 months	**Gross** Age equivalent
Play and Leisure Skills 3 years, 11 months	**Fine** Age equivalent Maladaptive behaviors clinically significant
Coping Skills 2 years, 3 months	

Alyssa, at the chronological age of almost 14, has development that is scattered. She functions like a 2-year-old in her interpersonal relationships—how she acts with others. Can you imagine living with a 14-year-old child who still throws temper tantrums, is defiant, is all about "me" and "mine," is still learning to potty-train, has no real defined interests, etc.? Her abilities to get dressed, complete chores and behave out in the community are more in accord with children of about ages 7 and 8. In talking with her, the extent of her vocabulary is small. Sentences are simple and only a few words in length. Her receptive and expressive language skills are only those of a young preschool-age child—at most. Socially, she is sadly a misfit. She lacks the art of conversation. Her overall immaturity is visible to her classmates. They are polite to her. Yet none of them invite Alyssa over or text her or friend her on Facebook. Alyssa's mom and dad have enrolled her in a wide variety of extra-curricular activities. She refuses to go. She is aware that the other kids don't want to sit next to her on the bench. They don't invite her out for pizza after games. At home, she chronically follows her parents around expecting them to entertain her. Homework requires a major effort on Alyssa's part as well as on the part of her mom and dad!

Alyssa is "young" when we compare her chronological age to her social and emotional age. Expecting Alyssa to act like a 14-year-old results in lots of frustration and disappointment for parents, brothers, sisters and Alyssa!

Neil, like Alyssa, is not performing at his chronological age of 6½ years old. His receptive skills—what he hears, his capacity to pay attention, and what he understands—lag 2½–3 years behind. He struggles to form relationships, to play and to move forward with rudimentary coping skills. First grade is off to a poor start. We can already see the developmental gaps at Neil's young age.

No matter what chronological age the adoptee arrives at, the expectation that he will "act his age" must be shed. This makes parenting and living with the adoptee who arrives after experiencing trauma in early childhood challenging. You are parenting a "little" child—on a chronic basis. This is partly why behaviors such as lying and stealing, for example, are common. These are the behaviors of the 3 or 4-year-old. Then, kids learn that Mom or Dad can evaluate situations. Mom and Dad can see the cookie crumbs on their face. So, they stop taking cookies without permission. The child who experienced early trauma stays "stuck," *per se*, in various developmental stages. The behaviors that go along with the age of the stuckness persist. Undesired behaviors persist until we help sons and daughters mature.

"Growing up" the "little" adoptee who has joined the family allows this child to develop in ways that will promote healthy functioning in the family, at school, with friends, etc. The family too, will develop and grow. Each member of the family assembles a tool box of ways to resolve the day-to-day challenges of being an adoption-built family. Complexity, annoyance, disappointment and so on are replaced with hope, empathy and optimism.

Chapter Summary

- Any adoptee—infant, toddler, preschooler, school age, tween or teen—can present with the residual effects of trauma, including attachment problems, because complex trauma starts early in life— in the prenatal period and shortly after birth. The myth of adopting a baby or young child to have a "healthy" child must be shed.
- Trauma includes (but is not limited to): abandonment, sexual abuse, physical abuse, witnessing domestic violence, neglect, multiple moves and prenatal drug and alcohol exposure. Poor nutrition pre- and post-birth, premature birth and low birth weight adversely impact youngsters too. Moms and dads must think through the experiences of the new arrival or the child who has lived with them for perhaps years. We can't just believe that "love will be enough," "time will heal all wounds" or "he'll grow out of it." We wouldn't want to wait to initiate chemotherapy or to administer insulin. Waiting is a luxury that can't be afforded when it comes to treating trauma either. Trauma festers as the child ages. The splintered foundation ultimately gives way. The child's functioning declines over time. Early intervention is essential!
- Common delays caused by complex trauma include: the inability to form intimate attachments and lags in the development of essential

skills like trust, compliance, cause-and-effect thinking, morals and values, self-confidence, reciprocity, emotional expression and regulation, coping skills, social and play skills, and so much more. Parents, armed with this knowledge, can recognize when help is needed.

- Fallout—post-adoption—is normal. While offering a home to a child in need extends untold positive benefits, it may also bring anger, exasperation, aggravation, sorrow, jealousy, woe, despondency and unhappiness. Negative feelings afflict adults and kids alike. Living with a child who stays perpetually "little" is challenging! Having knowledge of this in advance helps moms and dads circumnavigate such conditions. Prepared for the rough patches, the family can adapt and recover.

Endnotes

1   Cook, A., Blaustein, M., Spinazzola, J., & van der Kolk, B. (Eds.) (2003). National Child Traumatic Stress Network. p.5. http://www.NCTSNet.org
2   Sextortion is when a predator convinces a victim to send a sexually provocative photo or video to the predator. The predator then threatens the victim with public exposure if additional photos or videos aren't provided. See Weinberger, J. (2017). *The Boogeyman Exists; and He's in Your Child's Back Pocket (second edition)*. California: CreateSpace Independent Publishing Platform, p.140.
3   The National Child Traumatic Stress Network. (n.d.). About child trauma: Trauma types. www.nctsn.org/trauma-types/sexual-abuse
4   The National Child Traumatic Stress Network. (n.d.). Caring for kids: What parents need to know about sexual abuse. www.nctsn.org/sites/default/files/assets/pdfs/caring_for_kids.pdf
5   United States, Administration for Children and Families, US Department of Health and Human Services. (1998). Child maltreatment 1996: Reports from the states to the National Child Abuse and Neglect Data *System*. Washington, D.C., OH: U.S. Dept. of Health and Human Services, Administration for Children and Families, Administration on Children, Youth and Families, Children's Bureau.
6   Ava's writing is reproduced here as written.
7   Briere, J.N., & Elliott, D.M. (1994). Immediate and long-term impacts of child sexual abuse. *The Future of Children*, 4(2), pp.56–57, & 62. doi:10.2307/1602523; Kendall-Tackett, K.A., Williams, L.M., & Finkelhor, D. (1993). Impact of sexual abuse on children: A review and synthesis of recent empirical studies. *Psychological Bulletin*, 113(1), p.156. doi:10.1037//0033-2909.113.1.164; Putnam, F.W. (2003). Ten-year research update review: Child sexual abuse. *Journal of the American Academy of Child & Adolescent Psychiatry*, 42(3), pp.271–273. doi:10.1097/00004583-200303000-00006; Putnam, F.W. (2006). The impact of trauma on child development. *Juvenile and Family Court Journal*, 57(1), pp.1–2. doi:10.1111/j.1755-6988.2006.tb00110.x; Trickett, P., McBride-Chang, C., & Putnam, F. (1994). The classroom performance and behavior of sexually abused females. *Development*

and Psychopathology, 6(1), p.193. doi:10.1017/S0954579400005940; Noll, J.G., Trickett, P.K., & Putnam, F.W. (2003). A prospective investigation of the impact of childhood sexual abuse on the development of sexuality. *Journal of Consulting and Clinical Psychology, 71*(3), p.582. doi:10.1037/0022-006x.71.3.575

8   Trickett, P.K., Noll, J.G., & Putnam, F.W. (2011). The impact of sexual abuse on female development: Lessons from a multigenerational, longitudinal research study. *Development and Psychopathology, 23*(2), p.462. doi: 10.1017/S0954579411000174

9   Scannapieco, M. (2008). Developmental outcomes of child neglect. *APSAC Advisor, 20*(1), p.8.

10 Block, R.W., & Krebs, N.F., Committee on Child Abuse and Neglect, & Committee on Nutrition. (2005). Failure to thrive as a manifestation of child neglect. *Pediatrics, 116*(5), p.1235; Homan, G.J. (2016). Failure to thrive: A practical guide. *American Family Physician, 94*(4), pp.2–3.

11 Prado, E.L., & Dewey, K.G. (2014). Nutrition and brain development in early life. *Nutrition Reviews, 72*(4), p.267. doi:10.1111/nure.12102

12 *Ibid.*

13 National Research Council and Institute of Medicine, Committee on Integrating the Science of Early Childhood Development, Shonkoff, J.P., Phillips, D.A., & Board on Children, Youth, and Families, Commission on Behavioral and Social Sciences and Education. (2000). *From Neurons to Neighborhoods: The Science of Early Childhood Development.* Washington (D.C.): National Academy Press, pp.204–205.

14 Prado, E.L., & Dewey, K.G. (2014). Nutrition and brain development in early life. *Nutrition Reviews, 72*(4), p.272. doi:10.1111/nure.12102

15 Karr-Morse, R., & Wiley M.S. (1997). *Ghosts from the Nursery. Tracing the Roots of Violence.* New York: The Atlantic Monthly Press, pp.78–79.

16 Perry, B.D. (1997). 'Incubated in terror: Neurodevelopmental factors in the "cycle of violence"' in: *Children, Youth And Violence: The Search For Solutions* (J. Osofsky, Ed.). Guilford Press, New York, p.14.

17 *Ibid.*, p.11.

18 Teicher, M.H., Samson, J.A., Polcari, A., & McGreenery, C.E. (2006). Sticks, stones, and hurtful words: Relative effects of various forms of childhood maltreatment. *The American Journal of Psychiatry, 163*(6), p.997.

19 Barbell, K., & Freundlich, M. (2001). Foster care today: An examination of foster care at the start of the 21st century. Washington, DC. *Casey Family Programs*, pp.3–4.

20 Adam, E.K., & Chase-Lansdale, P.L. (2002). Home sweet home(s): Parental separations, residential moves, and adjustment problems in low-income adolescent girls. *Developmental Psychology, 38*(5), p.799. doi:10.1037//0012-1649.38.5.792; *Ibid.*, pp.799–800; Howard, K., Martin, A., Berlin, L.J., & Brooks-Gunn, J. (2011). Early mother-child separation, parenting, and child well-being in early head start families. *Attachment & Human Development, 13*(1), p.10. doi:10.1080/14616734.2010.488119

21 Lambert, B.L., & Bauer, C.R. (2012). Developmental and behavioral consequences of prenatal cocaine exposure: A review. *Journal of Perinatology, 32*(11), p.822. doi:10.1038/jp.2012.90; Lester, B.M., & Lagasse, L.L. (2010). Children of addicted women. *Journal of Addictive Diseases, 29*(2), p.10. doi:10.1080/10550881003684921

22 FASD: What everyone should know. (n.d.) *National Organization on Fetal Alcohol Syndrome.* https://www.nofas.org/wp-content/uploads/2014/08/Fact-sheet-what-everyone-should-know_old_chart-new-chart1.pdf

23 *Ibid.*

24 Center for Disease Control and Prevention CDC. (2018, July 17). Fetal alcohol spectrum disorders (FASDs): Basics about FASDs. https://www.cdc.gov/ncbddd/fasd/facts.html

25 https://www.cdc.gov/ncbddd/fasd/features/neurobehavioral-disorder-alcohol.html

26 *Ibid.*

27   Streissguth, A.P., Barr, H.M., Kogan, J. & Bookstein, F.L. (1996). Understanding the
     occurrence of secondary disabilities in clients with fetal alcohol syndrome (FAS)
     and fetal alcohol effects (FAE). Final report to the Centers for Disease Control and
     Prevention (CDC). Seattle: University of Washington, Fetal Alcohol & Drug Unit, p.28.
     http://lib.adai.uw.edu/pubs/bk2698.pdf; Streissguth, A.P., Bookstein, F.L., Barr, H.M.,
     Sampson, P.D., O'Malley, K., & Young, J.K. (2004). Risk factors for adverse life outcomes
     in fetal alcohol syndrome and fetal alcohol effects. *Developmental and Behavioral Pediatrics,*
     5(4), p.6.
28   Lester, B.M., & Lagasse, L.L. (2010). Children of addicted women. *Journal of Addictive*
     Diseases, 29(2), p.8. doi:10.1080/10550881003684921
29   Jansson, M.L., Velez, M.M., & Harrow, C. (2009). The opioid-exposed newborn:
     Assessment and pharmacologic management. *Journal of Opioid Management, 5*(1), pp.3–4.
     doi:10.5055/jom.2009.0006; Kocherlakota, P. (2014). Neonatal Abstinence Syndrome.
     Pediatrics, 134(2), p.e550. doi:10.1542/peds.e547-e561 http://pediatrics.aappublications.org/
     content/134/2/e547
30   Lester, B.M., & Lagasse, L.L. (2010). Children of addicted women. *Journal of Addictive*
     Diseases, 29(2), p.8. doi:10.1080/10550881003684921
31   Cain, M.A., Bornick, P., & Whiteman, V. (2013). The maternal, fetal, and neonatal effects
     of cocaine exposure in pregnancy. *Clinical Obstetrics and Gynecology, 56*(1), p.e1013.
     doi:10.1097/grf.0b013e31827ae167; Behnke, M., & Smith, V. C. (2013). Prenatal substance
     abuse: Short- and long-term effects on the exposed fetus. *Pediatrics, 131*(3), p.1013.
     doi:10.1542/peds; Minnes, S., Lang, A. & Singer, L. (2011). Prenatal tobacco, marijuana,
     stimulant, and opiate exposure: Outcomes and practice implications. *Addiction Science*
     and Clinical Practice, 6(1), pp.61–62.
32   National Institute on Drug Abuse. (2016, May). What are the effects of maternal
     cocaine use? https://www.drugabuse.gov/publications/research-reports/cocaine/
     what-are-effects-maternal-cocaine-use
33   Chasnoff, I.J., Schwartz, L.D., Pratt, C.L., & Neuberger, G.J. (2006). *Risk and promise: A*
     Handbook for Parents Adopting a Child from Overseas. Chicago, IL: NTI Upstream, p.31.
34   Minnes, S., Lang, A. & Singer, L. (2011). Prenatal tobacco, marijuana, stimulant, and
     opiate exposure: Outcomes and practice implications. *Addiction Science and Clinical*
     Practice, 6(1), pp.59–60.

CHAPTER 2

Tips to Grow Up the "Younger" Adoptee

Let's begin to apply the knowledge we gained in Chapter 1. Information is wonderful. We need to be able to use it to improve our day-to-day life. These first parenting tips lend to growing the "young" adoptee by starting at the social and emotional age of the child. This first set of tips improves the emotional climate of the home as well.

Using the Tips

In all the tips chapters some strategies are concrete tools for immediate use. Some are food for thought. Others are recommendations for additional resources or professional services.

All the tips chapters combined equal a menu of new approaches. I suggest earmarking the ideas that you feel comfortable implementing. Then, prioritize the two or three you feel will be most effective for your unique situation. Use these new strategies until they become routine. Then, move onto a few more.

As we implement tips, let's keep in mind that there are no "one-size fits-all-families" solutions. Each member of the family is unique. Each child who experiences trauma has a distinctive response. I say to folks in therapy that a part of my job is to offer an array of strategies. Moms and dads can select which parenting tools make sense within their family, which interventions go along with their values and which are safe within the context of their home.

Change the View

Comments made by folks entering therapy are, "When he opens his eyes, I feel like it's game on. The battles start right away!" "I dread when she gets off the school bus." "I hate coming home from work. Sometimes, I take a longer way home." Children who arrive via adoption can do a number on the parents' sense of self! The way parents come to view themselves and their situation contributes to the outcome.

Let's start changing our view now. I want parents to get up every morning believing they can handle whatever comes their way. To do this, we must remind ourselves that the child didn't ask to be abused, neglected, abandoned or exposed to drugs/alcohol. The youngster, tween or teen who joins the family by adoption is challenging to parent! There is no doubt about this! Yet, there is a person underneath all that baggage! We do get glimpses of the kind, smart, funny, talented kid who can emerge! With the right tools and services—you'll see more of this kid! Please also remind yourself that you didn't create your youngster's problems. Perhaps, to date, you feel like nothing you have done has worked. It is really that trauma renders "normal" parenting strategies ineffective. Hindsight isn't helpful. What matters is what you do from today forward. You're taking a good step by reading this book! New approaches! New view! The family will begin to thrive!

This is a Family Problem

The "young" arrival exhibits an array of undesired behaviors. Frequently, this scenario is chalked up to, "Boys will be boys!" "All kids do that!" Yet, the frequency, intensity and duration of these behaviors greatly exceeds those put forth by children developing within normal parameters. So, let's start shedding the myths now. On any given day, adoptive moms, dads, brothers and sisters deal with:

| Hoarding food | Rummaging through classmates' lunches for snacks | Overeating |
| | | Picky eating |

Acting in sexual ways

Sexting

Pornography

Throwing temper tantrums

Screaming and yelling

Being aggressive/ bullying

Being argumentative

Refusing to shower, wear deodorant, etc.

Wearing the same clothes for several days

Running away

Lying

Stealing

Refusing to get out of bed in the morning

Refusing to go to bed

Getting up in the middle of the night

Carrying out chores sloppily

Constantly losing/ breaking possessions

Writing or drawing on clothing, walls

Making poor eye contact

Mumbling

Using the possessions of others without permission

Going into parent's and sibling's bedrooms without permission

Swearing

Urinating in public

Enuresis (night-time bed-wetting)

Encopresis (daytime wetting self)

Smearing feces

Cutting themselves

Pulling out eyelashes

Pulling out teeth

Picking off toenails

Head banging

Rocking

Suicidal ideation

Suicidal threats

Behaving in a superficially charming manner

Cutting holes in clothing

This list is not exhaustive. The negative behaviors of the child joining a family through adoption cause the adoptee to become the "identified problem."

I believe that a primary job I have is helping each member of the family recognize that they must be part of the solution. Each family member will need to make changes for the adoptee to heal. I think what happens plays out as below—over and over and over:

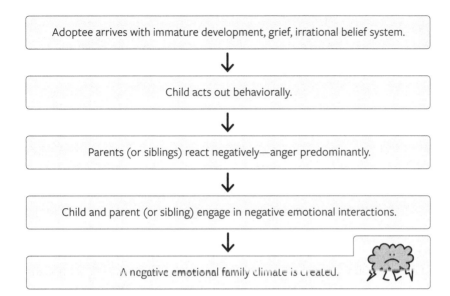

Figure 2.1: The arrival of a child with a trauma history can create a negative emotional climate in the family.

Moms, dads, brothers and sisters can learn to change the way they react. In turn, this leads to interrupting the unwanted behavioral problems of the arrival with an early history of trauma. We'll explore how we can change our reactions later in this book when we focus on emotional development. Suffice to say at this time, each member of the family can and must play a part in the recovery of the adoptee. We must grow our whole family post-adoption.

How Old is Your Adoptee?

There are many ways to hone in on the social-emotional age of your adopted child. Call our office and we'll arrange to conduct a Vineland Adaptive Scale. If your child has an Individual Education Plan (IEP) or has had a psychological, psychiatric or neuropsychological evaluation, developmental testing may already exist.

Reading books and websites about child development (see Resources) is quite helpful. Learning what is "normal" for given ages helps us determine the types of skills the traumatized adoptee is lacking. We can figure out how to fill these gaps. Let's focus our learning on the ages infant to 3- to 5-year-olds. Early trauma affects primary skills.

You can also observe your child in social situations. Visit the park or volunteer in the classroom. Observe what kids developing normally are doing. Sunday school classrooms offer the ability to observe kids of differing ages. Each time I am waiting in line at a store, or I'm at the mall, I take the opportunity to notice the kids. Everywhere you go, you can observe children.

If you have parented typically developing children, you have personal knowledge of child development that you can apply to this process as well.

I've included a few charts throughout the book to help you get started too!

Parenting "Younger": Chores, Privileges and More!

Treating boys and girls with early trauma "younger" is one way to repair the devastating impact that trauma leaves in its wake. We can apply this approach to many undesired behaviors.

First, place a Post-it® note in a conspicuous place to remind yourself that you live with a child who is "younger" than their chronological age. If you have photos of your child as a baby, toddler or preschooler, hang these on the fridge. A visual reminder helps keep expectations in check. Would I expect a 3-year-old to be able to feed the cat daily—on their own? Would I expect a 2-year-old to clean their room, put away laundry, hang up their clothes, set the table or empty the dishwasher—on their own? Can a 4- or 5-year-old handle electronic privileges—or need these privileges? Do I expect a little kid to say, "I'm sorry" and comprehend its full meaning? Would I ask a preschooler to babysit? If the answer to any of these questions is "no," don't assign these tasks. Or assign these chores/ give these privileges knowing that the chore may not be completed correctly or the privilege wisely used. Adjusting expectations in this manner lessens our frustration.

I'm not suggesting that we lower our expectations. Indeed, I hold children and teens accountable for their actions. I am putting forth that when we meet the child where they are developmentally, we are parenting in a manner that facilitates growth and healing. Some issues aren't so frustrating or as hard to decide about when we put them in context of the youth's social and emotional age, and when we adjust our approach to meet the child's developmental needs

A Few Examples...

Perhaps six or seven sets of clothing hanging in the closet are all that is needed. This makes it easier to pick an outfit each day. The selection can be rotated. This isn't a punishment. This is simply to make life better for everyone.

Offer a smaller variety of toys or art supplies at one time. This makes it simpler for children to choose what to select. Clean-up goes more smoothly. Next week, alternate the playthings.

One dad solved a mealtime dilemma as follows:

> **Vince**, dad to 6-year-old Finn, was often frustrated at dinner. This little one wouldn't eat in a timely manner. Most of his food wound up on the floor. He interrupted the conversation. Eventually he would have a melt-down and need to be removed from the table. The effort to have family dinner was wrecked time and time again. This issue was solved with the toddler game of airplane. You know, the fork is the airplane and the child's mouth the airplane hangar. The utensil spirals around until the food lands. Initially, this dad's response to this idea was, "He's 6!" Really, 6-year-old Finn was about 16 months old. Good dad that he is, he gave it a try. Much to his surprise, meal time improved immensely. A few months later, his son was participating in family dinner nicely—without the airplane game. This school-age youngster outgrew this need.

Carrying out chores together can work, rather than asking your child to accomplish chores by himself. Youngsters like to work side-by-side with their parents. Breaking a chore into pieces is often more effective than requesting completion of one large chore like "clean your room." Little children don't have the ability to carry out three- and four-part instructions and tasks. "Let's pick up your dirty clothes." "Let's change your sheets." "Go ahead and put your clothes in your dresser while I tidy up the closet." This approach may get the bedroom spic and span in no time.

Eventually, as we work with additional strategies yet to come in this book, the child will mature and take these tasks on solo.

We can also apply this same philosophy to privileges. Privileges are doled out as kids show the sensibleness to handle them. For example, a 14-year-old typically developing child may get to stay home alone when their parents go out to dinner. A 14-year-old adopted child may not. A college student or grandma may need to keep him company. No explanation needed. The child care provider just arrives. We don't explain to 4-year-olds why they're staying with a babysitter. We don't need to explain it to a 14-year-old who is 4 years old!

Driving is challenging:

Betty and Mark adopted two children who happened to be eight months apart in age. Their son, Craig, and daughter, Leah, reached driving age the same year. Craig obtained his driver's license right away. Leah drove the car for the first time a year later. Her level of responsibility finally matured. No. Leah wasn't happy about this. Yet, for her safety and the safety of others, this decision was essential. Leah was provided with the reasons for the delay. She was also offered an action plan to develop the skills necessary. Each time she complained that her mom and dad loved Craig more—her opinion of why he was driving and she wasn't—she was calmly directed back to her action plan.

Screens can cause serious problems in adoptive families. While technology is wonderful, it is often misused by children left immature due to a hard beginning. The device is removed from the tween or teen due to misuse. Then, it is given back. Then, it is misused. The cycle repeats and repeats and repeats. Life begins to revolve around the devices. Value is assigned to the device, instead of the people providing the device!

School-issued devices compound the problem of securing the adoptive home from unwanted and potentially dangerous screen behavior. Many moms and dads struggle to manage devices safely when there are multiple kids in the family.

I'd like to suggest a resource to assist families in making decisions about screens. The book is, *The Boogeyman Exists; And He's In Your Child's Back Pocket* by Jesse Weinberger (see Resources.) Weinberger also has a website and she speaks throughout the country. I find this written work offers sobering statistics based on Weinberger's own data collection and substantiated by research from other reputable organizations/individuals:[1]

- The new age of onset of pornography consumption is 8 years old. The new age onset of pornography addiction is 11 years old.
- Sexting begins in 4th/5th grade.
- Cell phone ownership among children starts solidly in the 3rd grade. Tablet ownership can begin as early as Kindergarten (ages 5–6).
- 37 percent of young people have experienced cyberbullying on a frequent basis.
- 88 percent of teens who use social media have witnessed cyber-bullying of another person, while 66 percent of teens who witness cyberbullying also witness others joining in.
- More than 50 percent of children, who are victims of cyberbullying never report the behavior to their parents.
- 36 percent of teen girls and 39 percent of teen boys say it is common for nude or semi-nude photos to get shared with people other than the intended recipients.
- Predators seek youths vulnerable to seduction, including those with histories of sexual or physical abuse, those who post sexually provocative photos/videos, and those who talk about sex with unknown people online. Thirty-three percent of sexual assaults occur when the victim is between the ages of 12 and 17.
- Children who spend more than one hour of unsupervised time per day online are far more likely to get victimized.

Over the past two years we have had clients enter services between the ages of 8 and 11, already engaging in pornography. Our clients have participated in or been on the receiving end of cyberbullying. Sexting and pursuing inappropriate sexual relationships online cause moms and dads to initiate services as well. For example:

Audria, adopted at age 2 internationally, now 16 years old, is obsessed with meeting older men online. She feels these men "understand her." She lacks an attachment to her adoptive family, and she is really about age 3 at the core. Clearly, her behavior could result in serious consequences to her and her family members. The family consulted an IT professional who helped Mom and Dad lock down all the devices in their own home. Audria is one of four children in this family. Removing all the devices doesn't make sense. Audria has a charming façade, and she continues to manipulate classmates to let her use their devices for a bit here and there. She has numerous Facebook, Instagram, Kik, etc. accounts. Supervision has increased. Audria is around a parent most of the time, and her oldest sister keeps an eye on her on the school bus and at lunch. Each member of the family takes time to engage Audria more. Audria's youngest sister is teaching her to play piano for example. The parents opted to install a security system in the home in case Audria had given any of these men "friends" the location of the home. Dad showed Audria's messages to the local police. While there wasn't much the police could do as the real identities of the men were concealed, they did review with Audria the type of problems she was making for herself and them. Audria was shocked that her parents would go to this length. She also didn't want her "boyfriends" in "trouble." Dad's and law enforcement's actions caused Audria to back off the screens. The family also entered an adoption-attachment-trauma-focused therapy. Audria's inability to form intimate relationships with her family and with peers caused a loneliness that she felt only these men could fulfill. As her connection to her family deepened, she matured. The screens took on less and less meaning over time. The precautions taken in this case weren't foolproof. I don't know if any parent can lock down an adolescent totally today. Yet, this family made a significant, concerted effort that eventually paid off.

Technology poses great benefits. Audria's case shows the serious complications that can arise. Audria is but one example of the array of technological dilemmas that happen. I like that Weinberg asks parents to make sure they are ready to handle the potential consequences. Then, she gives you ample examples of what can happen, an overview of the pros and cons of various social media platforms, and various safeguards to put in place. She encourages parents to make decisions that are in accord with values, not societal pressure. After you finish this book, make reading *The Boogeyman Exists* a priority.

Recently, a parent gave her teen son access to a cell phone. Within a matter of days, the history was replete with pornography. She removed the device. In therapy, she lamented that she wanted to be able to give him privileges and to have a more "normal" life. Certainly, there is grief that goes along with parenting children with a history of trauma. They often can't do or can't have the age-appropriate experiences their peers enjoy. It takes time to come to terms with this. Give yourself the space to work through the losses.

Prioritizing Behaviors: Think New Year's Resolution

Frankly speaking, there are kids for whom we need to work on serious behaviors first. Stealing, aggression and property damage can lead to getting arrested in the teenage years. So, for example, I have worked with many parents who—once every week or two—take a garbage can and clean their son's or daughter's bedrooms themselves. Others simply make sure there is no trash strewn about and close the door. These moms and dads have opted to make the bedroom a low priority. They've also stopped worrying so much about food issues and homework. Part of parenting an adoptee with a traumatic beginning is deciding which behaviors you really need to change, and which you can live with for now. As we mature the little adoptee, he will take on more initiative and responsibility himself. Many unwanted behaviors will be shed naturally.

Think New Year's resolution in this area. Each January 1, millions of us make our New Year's resolution. Each January 31, millions of us have let our resolutions go by the wayside. Changing behavior is no easier for a preschooler, grade schooler, tween or teen than it is for an adult. Working on a few behaviors or skills at one time will lead to better overall outcome. Yes. This means that in the interim, the child who arrived via adoption will be "getting away" with undesired behaviors. My experience is that as we get success, and as we get improved social, emotional, cognitive and brain development—as we grow up the little adoptee—this is a temporary situation.

Growing Up Young Children Takes Time

Work, grocery shopping, yard work, laundry, driving the kids to soccer, arranging play dates, meeting friends for dinner, completing homework, spending time alone with your partner, birthday parties, visiting extending family—where does the list end! Then, the addition of a child with an early history of trauma adds therapy, psychiatric appointments, tutoring, school meetings, occupational, physical and/or speech therapy! All children need quality and quantity time. The adopted arrival may require extensive time. I do work to make parenting suggestions that can be easily incorporated into the schedules of the families. However, "little" children require time and attention. The child who takes an extra-long time to mature requires parental supervision and guidance sometimes into the tween and teen years.

Carving out time means re-thinking priorities. It also means seeking out help. Below are a few ideas that come from parents I have worked with:

- Perhaps learning to say "no" more often is necessary. You can volunteer for the prom committee, but you don't have to be the chairperson. You can still do things you enjoy, perhaps on a smaller scale.
- Hiring a cleaning service can be helpful. No. They won't clean the house exactly like you do. But, they will do an adequate job. Really, what's a few dust bunnies in comparison to a healthy family? Ask your extended family for gift cards for a cleaning service, to restaurants that deliver or to landscaping services as Christmas or your birthday rolls around. One of our clients asked for some time to address the congregation before the church service. She told her fellow parishioners that she didn't expect them to understand what life was like with two children with mental health issues. She was hoping they could take her word for it and come give her a hand with painting and repairs needed at her home. The following Saturday, she received help with the repairs plus enough casseroles for a few weeks.
- Several of our clients have moved. One family re-located to a new house that was a detached condo. This reduced the time mowing the grass, trimming the bushes and so on. Instead, the family spends time on the common areas playing.

- If you haven't already taken the Crock Pot™ out of the pantry, now may be the time to do so. It is quick to throw some meat and veggies into the Crock Pot™ and let them simmer all day. Paper plates a couple of nights per week reduces clean-up time as well as decreases time arguing about who should load the dishwasher!
- College students studying psychology, social work, education, etc. often need to accumulate hours of experience. Post some notices on your local college campus today. They earn hours in exchange for spending time with your traumatized child.
- One or two nights per week all the kids can go to their rooms 30 minutes early. No one is expected to go to sleep. They are simply going to their rooms. Mom and dad can get a little time alone.
- One mom and dad, at our office, snuck out to the garage with a thermos of coffee on occasion. By the time their kids found them, they had gotten to enjoy a peaceful cup of java and some conversation!
- Many families have found retired folks in their neighborhood to help as the kids get home from school, or to help transport their sons and daughters to extra-curricular activities and back home. These older neighbors have enjoyed feeling useful. Parents have some time to go to the gym, read, shop, walk the dogs—anything that is enjoyable.

Think about some ways your family can free up some time here and there. Have the kids brainstorm a list. Give prizes for the ideas that pan out. Notice I am thinking in small increments of time—15 or 30 minutes. Certainly, weekend getaways and vacations are wonderful! Yet, small breaks each day can refresh and rejuvenate a busy, stressed out parent. Or, an extra 15 to 30 minutes—here and there—with any of your children adds up to a lot of quality time!

Chapter Summary

- The way Mom and Dad view themselves, their situation and the child who arrived via adoption leads to outcome. Parents need to see themselves as adept. They need to see the adoptee as vulnerable, rather than as a bundle of behaviors causing chaos in their home.
- The arrival of a challenging adoptee means that the entire family

becomes part of the solution. Mom, dad, brothers and sisters need to work together to develop and implement strategies that facilitate the cognitive, social, emotional and brain development of the new addition. The family built by adoption must grow the whole family.

- Gauging the age at which the child functions in comparison to the chronological age is essential. Concrete reminders strategically placed about the house help parents keep their expectations in check. Expecting a "little" child to act his chronological age only leads to frustration for each member of the family. Anticipating and planning for the adopted child to act younger allows the daily routine of the family to go more smoothly. Chores and privileges correspond to the skills and abilities of the child, tween or teen arriving after abandonment, neglect and/or abuse.

- Prioritizing which issues the adopted youngster needs most takes thought. Yet children, like adults, struggle to make more than a few conduct or developmental changes simultaneously. Learning to live with an unkempt room, messy mealtimes, a disarray of toys and clothes and so on, may be a necessity for a time.

- All children require time. The child with a history of trauma may require support and direction daily and into older ages. The adopted arrival consumes parental time. Finding opportunities for parents to make time for themselves as individuals and as a couple, and for parents and each child to spend time together is essential. This matter may best be accomplished as a family endeavor.

- Learning to tolerate school and societal pressures is a part of all parenting. This situation is amplified in adoption-built families. Parents will need to develop the vigor to make choices that are safest and most suitable for their unique family.

Endnote

1   Weinberger, J. (2017). *The Boogeyman Exists; And He's In Your Child's Back Pocket* (second edition). California: CreateSpace Independent Publishing Platform. Vanning, K. (2010). *Child molesters: A behavioral analysis.* National Center for Missing & Exploited Children. https://www.icmec.org/wp-content/uploads/2015/10/US-NCMEC-Child-Molesters-A-Behavioral-Analysis-Lanning-2010.pdf. Sabina, C., Wolak, J. & Finkelhor, D. (2008). The nature and dynamics of internet pornography exposure for youth. *CyberPsychology & Behavior*, 11(6), pp.1–3. doi: 10.1089/cpb.2007.0179. Enough is Enough: Making the Internet Safer for Families and Children. (2014). Cyberbullying statistics. https://enough.org/stats_cyberbullying

A Bit About The Brain: When The Path Most Traveled Is Accompanied By Toxic Stress

Why a chapter on the brain? Because brain growth and functioning are influenced by the experiences encountered in the womb and in the first years of life. The brain begins forming very early in prenatal life just three weeks after conception.[1] Between conception and age 3, it has reached 80 percent of its adult volume! The first year of life is perhaps the most dynamic in terms of brain growth![2] Where was your child in the first year to few years of life? What was their prenatal experience like?

Building Up the Brain

The brain grows from the bottom to the top. Areas that control more life-sustaining functions like heart rate and breathing come online first. Areas that perform more sophisticated tasks, like thought, develop over time.[3] There is an order in which the parts of the brain grow. Via this pattern of growth various parts of the brain learn to work together. If the brain is unable to prepare itself properly—either by maturation or experience—learning,[4] eschewing morals and values, attaching, attending, making friends, playing, etc. will be impaired. Early trauma interrupts the brain's ability to organize itself.

Brain Structures for Baby Tasks

Structures like the brainstem control the baby's tasks like sleeping, waking, breathing, crying, feeling temperature, hunger, wetness, pain, vomiting, sneezing, posture, balance, motor control, urinating and defecating.

I was happy when I read *The Body Keeps the Sore* by Bessel van der Kolk because he said, "It is amazing how many psychological problems involve difficulties with sleep, appetite, touch, digestion and arousal."[5] Pee and poop issues abound in adoptive families! Kids urinate on the carpet, in the heat ducts, in the middle of outings. One teen I worked with was still pooping herself in fifth grade. Little pieces fell out of her pants as she walked in the school hallway. She seemed oblivious to the odor and health hazard this created. Other kids will not wipe themselves. Picky eating and overeating are common. It is difficult to give and receive affection as touch feels aversive or abrasive. Falling asleep, staying asleep and waking can be problematic. Some children wander the house at night eating, watching television or using electronic devices. Others have intense nightmares or sleepwalk.

The hypothalamus adapts the body to the environment and helps us survive. Specifically, it plays a role in things like stress reaction, sweating, fat burning, thirst, rage, pleasure, tranquility, parenting behavior and sexual activity. The brainstem and the hypothalamus together also control the energy levels of the body—the arousal. They coordinate the functioning of the heart and lungs, the immune system and the endocrine system.[6] The endocrine system produces hormones that contribute to physical growth, metabolism, and sexual development and functioning.

Lucy was sitting in the waiting room while her parents spoke with the therapist. Another family arrived for an appointment. Shortly, their therapist informed me that there was a complaint that such a young child was left in the waiting area by herself. I went to check, and Lucy was sitting reading a magazine. Lucy is only 4'6" at 15 years of age. Her physical growth is stalled. She looks like a much younger child. I assured the concerned family that Lucy was of an age to manage in the waiting room.

We do see many children who are small in height and weight for their chronological age. We also work with many children with an array of sexual behaviors at discord for their age.

The Stress Response System: Red Alert!

At birth the brain contains hundreds of billions of nerve cells—neurons—
that branch out forming neural networks like a tree grows from a sapling
to a mighty oak. During the first six months after birth the growth of
these neural networks becomes extremely active as sensory input—sights,
sounds, smells, tastes, strokes, pats, kisses—bathe the infant brain.[7]
Neurons connect and communicate with other neurons. Neurons in our
cerebral cortex—our gray matter—must talk to other neurons in various
parts of the gray matter. This communication helps us with memory,
attention, perception, cognition, awareness, thought, language and consciousness. White matter connects the different parts of gray matter—like
a subway gets you from home to the office or a coffee shop or a clothing
store. White matter puts us in the express lane because of myelin. Myelin
sheaths—made of glial cells—encase neurons, enhancing the speed at
which neurons can communicate. The brain favors and strengthens the
connections—pathways—most needed by a child in their environment.[8]
Taking the same subway route repeatedly carves a corridor in the brain.

Traumatized children experience toxic stress. This type of stress
includes strong, frequent, or prolonged activation of the body's stress
management system.[9] These events are chronic, uncontrollable, and/or
experienced without a caring parent acting as a buffer.[10] When the path
most traveled has been replete with toxic stress, boys and girls—age infant
through adolescents—enter the adoptive family with a brain that's on
chronic red alert. We've already looked at neglect, abuse, abandonment,
orphanage residence and multiple moves as traumas that create toxic
stress. It is also important to point out that maternal stress during pregnancy can lead to the infant exhibiting reactivity to stress. In fact, fetuses
who experience higher maternal stress in the womb are more fearful and
more reactive to novelty as infants and young children.[11] These children
are at higher risk for affective problems like depression and anxiety as
tweens and teens.[12] I would certainly believe that many children who
come to our office had birth mother's living in stressful life situations.

Toxic stress over-sensitizes—carves a corridor—in the brain structures
related to fear, anxiety and impulsive responses. Fewer neural connections

are devoted to reasoning, planning and behavioral control.[13] The stress response system activates more often and for longer time periods. Simple day-to-day routines can be interrupted, as can cherished family outings, when the brain is overreactive in this manner:

> **Ed** entered his adoptive family at age 8. He had been removed from his birth family due to domestic violence and neglect. One evening, shortly after his placement, the family prepared to attend the annual church dance. This event is the highlight of the year for this church. The proceeds fund the many charitable causes on whose behalf the congregation proudly works.
>
> Upon arrival at the church, Ed noticed a group of adults standing outside a nearby convenience store smoking. His thoughts raced from the smoking of cigarettes to the smoking of drugs he had witnessed in his birth home. Drugs led to violence. Drugs led to Ed hiding in his closet to escape the screaming and hitting that occurred when his birth parents were high. Ed took off, running into the church where he positioned himself in the janitor's closet. It took much coaxing before Ed was willing to re-join his family and move on to the dance. Still, he was clearly anxious the entire evening. He kept asking, "When are we going home?" "Can we go now?" "Are we going soon?" It was difficult for Ed's family to relax and enjoy this much looked forward to event. The family left early—bewildered, confused and disappointed.

The traumatized brain operates differently than the brain that was nurtured and stimulated in utero and after birth. In this vignette, Ed was stuck in his past. He couldn't shift his focus to the fun occasion. He couldn't discern the difference between the people in his life now and those of the past. Ed couldn't trust that he was safe at the church with his family. He couldn't experience the enjoyment of a new experience. This is just one instance with Ed. Ed's difficulties are shared by many children with poor early beginnings. Ed's difficulties have roots in his brain.

Your adoptive parenting journey must include knowing about the brain! The more familiar you are with brains of kids like Ed, the more your child can heal and grow!

Limbic Circuitry: Threats Abound!

The para-limbic and limbic circuity is part of the stress response system and is one seat of emotions, the monitor of danger, the judge of what is pleasurable or scary, and it decides what is important for survival.[14] These mechanisms keep us safe. Memory formation and memory integration occur in the limbic circuits. It also has as tasks motivation, olfaction, sensory processing, attention, time perception, instincts and motor actions. We must be able to run from danger!

Many adoptees with early histories of trauma have limbic circuitry that is always on red alert. Threats—real or perceived—are everywhere to these boys and girls! From the brain's—child's—view, past trauma could occur again any moment. Joining a new family, trusting a new family, embracing learning, being curious and motivated, seeking fun and so on are dampened by the need to be in a chronic state of alarm—survival mode! Growth is immobilized because new experiences cannot be embraced and integrated into daily life! Children with histories of trauma remind me of deer. I am from Pennsylvania where deer are plentiful. They are hunted at a designated time of year, causing them to be wary of their environment. The snap of a twig can send the herd running off!

The limbic circuitry is comprised of various structures. For example, the thalamus takes in and distributes sensory information. We become aware of what is going on around us. The hippocampus, the seat of memory, compares our current experience of what is happening to past experiences. The amygdala, a para-limbic structure, decides whether the current situation is a danger. We've all had the experience of burning a pot on the stovetop. We smell burning or there may even be smoke. Our breathing, blood pressure and heart rate increase! Hormones like cortisol and adrenaline are released! The autonomic nervous system is now primed and prepares us for flight, fight or freeze. We think there is a fire! Some of us grabbed the pot without a potholder—fight! Ouch! Some of us arrived in the kitchen and took on a deer in the headlights look—freeze and flight. We simply couldn't act.

Trauma increases the risk of interpreting whether a situation is dangerous or safe.[15] Traumatized children think "fire" most often. Extreme exposure to toxic stress alters the stress response system. It responds to events that might not be stressful to others. The stress response system activates more frequently and for longer periods than is necessary, like revving a car engine for hours every day.[16] In order to get along with others, you must be able to gauge whether their intentions are benign or dangerous.[17]

> **Pete**, now 15 years old, was adopted when he was 2½ from a South American orphanage. Each time his adoptive parents asked him to complete a chore, he became extremely defensive, disrespectful and argumentative. His face reddened. Eventually he stomped to his room and slammed his door. His parents, Marsha and Bob, were beside themselves! This pattern of behavior had been going on for years. Pete agreed to make a drawing of what he thought life was like in his orphanage. These were the only directions he was given. Figure 3.1 shows his drawing, which makes clear that Pete felt "all alone" and that the institution was an environment in which it was "me vs. everybody." "Everybody" is the orphanage staff. Pete, to this day, continues to act as if it is Pete against Marsha and Bob. Pete was physically removed from his orphanage. Psychologically, his amygdala hijacks his brain in his day-to-day encounters with adults. He feels at battle with adults. His response is "fight."

Figure 3.1: "All alone. Me vs. everybody. Why?"

The limbic system, which is designed to help us cope in our social relationships and our environment, often does the opposite for children exposed to early childhood trauma. Children and teens live in the throes of a stress response system on red alert. They have no sense of time passing or of a past at all. It is as if the abuse/abandonment could happen again at only a moment's notice.[18]

The Intelligent, Calming Frontal Lobes

The frontal lobes develop slowly over time—through our infancy, pre-school years, school-age years and into our twenties, and their development is influenced by the quality or lack of quality of interactions between infants and parents. The frontal lobes are an exciting place in the brain. With frontal lobe functioning we can plan anything, and we can design the steps to execute our plans. We have abstract thinking. We can use language—we can communicate as a group! We can predict the positive or negative outcomes of our decisions. We can decide whether to take the action. We have choice! We can absorb information, assign it meaning, form opinions and alter our opinions as we receive new information. We can go to school, sit still and learn about all kinds of subjects. We have creativity. We develop hobbies. We learn to structure our time to carry out responsibilities like work, grocery shopping, homework, dance practice and so on. We also make downtime plans to relax, to pursue a hobby or to volunteer on behalf of a cause. We enjoy getting together with friends and family. We seek to relate and to be social. We have empathy. We can put ourselves in other's people's shoes to see how they feel. We learn to make decisions in relation to others. We avoid hurting other's feelings. We comfort folks going through hard times, and we celebrate their joyous times. We can reflect on ourselves as well as we can understand the beliefs and intentions of others. We get along better with others when we can gauge their intentions as benign.[19] We can simulate scenarios. We can see ourselves attending a birthday party or a job interview. We can imagine how interactions with the other party goers or the interviewer might play out. This is referred to as theory of mind, and it leads to the ability to successfully navigate social interactions—social cognition. We begin to see ourselves functioning in the future perhaps as a nurse, a doctor, a wife, a husband, a mother or a father. The frontal lobes offer us infinite possibilities!

The frontal lobes also play a primary role in emotional regulation. Right frontal brain structures help us manage our emotions. The right hemisphere of the brain develops over the first 1–18 months of life. The emergence of language, at about 18 months old signals the left hemisphere coming online.[20] We can now use words to describe our thoughts and feelings. Language allows children to grow out of having angry outbursts—the "terrible twos"! Learning to calm the intensity of one's feelings is a process that starts in infancy. As a baby's cries are consistently met by a loving parent providing a warm bottle, a clean diaper, lullabies or soothing talk and rocking, the infant calms. Eventually, the skill of calming is transferred from mother to child. The youngster develops the ability to calm himself.

Many children arrive in their adoptive families lacking the type of nurturing experiences that build a healthy brain. Brain wiring requires an intricate dance between nature and nurture.[21] So, the adoptee's reactive limbic system prevents emotional regulation. These kids are prone to emotional dysregulation! Trauma intrudes on their daily life and freeze, flight, or fight prevails.

Our frontal brain structures like the anterior cingulate, the insula, the right and left frontal and pre-frontal cortexes and the medial pre-frontal cortex(MPFC), which is our main "watchtower,"[22] have the capacity to quell the over-reactivity of the amygdala. These structures turn on and help us remain calm. We turn the stove off and maybe move the pot to the sink. *Trauma renders the frontal inhibitory capacities of the brain ineffective. So, the stress response system remains dominant.*

A final concept covered in this segment is that the dorsolateral pre-frontal cortex (DLPFC) is the "timekeeper" of the brain. Summarizing from *The Body Keeps the Score* by Bessel van der Kolk:

> The DLPFC tells us how our present experience relates to the past and how it may affect the future—you can think of it as the timekeeper of the brain. Knowing that whatever is happening is finite and will sooner or later come to an end makes most experiences tolerable. The opposite is also true—situations become intolerable if they feel interminable. Trauma is the ultimate experience of "this will last forever."[23]

We must help the child with a history of trauma learn that the terrible events she experienced belong to the past:

> **Marie** came to my office with her parents, Amber and Mike, when she was 14 years old. Marie was placed with Amber and Mike as a foster child at age 4. They adopted her at age 6. Marie had displayed an array of negative behavior over the years. After asking a few basic questions designed to get acquainted, I asked Marie how she came to live with this family. She responded, "Oh, I am only living with these people until my birth mom comes back. She went to the hospital. But, she told me she'd be back for me." Amber and Mike were stunned by Marie's statements. Overall, Marie was correct. Her birth mother had gone to the hospital—ten years ago! Marie was removed from her birth parents' home—at age 4—due to an incident of domestic violence during which the birth mother was injured. From the ambulance gurney, she reportedly yelled to Marie and her three siblings that she would "come and get them" after she "got all fixed up." Marie and her three siblings were taken to social services. Marie sat at social services as—one by one—each brother and sister was picked up by a different family. Marie was the last to get a home that day. She went home with Amber and Mike.
>
> Ten years later, she was still convinced that her birth mother would return. Overwhelmed, Marie had no ability to make sense of what had happened to her. She remained totally stuck, unable to allow herself to move beyond that day. The grief of losing her birth mother, birth father and three younger siblings was too much to even think about. Can you use your empathy to think about what this day was like for Marie?

I meet many younger and older children like Marie. It is easier to believe that you are "going back" than to believe you have lost everyone you knew even if the care you received was abusive and/or neglectful. Each of these children misses so much living in this state of "stuckness." The warm feelings that go along with close family connections escape the adoptee with an early history of trauma. So, each member of the adoptive family is short-changed.

Fortunately, knowing that the brain develops in the bottom to top manner allows us to design interventions that help the adopted child achieve posttraumatic growth. Knowing how trauma affects various brain structures creates the opportunity to develop approaches that can improve the overall functioning of the brain. We can help the brain work better bottom-up or top-down.

The Ins and Outs of the Brain

Is the Input System up to Speed?

Earlier I noted that the brain takes in sensory information each day. We can feel the difference between sandpaper and denim. We can smell bread baking or burgers grilling. When we hear the teacher start to talk, we attend. A bee stings! Lotion soothes. A friend looks sad, so we offer a hug and a kind word. A car pulls out in front of us; we swerve instantly to avoid an accident. Our sensory input—our input system—guides us through all our interactions each day!

We think of the brain as chemical and electrical. The electrical nature of the brain leads to how well our brain processes the sensory input. Various wave forms—Delta, Theta, Alpha, Beta and Gamma contribute to optimal mental functioning. Each has a unique purpose, shape and speed—slower or faster depending on the tasks it contributes to.

For example, Delta is a slower energy. Delta helps with physical growth and restoration. It plays a role in complex problem-solving.[24] In our work at our office, most children and teens present with excess Delta. An imbalance of Delta leads to sleep disturbance, poor impulse control and poor judgement.[25] Delta waves are also involved with the ability to integrate and "let go of" things.[26] This slower wave form inhibits a child's ability to be group minded. The focus is internal, "offline." Learning disabilities may result.

Theta, when normal, promotes learning, memory, creativity and intuition. Theta is a state between sleeping and waking—a daydream-like or spacey or fantasy-prone place. Theta is dominant when kids are entering the preschool ages of 2–5. This is the time of imaginary play and imaginary friends. We all daydream and this often offers a fun mental break. I notice that traumatized children too frequently space out when Delta and Theta are excessive. Trauma is more tolerable when the brain escapes to a place of fantasy. Eleven-year-old Susan stated in a therapy session that she imagined a world of unicorns when her birth parents engaged in domestic violence. The unicorns were "pink and pretty" and they made her feel less "alone." Theta—in imbalance—can make it difficult to control attention, behavior and emotions.[27] Excess Theta makes it impossible to mature.

Alpha is associated with a calm, relaxed and alert state. In this state, you can move quickly and efficiently to accomplish the task at hand. Alpha is one of the brain's most important frequencies for learning, using information and seeing the world positively. Rarely has there been a client at our office who has efficient Alpha. Most present with Alpha deficit. There are some with excess Alpha. Whether too much or too little, the array of problems can include depression, rumination—repetitively thinking about a situation, defiance, agitation, fatigue, anxiety, poor retention of information and drug and alcohol problems. Alcohol and marijuana increase Alpha waves and thus offer good feelings for those with too little Alpha.[28]

Alpha is the "dominant" frequency. It is a like a drum beating out a rhythm. It keeps a pace or a speed that allows the brain to constantly sample the sensory input and turn it around into output. This is processing speed. Processing speed is the time it takes to receive information and formulate a response with reasonable accuracy—to output information. Processing speed increases 1 hertz (Hz) per year through age 10.[29] A processing speed of "10Hz" is preferred by age 10.[30] Figure 3.2 shows the processing speed of a 15-year-old youth. He is a client at our office. His processing speed reflects one pattern we often see. The numbers reflect his processing speed from frontal brain areas, to central brain areas and then to brain areas located at the back of the head. A processing speed of "7" is too slow. The areas that are functioning slowly are immature. They view the world like a "young" child. The areas registering a "12" or "13" are too fast. Whether too slow or too fast, errors are made interpreting incoming sensory information. These errors impair academic learning, the ability to maintain a positive mood and the ability to get along socially. Can you imagine if the tires on your car each rotated at a different speed? It would be very hard to get anywhere! Trauma skews the way the brain can utilize its energy.

Earlier I mentioned white matter and the process of myelination. The brain exposed to early trauma is comprised of less white (and gray) matter. The myelin sheath that speeds up communication between neurons is deficient. This brain dominated by a slower energy spectrum can't get up to speed and neither can the brain that can't carry out the process of myelination. Myelination is a sign of brain maturity.

	Site	Overall	7-14 Hz
▶	01: DorsoL	2.125	7
	02: DorsoR	2.125	7
	03: Broca	2	7
	04: Orbital L	2.125	7
	05: Orbital R	2	7
	06: Cing L	2.375	7
	07: Cing R	2.25	7
	08: Motor L	2.125	7
	09: Motor R	2.125	12.5
	10: Somato L	2.25	12.125
	11: Somato R	2	12.125
	12: Audit L	22.625	12.125
	13: Audit R	2.125	13.875
	14: VisTemp	2	12.125
	15: VisTemp	2.125	13.875
	16: VisPar L	2	12.25
	17: VisPar R	1.875	12.125
	18: VisOcc L	2	12
	19: VisOcc R	1.875	11.875
✳			

Figure 3.2: Processing speed (far right column) of 15-year-old boy as described in the section above.

As you view the chart, keep in mind that the frontal brain areas are too slow. Let's recall what we learned about the front of the brain earlier in this chapter. It is key to emotional regulation—it helps us switch off the limbic system. It helps us with our cognitive control—selecting behaviors that accomplish our goals. It encourages our social cognition—perceiving, attending to, remembering, thinking about and making sense of the people in our social world.[31] Many of the frontal tasks are referred to as executive functions and fall into categories like:

- **Working memory**, which helps us hold onto information long enough to use it. For example, you realize leaving the house that you forgot your grocery list. You think you can remember the items on the list so, you proceed without the list. Once at the grocery store, you realize that you can't recall all the things you need. In a classroom, kids must remember sounds long enough to sound out a word. They need to remember the steps to solve a math problem and what numbers to plug into each step. Problems with working memory make this hard! Following a three- or four-part set of instructions likely isn't going to happen. Executive function keeps us from being impulsive!

- **Cognitive flexibility** also comes from executive function. Daily, we must be able to prioritize and re-prioritize our tasks. We need to learn new perspectives and new ways to solve problems.
- **Inhibitory control**, which is being able to process thoughts and responses. "I'd like to eat the cookies Mom just finished baking for the church bake sale—but, I won't! This would make Mom mad! These cookies are for a fundraiser. I can eat a different snack."

Skills specifically associated with executive functions include:

- Making plans and following through with the tasks needed to carry out the plans.
- Reasoning.
- Recognizing the positive and negative actions of our decisions; taking the steps necessary to avoid undesirable consequences.
- Planning for the future.
- Setting goals and completing the steps needed to achieve the goal.
- Managing time.
- Being able to cope with changes in routine; being able to transition from one task to another.
- Filling our unstructured time wisely.
- Shifting our focus to the task at hand.
- Telling a story concisely from beginning to end.
- Frequently, I hear comments like, "He is so lazy!" "He is so smart! He just won't apply himself." "She knows the 'right' thing to do. She just won't do it." Parents and professionals alike need to re-think these notions. It is not easy to move along in life when your

fore-brain will not get up to speed! The more primitive areas of the brain are racing along at "12" and "13"—like back-seat drivers—these structures cannot put on the brakes. Impulsivity, flawed logic, poor decisions and so on are steering this youngster down a troubled path! Trauma residue is not a good passenger to have on board any child's, tween's or teen's life journey!

If you are doing work that demands that you use your brain, then Beta is the frequency you need to concentrate, to be focused and to be alert. The three Rs—reading, writing and arithmetic—go better with Beta. Beta helps us solve problems, use our judgement and make decisions. Beta helps us engage with others and the world around us. Excess higher frequency Beta leads to an inability to calm oneself emotionally—flight and fight prevail. Boys and girls are hypervigilant, anxious and always scanning the environment for danger. Beta is important to working memory.

Excess Beta can also be reflective of muscle tension. When the body is stressed, muscles tense up. Muscle tension is almost a reflex reaction to stress—the body's way of guarding against injury and pain. Chronic stress causes the muscles in the body to be in a constant state of guardedness. When muscles are taut and tense for long periods of time, this can promote stress-related disorders like tension or migraine headaches.[32] We certainly see few kids who can genuinely relax their neck and shoulders at our office. Again, like deer, traumatized children are always threat-ready.

Gamma is the frequency that is currently of interest. Research is needed to help understand the role of Gamma in this population.

Can We Talk? Communication Among Brain Sites

Brain areas like those mentioned in this chapter—medial pre-frontal cortex, anterior cingulate, insula, etc.—perform functions unique to them. They also carry out tasks jointly, or they are involved with several other brain sites as part of a network. Trauma leads to some areas communicating together too slowly or the areas talking excessively, "hypo-connectivity" and "hyper-connectivity," respectively. When there is hyper-connectivity, a greater than normal number of brain areas are activated at one time. Vice versa, when there is hypo-connectivity, fewer numbers of sites turn on. So, sites that are partners or structures that are involved in networks are rendered unable to perform their functions. We'll use our next section to exemplify this concept of connectivity further.

Networks to Tune Into!

The brain is also comprised of networks—multiple brain regions that interact together. The Default Mode Network (DMN) is a network that adoptive parents need to know about. It develops in infancy and through about age 9.[33] So, it too is vulnerable to the impact of adverse experiences. The DMN is most active when we are left to think on our own, undisturbed—when our mind can just wander.[34,35] We get to fantasize, imagine and daydream. We "default" to our own private mental world. In this default state our focus is mostly on ourselves! The areas that comprise the DMN are the "watchtower" we learned about earlier—the MPFC, the anterior and posterior cingulate, the temporal lobes, the precuneus, medial parietal lobes and the temporoparietal junction. These areas house autobiographical memory and are key to developing a sense of self. The mind-wandering generated by the DMN helps us develop our sense of self. We process our past experiences and we integrate our experiences so that we have one continuous sense of self over time.[36] We also use our past experiences to explore and predict future social situations and events. The DMN helps us answer questions like, "Who am I?," "What do I value?," "What is moral?," "What matters to me?" and so on. Via the DMN, we can relate with others. We can see their perspective in relation to ourselves—self-reference.[37]

Trauma can have negative lasting effect on the sense of self. When traumatized kids' brains wander, the DMN is off. The process of defining, "Who am I?" is also off. The connectivity or communication of the parts of the DMN is diminished due to trauma.[38] This youngster can't form accurate beliefs about themselves.[39] This child has less recall of autobiographical memory. This is memory that relates to ourselves, including knowledge of the kind of person we were, are and will be.

Your Attention Please! Networks as a Model of Attention

Networks offer a paradigm regarding the attentional abilities of the brain that develop after adverse experiences. Two other networks are the Salience Network (SN) and the Central Executive Network (CEN.) We can think of the SN as the conductor. The SN—the conductor—pulls us away from our world of fantasy or day-dreaming when something more relevant or urgent needs our attention—the teacher instructs the students to take out their math books. The conductor directs us to depress our DMN, and it guides us to use our CEN—the network involved in learning and memory.[40] With the CEN playing, we can use our cognitive processes to solve tasks or to carry out a goal.[41] We shift from our internal world to attend and focus, like orchestral musicians know when to play and when to be quiet.

This process of shifting networks is confounded for the traumatized brain. For example, emotions contribute to where we focus our attention. We have already learned that the traumatized brain struggles to regulate its emotions. There are brains that go to heightened emotional states quickly! There are brains that are detached or numb of emotions. Repetitive traumatic experiences shut down feelings. The SN conductor, in the brain exposed to early trauma, doesn't always select the most urgent priority as its focus. When you are sad, angry or anxious, are you able to focus on the task at hand?

As a second example, the brain with an early history of trauma will have a harder time shifting from the DMN to the CEN.[42,43] The brain that is affected adversely by trauma wants to stay engaged with the DMN when it needs to solve a problem, be attentive or decide to put something to memory. This failure to turn off the DMN leads to attentional problems and poor performance.[44] So, we now have a network model to help explain why boys and girls struggle to focus post-trauma. We'll learn four ways to influence the brain to attend (and much more) in the upcoming chapter. I think Nate provides a common example of this inability to shift gears—networks—to the task at hand.

Nate arrived in his foster home when he was about 4 years old. Nate witnessed the murder of his younger sibling at the hands of his birth parents—a most horrible atrocity. Nate was adopted by his foster dad, Greg. Over the years that I worked with Greg and Nate, I received many calls from history teachers, gym teachers, lunch room aides, coaches, Sunday school teachers, extended family and so on. No matter what activity Nate was participating in, he chronically relayed the story of his sister's death. In the middle of basketball practice, he interrupted the drill instruction to tell this story. In health class, he interrupted mouth-to-mouth resuscitation to tell this story. Family holiday celebrations were disrupted by Nate telling the story. Nate was stuck in his internal thought process. He simply was so overwhelmed by this experience that his brain could not put itself in any other location. The calls to me were from folks genuinely concerned about how they had reacted to Nate and about how his teammates or classmates had reacted. Certainly, Nate's story is not a tale of familiarity to most.

The trauma of abandonment, of being alone as a baby, being beaten or raped, witnessing horrific violent acts, being moved abruptly, overwhelm children—for years to come. Many are like Nate in that they replay their trauma to all who will listen. Key here is that Nate never actually processed his experiences until he entered services. He never put the trauma in a context that allowed him to develop as a person. He defined himself as a victim of a horrific act of violence. This is the only way he viewed himself. He related to others via this mindset. There are other kids who never mention their thoughts about their trauma. Current research that is focused solely on the adolescent brain shows that the networks "switch out," rather than "on or off."[45] When this switching out occurs, traumatic memory is suppressed. If your adopted arrival never talks about his early childhood, this may be why. It isn't that he has resolved it or that he has come to understand his abuse or neglect. His brain isn't allowing him to think about it.

Chapter Summary

- Brain growth starts before birth and is most explosive in the first year of life. Neurons branch out into neural networks. Brain areas communicate with one another facilitating memory, attention, perception, cognition, awareness, thought, language and consciousness. White matter and gray matter facilitate communication in the brain akin to a speeding subway train getting us from one stop to the next. The brain favors and strengthens connections—corridors—most needed by a child in their environment.

- Toxic stress creates a brain that is mapped for red alert. Toxic stress over-sensitizes—carves a corridor in—the brain structures related to fear, anxiety and impulsive responses. Fewer neural connections are devoted to reasoning, planning and behavioral control. The stress response system activates more often and for longer time periods. The traumatized brain develops in an environment in which it needs to survive neglect, abuse and abandonment. It is not always a brain that can direct itself to settle into the calm, loving interactions of the family or the classroom filled with opportunity to learn and make friends.

- Frontal lobes help us to be social—to seek out relationships and to enjoy close connections. They guide our behavioral choices, dampening impulsivity. They are home to our executive functions. We can plan, organize, set goals, envision the future, enjoy free time, pursue education, empathize, experience feelings, form opinions and continue to grow as humans throughout our life-span. The child who arrives in the adoption-built family can't fully appreciate relationships and learning. The frontal lobes won't override the stress response system. He remains on red alert! The quality of life is diminished by early adverse happenings.

- The brain has ins and outs. Incoming sensory information bathes our brain constantly—taste, touch, smell, sight and sound—allows us to interpret the meaning of what is going on around us. We create output—opinions, conversation, ideas, a good grade on a test, a completed science project, an athletic victory or a musical performance. The brain must get up to speed for input and output to flow adequately. The various brain structures need connectivity or communication so that each can perform its tasks. A brain that functions in the Alpha range is a brain that operates like a well-running machine. In Alpha, the brain can accomplish tasks smoothly and efficiently. Slower energy forms tend to dominate the brain exposed to trauma. This makes it hard for the brain to mature and perform as it should.

- The Default Mode Network helps us form our sense of self. Via this network, we can see ourselves in relation to others. It is most active when we are free to let our mind wander. In traumatized individuals, this network turns off when the brain idles. Children, teens and tweens who suffer neglect, abuse, maternal depression, orphanage residence or prenatal maternal stress, lack the capacity to explore themselves. Recall of their experiences is decreased or suppressed. Their identity development is thwarted or skewed negatively.

- The Salience Network and the Central Executive Network offer a paradigm through which to view how the brain prioritizes the tasks to be attended to. The inability of these networks, and the Default Mode Network, to turn on and off as needed creates focus problems for younger and older kids.

Endnotes

1   Frequently Asked Questions About Brain Development. (2017). Zero to Three. https://www.zerotothree.org/resources/series/frequently-asked-questions-about-brain-development

2   Gilmore, J.H., Lin, W., Prastawa, M.W., Looney, C.B., Vetsa, Y.S.K., Knickmeyer, R.C., Evans, D.D., Smith, J.K., Hamer, R.M., Lieberman, J.A., & Gerig, G. (2007). Regional gray matter growth, sexual dimorphism, and cerebral asymmetry in the neonatal brain. *The Journal of Neuroscience, 27*(6), p.1255. doi:10.1523/JNEUROSCI.3339-06.2007

3   Perry, B.D. (2000a). The neuroarcheology of childhood maltreatment: The neurodevelopmental costs of adverse childhood events, pp.1–2. https://pdfs.semanticscholar.org/35bf/24c5d43f42a3c8f5e91b81db933372b54c27.pdf

4   Healy, J.M. (2004). *Your child's growing mind*. New York: Random House, p.20.

5   Arousal: the state of being awake, alert and attentive. Children who have experienced early trauma have difficulty maintaining arousal. They are often over-aroused.

6   van der Kolk, B.A. (2014). *The Body Keeps The Score. Brain, Mind And Body In The Healing Of Trauma*. New York: Penguin Group. p.56.

7   Healy, J.M. (2004). *Your child's growing mind*. New York: Random House, p.17.

8   Ibid., p.19; Perry, B.D. (2004). Maltreatment and the developing child: How early childhood experiences shapes child and culture, p.1. http://www.lfcc.on.ca/mccain/perry1.html

9   Shonkoff, J.P., Boyce, W.T., & McEwen, B.S. (2009). Neuroscience, molecular biology, and the childhood roots of health disparities: Building a new framework for health promotion

and disease prevention. *Journal of the American Medical Association, 301*(21), p.2256. doi:10.1001/jama.2009.754; Zhang, T., Parent, T., Weaver, I., & Meaney, M. J. (2004). Maternal programming of individual differences in defensive responses in the rat. *Annals of the New York Academy of Science, 1032*(1), pp.85–103.

10　Shonkoff, J.P., Boyce, W.T., & McEwen, B.S. (2009). Neuroscience, molecular biology, and the childhood roots of health disparities: Building a new framework for health promotion and disease prevention. *Journal of the American Medical Association, 301*(21), p.2256, doi:10.1001/jama.2009.754; Zhang, T., Parent, T., Weaver, I., & Meaney, M. J. (2004). Maternal programming of individual differences in defensive responses in the rat. *Annals of the New York Academy of Science, 1032*(1), p.97.

11　Davis, E.P. & Thompson, R.A. (2014). Prenatal foundations: Fetal programming of health and development. *Journal of Zero to Three, 33*(4), p.8; Davis, E.P. & Sandman, C.A. (2012). Prenatal psychobiological predictors of anxiety risk in preadolescent children. *Psychoneuroendocrinology, 37*(8), p.1225. doi:10.1016/j.psyneuen.2011.12.016

12　Davis, E.P. & Sandman, C.A. (2012). Prenatal psychobiological predictors of anxiety risk in preadolescent children. *Psychoneuroendocrinology, 37*(8), p.1225. doi: 10.1016/j.psyneuen.2011.12.016

13　National Scientific Council on the Developing Child. (2005/2014). Excessive stress disrupts the architecture of the developing brain: Working paper 3. Updated Edition, p.2. http://www.developingchild.harvard.edu; Shonkoff, J.P., Boyce, W.T., & McEwen, B.S. (2009). Neuroscience, molecular biology, and the childhood roots of health disparities: Building a new framework for health promotion and disease prevention. *Journal of the American Medical Association, 301*(21), p.2256. doi:10.1001/jama.2009.754; Zhang, T., Parent, T., Weaver, I., & Meaney, M. J. (2004). Maternal programming of individual differences in defensive responses in the rat. *Annals of the New York Academy of Science, 1032*(1), p.86.

14　van der Kolk, B.A. (2014). *The body keeps the score. Brain, mind and body in the healing of trauma.* New York: Penguin Group. p.56.

15　*Ibid.*, p.62.

16　National Scientific Council on the Developing Child. (2005/2014). Excessive stress disrupts the architecture of the developing brain: Working paper 3. Updated Edition, p.2. http://www.developingchild.harvard.edu

17　van der Kolk, B.A. (2014). *The Body Keeps The Score. Brain, Mind And Body In The Healing Of Trauma.* New York: Penguin Group. p.62.

18　Fisher, S.F. (2014). *Neurofeedback In The Treatment Of Developmental Trauma: Calming The Fear-Driven Brain.* New York: W.W. Norton & Company. p.64.

19　van der Kolk, B.A. (2014). *The Body Keeps The Score. Brain, Mind And Body In The Healing Of Trauma.* New York: Penguin Group. p.62.

20　Fisher, S.F. (2018, March 11). The Fear Driven Brain [Telephone interview].

21　Eliot, L. (2000). *What's Going On In There?: How The Brain And Mind Develop In The First Five Years Of Life.* New York: Bantam Books. p.29.

22　van der Kolk, B.A. (2014). *The Body Keeps The Score. Brain, Mind And Body In The Healing Of Trauma.* New York: Penguin Group. p.62.

23　*Ibid.*, p.69–70.

24　Lubar, J.F., Angelakis, E., Frederick, J., & Stathopoulou, S. (2001). The role of slow-wave electroencephalographic activity in reading. *Journal of Neurotherapy, 5*(3), p.23.

25　van der Kolk, B.A. (2014). *The body keeps the score. Brain, mind and body in the healing of trauma.* New York: Penguin Group. p.320.

26　Warner, S., Ph.D. (2013). Cheat Sheet for Neurofeedback. p.21. http://www.stresstherapysolutions.com/uploads/STSCheatSheetoftheBrain.pdf

27　*Ibid.*, p.19.

28　Fisher, S.F. (2014). *Neurofeedback in the treatment of developmental trauma: Calming the fear-driven brain.* New York: W.W. Norton & Company. p.198.

29 Fisher, S.F. (2018, March 11). The Fear Driven Brain [Telephone interview].
30 Fisher, S.F. (2014). *Neurofeedback in the treatment of developmental trauma: Calming the fear-driven brain*. New York: W.W. Norton & Company. p.94.
31 Moskowitz, G.B. (2005). *Social cognition: Understanding self and others*. New York: Guilford Press, p.3.
32 American Psychological Association. (n.d.). Stress effects on the body. http://www.apa.org/helpcenter/stress-body.aspx
33 Daniels, J.K., Frewen, P., McKinnon, M.C., & Lanius, R.A. (2011). Default mode alterations in posttraumatic stress disorder related to early-life trauma: A developmental perspective. *Journal of Psychiatry & Neuroscience, 36*(1), pp.56–58. doi:10.1503/jpn.100050
34 Buckner, R.L., Andrews-Hanna, J.R., & Schacter, D.L. (2008). The Brain's Default Network: Anatomy, Function, and Relevance to Disease. *Annals of the New York Academy of Sciences, 1124*(1), p.1. doi:10.1196/annals.1440.011
35 Bluhm, R.L., Williamson, P.C., Osuch, E.A., Frewen, P.A., Stevens, T.K., Boksman, K., . . . Lanius, R.A. (2009). Alterations in default network connectivity in posttraumatic stress disorder related to early-life trauma. *Journal of Psychiatry & Neuroscience, 34*(3), p.188.
36 Lanius, R.A., Frewen, P.A., Tursich, M., Jetly, R., & Mckinnon, M.C. (2015). Restoring large-scale brain networks in PTSD and related disorders: A proposal for neuroscientifically-informed treatment interventions. *European Journal of Psychotraumatology, 6*(1), p.7. doi:10.3402/ejpt.v6.27313
37 *Ibid.*, p.7.
38 Daniels, J.K., McFarlane, A.C., Bluhm, R.L., Moores, K.A., Clark, R., Shaw, M.E., . . . Lanius, R.A. (2010). Switching between executive and default mode networks in posttraumatic stress disorder: Alterations in functional connectivity. *Journal of Psychiatry & Neuroscience, 35*(4), p.259. doi:10.1503/jpn.090010
39 Lanius, R.A., Frewen, P.A., Tursich, M., Jetly, R., & Mckinnon, M.C. (2015). Restoring large-scale brain networks in PTSD and related disorders: A proposal for neuroscientifically-informed treatment interventions. *European Journal of Psychotraumatology, 6*(1), p.6. doi:10.3402/ejpt.v6.27313
40 Menon, V. (2011). Large-scale brain networks and psychopathology: A unifying triple network model. *Trends in Cognitive Sciences, 15*(10), pp.495–496. doi:10.1016/j.tics.2011.08.003
41 *Ibid.*, p.495.
42 Lanius, R.A., Frewen, P.A., Tursich, M., Jetly, R., & Mckinnon, M.C. (2015). Restoring large-scale brain networks in PTSD and related disorders: A proposal for neuroscientifically-informed treatment interventions. *European Journal of Psychotraumatology, 6*(1), p.3. doi:10.3402/ejpt.v6.27313
43 Daniels, J.K., McFarlane, A.C., Bluhm, R.L., Moores, K.A., Clark, R., Shaw, M.E., . . . Lanius, R.A. (2010). Switching between executive and default mode networks in posttraumatic stress disorder: Alterations in functional connectivity. *Journal of Psychiatry & Neuroscience, 35*(4), pp.263–264. doi:10.1503/jpn.090010
44 *Ibid.*, pp.263–264.
45 Patriat, R., Birn, R.M., Keding, T.J., & Herringa, R.J. (2016). Default-mode network abnormalities in pediatric posttraumatic stress disorder. *Journal of the American Academy of Child & Adolescent Psychiatry, 55*(4), pp.325–326. doi:10.1016/j.jaac.2016.01.010

CHAPTER 4

Tips to Re-route the Brain Down New Paths

The brain can learn new ways of communicating and moving information about and in and out. I've selected a few areas for food for thought and four therapies/activities as "tips" to re-route the pathways in the brain. Those selected are based on my familiarity with these methods and/or research supporting their effectiveness. First, some good news!

Good News! You—Mom and Dad—Make a Difference!

Research shows that supportive, responsive relationships with caring adults—formed as early in life as is possible—can prevent or reverse the damaging effects of toxic stress response.[1] You, Mom and Dad, are the best remedy! Know this even on days when it doesn't seem like it!

Today is a Good Day to Get Help!

I mentioned in the Introduction that I wish we would take trauma as seriously as medical diagnoses like cancer, diabetes or cystic fibrosis. Above, the statement includes "as early in life as is possible." We wouldn't wait to see if the child "grows out of" chronic or acute medical conditions. We would seek medical help immediately. Early intervention is key with trauma as well. Even if the help you need is a drive or a flight away, make an appointment today. Those adopting infants and young children, please definitely heed this advice.

Knowledge is Key!

Read! Read! Read some more! Talk with other adoptive parents. Keep learning over time. I can't tell you the number of parents I meet whose child received a diagnosis of Attention-Deficit/Hyperactivity Disorder, Oppositional Defiant Disorder or Disruptive Mood Dysregulation Disorder (Now used for children instead of Bipolar Disorder) and years later the treatment protocol is the same. Yet there is little to no symptom relief. We live in an exciting time for families whose composition is comprised of a child with an early history of complex trauma. There has been an ongoing boom in trauma and neuroscience research for the past decade. It's not slowing down! The more we know, the more we create new approaches. We can add therapies to your existing regime or switch to new services. We can continue to take healing steps forward when we are armed with current knowledge. Leave no reasonable stone unturned in your quest to "grow up" your adoptee. Realize that no matter the age of your child—infant, toddler, preschool-age, school-age youngster, tween or teen—help does exist! Again, the sooner the better. But it's never too late to get started!

Knowledge helps you to be patient on a more regular basis. You learn what is happening in the inner world of a child of trauma. You can more readily learn to accept that the adoptee will likely exhibit actions that you don't like each day. Yet you can be with the child through all the moments of the day. You can determine what your child needs if the day sours. The more you know, the more you can fight the disease—trauma—instead of the child.

Plasticity: The Brain Can Learn and Grow

The brain is plastic. It can learn to strengthen, or to create new abilities.[2] Brain plasticity continues throughout life. The neural networks specialized for learning, in particular, continue to adapt their architecture in response to experience, and they do so throughout the adult years.[3] Even the networks formed during sensitive periods maintain a degree of flexibility. When we speak of sensitive periods, we are referring to the fact that development follows a schedule. We learn to roll over, crawl and walk in a sequence. Most of us complete this sequence by the time we're around 1 year of age. We master certain skills at certain times. Most of our adult conversational language is in place by the time we are 6 years old. It's hard to learn a second language at older ages! The sensitive period has passed. While we can master a second language, it will be harder and may require more effort. The same is true for other skills. They can be acquired, but a greater effort will be expended.

Activities and Therapies that Encourage the Brain to Heal and Grow

Neurofeedback

When you take your child's temperature with a thermometer, you have used a "device" to obtain feedback about your son's or daughter's condition. You can now make choices about a course of treatment—medication, a visit to the family physician, etc. When you weigh yourself, you use a scale. This device signals whether you are at your optimal weight or that perhaps a diet is in order.

Neurofeedback (EEG Biofeedback) obtains information via a device—a computer with specialized software. We can learn how the brain distributes its electrical energy, and we can learn how brain sites communicate. Then, we can provide the brain with feedback so that it can make the best use of its energy as well as help brain sites talk to each other in healthier ways. These sites can then perform their individual functions, their joint functions and their network functions with greater efficiency. We can encourage the brain to process information faster or slower. We can help the brain quell the overreactive stress response system.

A typical neurofeedback session includes placing electrodes on the designated brain sites we wish to influence. Brain activity is monitored on a computer screen. The child is watching Netflix, a DVD or playing a specially designed game on a monitor. When the brain creates an optimal rhythm, it is rewarded with sounds and the movie or game plays normally. When the brain falls out of rhythm, the movie fades or the game stops. The auditory reward slows. The brain will seek to regain an optimal rhythm. The brain sites being trained will eventually learn to enhance their performance—to establish a new pathway—with enough repetition.

We prefer to utilize a QEEG—quantitative electroencephalogram—at the start of the neurofeedback service. I like to think of the QEEG as a GPS. It helps us determine which brain waves are out of balance, which sites need to talk to each other to a greater or lesser degree, how the networks are working and whether the brain is up to speed. The QEEG maps a clear course of neurofeedback protocols. A protocol is akin to a medication. A medication has a name and a dosage. A protocol has a name. For example, if we want to improve the functioning of the Default Mode Network(DMN) we learned about in the previous chapter, we'll train AFZ-PZ. These are the names of the medial pre-frontal cortex and the posterior cingulate—two main hubs of the DMN. We'll ask the brain to make less of the frequencies, 4–7, Theta. This will help mature the brain. We'll also encourage AFZ-PZ to work together in Alpha, the rich energy form needed to process information efficiently.

We offer an in-home model of neurofeedback. Families purchase the software, computer, electrodes and supplies. We teach moms and dads how to operate the software and monitor the brainwaves during each session. Conducting neurofeedback at home allows for greater frequency of neurofeedback sessions. It also makes this service more cost-effective.

Yoga: "May I have the attention of your breath please!"

The autonomic nervous system (ANS) plays a role in preparing the body for "flight, fight and freeze" as I mentioned in the preceding chapter. This is accomplished via the sympathetic nervous system which is one part of the ANS. The parasympathetic nervous system—another part of the ANS—is dubbed "the relaxation response" or "rest and digest" for its role in overseeing the bodily functions like sleep, digestion, blood pressure and heartrate. The parasympathetic nervous system helps us calm down after stressful events. It is important to our psychological and physical well-being. When these two sub-systems of the ANS work in balance we have good heartrate variability (HRV).[4] The way we inhale and exhale—our breathing—influences our HRV.[5] When we have a "good" or "high" HRV, we can respond to incoming information in a calmer manner. We think about a difficult exchange with our wife or boss. We can form a thought-out response, rather than an impulsive, emotional comeback. For those with a poor HRV, overreaction occurs frequently!

John is now age 10. He was recently adopted. Prior to joining his forever family, he experienced physical abuse at the hands of his birth father. He witnessed violent exchanges between his birth parents too. After he was removed from his birth home, he was separated from three siblings. He bounced from foster home to foster home due to his own aggression. His first summer started with his new parents. Vacation Bible School (VBS) was on the agenda. Day one, the staff announced that weekly awards were given to the participants who exhibited kindness. Day three of VBS, John shoved a boy to the ground because he felt this boy took "my magic markers." Supplies were there for all to share. On day five, Friday, John didn't receive an award. His response was to grab the certificates from the four award winners and rip them to pieces! Some kids shrieked! Others ran and hid! John has an overreactive stress response system and a poor HRV—a poor balance between his sympathetic and parasympathetic nervous system. John, like many traumatized kids, has a hard time handling the disappointments and frustrations of life!

Yoga includes learning to gain control over your breathing. With practice, this leads to improving the functioning of the ANS and improved HRV. Reactions of flight, fight and freeze can diminish.

Yoga also includes meditations and body postures. The postures and meditations can help those with histories of trauma feel what is going on in their bodies or notice how different muscles react from pose to pose. There is an ability to become aware of inner sensations. Emotional regulation flows from body awareness.[6] Knowing one's body fosters a sense of what is safe and nourishing. Otherwise, reliance on external regulation—drugs (prescription and non-prescription), alcohol, constant reassurance or complying with the requests of others—prevails.[7]

Samantha was adopted at age 2 after sustaining neglect. She's now 14 years old. She's developed a pattern over the years of saying, "I'm so stupid," each time she receives even a minor correction. Making an error makes Samantha anxious about herself. Her parents, coaches and teachers tend to respond by telling her, "She's a wonderful kid." Then, they list all her virtues. Samantha's way of acting causes her to receive validation that she's okay. Rather than feeling this herself internally, she only knows it when others tell her. This quells her anxiety.

Those with histories of trauma lack body awareness. For example, a former client, now in her twenties, recently called me in a panic. She said, "I feel like I'm walking around with only half my body. I don't know what happened to the other half. I feel like I can't really feel it. I've been clumsy at work and my co-workers are getting annoyed with me. This is giving me more stress." It is common to hear statements like this when working with traumatized youngsters, tweens and teens. Some have bodies that don't stop talking. My colleague sees a teen with a horrific history of sexual and physical abuse. She moans all the time—loudly. She can only talk about her current headache, pain in her leg and stomach ache. It's so sad. She has no friends. Her parents and siblings struggle to be around her too. Like many traumatized children (and adults) each of these young women copes with their experiences and emotions by hiding from them. They can't bring themselves to become aware of what is happening in their inner world. It is too painful, too frightening! Negative symptoms manifest instead.

Once in touch with the body, the traumatized person learns what she feels and why she feels the way she does. This fosters emotional regulation. Body awareness enhances your ability to get to know yourself.[8] We must know what our body needs, what makes us feel better or worse, if we are to know ourselves. If your spouse asks you how you feel, you may reply "tired," "hungry," "tense," "hot" or "relaxed." This is interoception—the ability to take stock of our inner sensations and to feel emotions.[9] We can choose to eat, change clothes or take a nap. We take action that makes us comfortable. Interoception leads to agency—a sense of overseeing one's life and knowing that there are steps we can take to improve our circumstances. Those of you reading this book who live with a traumatized adoptee know that these kids want control! They try to control every situation all day long! I jokingly say that it's like Chinese Water Torture. Drip! Drip! Drip! Parents eventually want to explode! The control your child needs to learn is that of agency. Yoga opens the self-system and with it the possibility of taking control of one's life, rather than stuffing the freshly washed and folded clothing under the bed for the zillionth time! Drip! Ugh!

Seek out yoga instruction to help your adoptee with a history of trauma. Everyone in the family will be able to breathe better when this son, daughter, brother or sister is on the road to recovery.

Let's be Mindful

If you search YouTube, Amazon or Google, you'll see a ton of CDs, videos, apps, coloring books and books that help incorporate being mindful into your family life or a classroom. My favorite children's book about being mindful is, *Sitting Still Like a Frog: Mindfulness Exercises for Kids (and Their Parents)* by Eline Snel (see Resources). This book includes a CD of eleven mindfulness meditations with titles like *Attention to the Breath*, *The Conveyor Belt of Worries*, *Sleep Tight*, *First Aid for Unpleasant Feelings* and the *Pause Button*.

Mindfulness is *living* in the present moment. *Presence* comes when we are attentive, when we are in touch with our experiences in each moment.[10] Mindfulness is like a "pause" button from the hustle and bustle of modern childhood (and parenting)! Kids get to catch their breath and focus on their inner world. Kids learn how to ground themselves. Mindfulness is an approach to help kids cope with feelings, impulses, intrusive thoughts, self-esteem and stress. Mindfulness facilitates qualities like kindness, empathy and compassion.[11]

As in yoga, mindfulness includes attention to the breath. Snel uses a frog analogy. Frogs sit on their lily pad breathing, taking in their surroundings—and then they react. Children can learn to calm down and formulate a response. The frog analogy is so easy to relate to.

Sensory activities are included in being mindful. The senses play a key role in the development of mindful attention.[12] Everything you see, hear, smell, touch and taste you perceive in the moment.[13] Exercises to relax the body and ways to decipher the signals of the body are included. Learning to be mindful, like yoga, facilitates body awareness. What are those knots in your stomach telling you? Why are your shoulders stiff? When we pay more attention to our body, things like feeling full or feeling pain come more into awareness. Do you parent a child who overeats? Do you parent a child who can tolerate intense pain with barely an ouch, yet runs screaming through the house over a hang nail? Do you parent a child who urinates on themselves at older ages? How about kids who don't know they need to go to the bathroom until the very moment they have to go? These are but a few examples of the types of out of kilter sensory issues/lack of body awareness issues that are common to children with histories of trauma.

> **Mary**, age 8, and the neighborhood kids were out having a blast climbing a large oak tree. Mary lost her footing and fell. Right away, her peers noticed that her arm was bleeding, and they thought they could see bone. One girl ran to get Mary's mom. Mary's mom came running! Quickly, she gathered Mary to go to the ER. Mary's arm was broken. Throughout, Mary barely winced. There were no tears. The ER Dr. said repeatedly how she had never seen anyone with a broken bone be so calm!

Over the years, I've had the experience of working with kids who have suffered broken ear drums and complained only of an earache. Or kids with full-blown pneumonia who barely showed any symptoms! The pneumonia came to light when the young man passed out in math class! I've had the experience of hearing a blood curdling scream coming from our waiting room, only to learn this was the result of a papercut! Countless parents have spent small fortunes at the ER or for medical testing because it truly can be difficult to tell when the child is having a genuine medical issue! Mindfulness is one approach to help kids with these types of body unawareness and sensory issues learn to tune in to the signals of their bodies with greater accuracy.

Learning to be mindful is another way to help a traumatized child develop interoception, agency and sense of self. Regarding the latter, meditation improves the insula and the medial pre-frontal cortex—the watchtower—we previously learned about.[14] These brain areas are parts of our self-system, as well as parts of the Default Mode Network. They help us define our self and ourselves in relation to others.

Sitting Still Like a Frog is filled with all kinds of practical and fun exercises to help kids take in all the sensations around them. There are mindfulness activities to identify and deal with emotions—*Your Personal Weather Report*—and much more! Being able to notice our emotions allows for the development of dealing with feelings without yelling, screaming, slamming doors, stomping off, swearing or throwing things. Moms and dads can carry out these activities with all their kids. We easily adapted this book into a six-part group for our school-age, tween and teen clients. Community-based classes are cropping up in cities everywhere. Training programs are available for professionals who wish to offer mindfulness as a service. Schools are reaping benefits by incorporating mindful practices in the classroom.

A growing body of research demonstrates that being mindful reduces stress,[15] anxiety[16] and depression.[17] Quality of sleep improves.[18] The Default Mode Network operates better when mindfulness is utilized.[19] Gray matter increases too.[20] Quality of life and general well-being result when we utilize a mindful approach to daily life.

Improving Sensory Input

Piggy-backing with the above, some children will arrive in the adoptive home with a Sensory Processing Disorder (SPD). In SPD, the brain has a hard time receiving and responding to information that comes in through the senses—sight, sound, touch, taste and smell.[21] The proprioceptive and vestibular senses give us our perceptions of speed, movement, pressure on our joints and muscles, and the position of our bodies.[22] You're using vision to see the words on this page. Your vestibular system is telling you if you are sitting upright or laying down. Your proprioceptive system is helping you decide how much resistance is needed to hold up the book.[23] SPD is chronic and disrupts kids' lives socially, academically, behaviorally and physically. You must gauge the position and speed of a baseball to hit it or catch it. You need to feel heat or cold correctly to dress appropriately for the weather. You need to filter out the humming of fluorescent lights to focus on your spelling words. Playing with other kids on the playground requires tolerating the feel of the sand in the sandbox, or the mud for mud pies.

In her book, *Sensational Kids: Hope and Help for Children with Sensory Processing Disorder*, Lucy Jane Miller describes several forms of SPD. There are those boys and girls who under-respond—exhibit less of a response to sensory information than the situation demands or take longer to react. This is the child who may not recognize the need to go to the bathroom. There is the over-responder—responds to sensory messages more quickly and for a longer time. Children who are over-responsive to touch complain, "You're hurting me!" when getting their hair brushed. Being hugged or held results in being physically pushed away. One adolescent we worked with was always hanging off the back of the couch upside down! There are sensory-seeking children. There is no satisfying the need for sensory input in this subtype of SPD! The quest for sensory input is often in socially unacceptable ways or ways that are unsafe.

Andrew joined his adoptive family as a newborn. He's now age 9 and he loves playing video games. In fact, Andrew will play so intensely that he urinates on himself. He'll arrive at the dinner table soaked in urine. Andrew seems oblivious to the odor. He doesn't mind being wet.

Charlie was adopted as a toddler. Even when he was 16 months old, he licked everything and everyone! If company came over, Charlie wanted to lick their arms and hands. If the family went to a store, Charlie tried to lick the shelves, floor or any items he could reach from the shopping cart. As he aged, licking continued. In Kindergarten, he licked the teacher, his classmates and the classroom walls. If the family dined out, Charlie tried to lick the patrons as the family was seated. If Charlie, now age 11, went to watch his older brother play football, he licked the folks in the stands. He also licked the bleachers. Obviously, this was embarrassing! Charlie's parents and siblings went to less places over time.

Each of the above children (and their families) was helped by SPD treatment. If your child struggles with the feel of their clothing, the texture of foods, transitions, loud noises, knowing the difference between full and hungry, smells being too powerful or distracting, crashing and banging into things, balance, handwriting, messy play materials (finger paint, Play-Doh), an excessive need to spin or swing, licking or chewing non-food items, getting dressed, then your adoptee may be exhibiting signs of SPD. The Resource section includes books and websites that explain this disorder in more detail and offer more expansive symptom checklists. SPD treatment is usually conducted by an Occupational Therapist with specialized training.

Chapter Summary

- Parents are the primary healing resource. They can offset the impact of the toxic stress residue created by trauma. The brain can learn to strengthen itself and to create new abilities due to its plasticity. Yet, it takes more effort to acquire a new skill once sensitive periods have passed. Early intervention is a key, as is ongoing education. The more parents learn about the impact of trauma, the wider their array of parenting and treatment interventions. Leaving no stone unturned in healing the child who arrived via adoption is critical to optimal outcome.

- Like a scale or a thermometer, neurofeedback makes use of a device—a computer with specialized software. Via auditory and visual feedback, the brain is provided with the information it needs to function in healthier ways. The brain can make the best use of its electrical energy. Brain sites can learn to communicate in the rich Alpha wave form needed for processing information efficiently. Thus, brain sites can perform their individual, joint and network tasks. Processing speed improves. The overreactive stress response system is calmed. This neurotherapy can be conducted at home with supervision. Neurofeedback is an efficacious tool to help heal the child with a history of trauma.

- Yoga and mindfulness meditation are activities that utilize attention to the breath. The way we breath influences our heartrate variability. A high or good heartrate variability allows for calm, thoughtful responses in our day-to-day interactions with others. Each contributes to body awareness so that trauma survivors can get to know themselves better. Each improves agency—a sense of overseeing one's life and knowing that there are steps individuals can take to improve their circumstances. Whether your child, tween or teen prefers to sit like a frog or perform postures, these two pursuits improve brain health and much more.

- Sensory Processing Disorder treatment improves the brain's ability to take in sensory input. The better kids can take in the sights, smells, sounds, tastes and feel of the world around them, the better their brain can turn this information into output. Academic learning, relationships, creative pastimes and athletic endeavors are enhanced. Find an Occupational Therapist today who can help your child experience his world in a whole new way!

Endnotes

1   National Scientific Council on the Developing Child. (2005/2014). Excessive stress disrupts the architecture of the developing brain: Working paper 3. Updated Edition, p.4. http://www.developingchild.harvard.edu

2   Merzenich, M. (2013). *Soft-wired: How the New Science of Brain Plasticity can Change Your Life*. San Francisco: Parnassus Publishing, p.9.

3   National Scientific Council on the Developing Child (2007). The timing and quality of early experiences combine to shape brain architecture: Working paper #5, p.4. http://www.developingchild.net

4   van der Kolk, B.A. (2014). *The Body Keeps the Score. Brain, Mind and Body in the Healing of Trauma*. New York: Penguin Group, p.267.

5   *Ibid.*

6   *Ibid.*, p.97.

7   *Ibid.*

8   *Ibid.*, p.273.

9   Mahler, K. (n.d.) What is interoception and how does it affect those with autism? *Autism Awareness Centre*. https://autismawarenesscentre.com/what-is-interoception-and-how-does-it-impact-autism/

10 Snel, E. (2013). *Sitting Still like a Frog: Mindfulness Exercises for Kids (and Their Parents)*. Boston: Shambhala Publications, p.3.

11 *Ibid.*, p.xiv

12 *Ibid.*, p.29.

13 *Ibid.*

14 Jang, J.H., Jung, W.H., Kang, D., Byun, M.S., Kwon, S.J., Choi, C., & Kwon, J.S. (2011). Increased default mode network connectivity associated with meditation. *Neuroscience Letters, 487*(3), p.359. doi:10.1016/j.neulet.2010.10.056

15 Goyal, M., Singh, S., Sibinga, E.M., Gould, N.F., Rowland-Seymour, A., Sharma, R., . . . Haythornthwaite, J.A. (2014). Meditation programs for psychological stress and well-being. *JAMA Internal Medicine, 174*(3), p.364. doi:10.1001/jamainternmed.2013.13018

16 Roemer, L., Orsillo, S., & Salters-Pedneault, K. (2008.) Efficacy of acceptance-based behavioral therapy for generalized anxiety disorder: Evaluation in a randomized controlled trial. *Journal of Consulting and Clinical Psychology, 76*(6), p.1088. doi: 10.1037?a0012720

17   Goyal, M., Singh, S., Sibinga, E.M., Gould, N.F., Rowland-Seymour, A., Sharma, R., . . .
     Haythornthwaite, J.A. (2014). Meditation programs for psychological stress and well-
     being. *JAMA Internal Medicine, 174*(3), p.364. doi:10.1001/jamainternmed.2013.1301
18   Black, D.S., O'Reilly, G.A., Olmstead, R., Breen, E.C., & Irwin, M.R. (2015). Mindfulness
     meditation and improvement in sleep quality and daytime impairment among older
     adults with sleep disturbances. *JAMA Internal Medicine, 175*(4), p.499. doi:10.1001/
     jamainternmed.2014.808
19   Jang, J.H., Jung, W.H., Kang, D., Byun, M.S., Kwon, S.J., Choi, C., & Kwon, J.S. (2011).
     Increased default mode network connectivity associated with meditation. *Neuroscience
     Letters, 487*(3), p.359. doi:10.1016/j.neulet.2010.10.056
20   Hölzel, B.K., Carmody, J., Vangel, M., Congleton, C., Yerramsetti, S.M., Gard, T., & Lazar,
     S.W. (2011). Mindfulness practice leads to increases in regional brain gray matter density.
     Psychiatry Research: Neuroimaging, 191(1), p.41. doi:10.1016/j.pscychresns.2010.08.006
21   WebMD. (n.d.) Sensory Processing Disorder. https://www.webmd.com/children/
     sensory-processing-disorder#1-2
22   Miller, L.J. (2006). *Sensational Kids: Hope and Help for Children with Sensory Processing
     Disorders (SPD)*. New York: Penguin Group, p.5.
23   *Ibid.*

CHAPTER 5

Attachment: Mirroring the Family's Values

There is immense joy when an infant is born to healthy parents. The baby is held, caressed, stroked, rocked, kissed and hugged from the moment of birth. Even during the pregnancy, parents, siblings and extended family members talk to the baby and caress the baby bump! This abundant attention sets in motion a healthy attachment. This loving connection, in turn, is the context for our social, emotional, cognitive, physical and brain development. Our attachment to nurturing parents causes all facets of our human development to grow.

Hugs and kisses continue as children grow in all kinds of situations— before getting on the school bus or while bandaging a boo-boo, snuggling while watching television or reading books, pats on the back for accomplishments, stroking hair as a gesture of affection, and lots of kisses and caresses just out of love!

Via consistent and predictable parental nurture and support—thousands of repetitions of the cycle of needs—these sons and daughters develop a *secure attachment*. The cycle of needs is also referred to as "serve and return."[1] The first signs of attachment appear at age 7–8 months.[2] The sensitive period needed to form enduring attachment to our care giver is 10–12 months to 18 months.[3] The securely attached child trusts his parents to meet his needs, "My parents are always there for me." He feels good about himself, "I am worthwhile." He seeks out his parents when he needs help or comfort, "I can rely on my parents." He has developed the skills to navigate life. He can generate solutions, handle stress, regulate emotions, follow directions and attend to tasks at hand.

He demonstrates empathy and remorse, "I have hurt Mom's feelings. I need to make this right." He strives to have fun. He explores his environment. He seeks parental praise for a job well done, "I want to please my parents." "I want my parents to be pleased with me." He enjoys intimacy. He seeks out companionship, "I want to be around others." He can do all these things within relationships with parents, his brothers and sisters, peers, teachers, coaches, neighbors, etc. He applies his secure model of attachment to all human interactions.

Figure 5.1: Cycle of needs.

In adulthood, this secure attachment will allow him to continue to have close interpersonal relationships. He will feel love and give love. He will understand his past—emotional baggage will not interfere with his capacity to interact in his marriage, with his children, in his career and in his community. All things are possible with a healthy attachment!

Loving, nurturing experiences with our parents create a positive internal working model. This internal working model is a set of beliefs about ourselves, others and the world. It influences our expectations about ourselves, others and the community at large. A securely attached person acquires two main beliefs

"I am a good, worthwhile or valuable person."
"I can trust others. Relationships are safe and fulfilling"

Inopportunely, and as we learned previously, many adoptees arrive in the family having been deprived of *enormous* amounts of emotional and physical nurturing in the weeks, months or years prior to the child's adoption.

Their style of attachment and their ability to navigate relationships reflect their traumatic experiences and is *insecure*. Their internal working model is:

"I am bad, dumb, stupid, or shameful. I am not a lovable person."
"I can't trust others. Relationships are scary, lonely and unrewarding."

Please see below for a description of these insecure attachment styles. Do you recognize your child in these styles of insecure attachment?

Insecure Attachment Styles

Four main styles of insecure attachment develop when a care giver and an infant don't attune well.

Avoidant Attachment

This child's model of relationships is that parents or others are not all that useful in meeting needs. So there is no point in seeking assistance. Connecting is limited; this adoptee refrains from engaging in meaningful interactions. There is little willingness to explore the environment or to play. The desire—early in life—to have an emotional connection was so frustrating that this child learned to tune out to survive the rejecting, neglecting relationship. Family members of children with avoidant attachment commonly report:

- "He never asks for any help."
- "She takes what she wants without asking."
- "He stares when he wants something. He won't ask."
- "She never asks politely. It is always a demand: 'I'm thirsty.'"
- "He is always bored. He can never think of anything to do."
- "She doesn't play."
- "We came home from our birth son's band concert. He didn't even act like he noticed we had been gone."
- "He can be alone in his room so long that we forget he is there."
- "As soon as someone starts talking, she glazes over."

- "He's always where the family isn't. If we're watching a movie, he's in his room. If we're in the front yard cleaning up, he's behind the house."
- "She wanders off when we are shopping, or she walks way ahead of us."

Ambivalent Attachment

This attachment style has two subtypes. One is demonstrated by a child who is anxious or "clingy." This child fears the parent may disappear at any moment. These children display considerable distress when separated from parents, although they often aren't comforted when the parent returns. In fact, the returning care giver may be met with anger and a rejection of their efforts to re-connect with the adoptee. The focus of this child is on the parent. He wants to dominate the parent's time and attention.

Parents of these ambivalently attached children may arrive at therapy saying:

- "I can barely go to the bathroom. She is at the door wondering if I am in there!"
- "We try to go out with friends and he acts so 'bad' the babysitter or our other kids call. We have to return home."
- "She follows me throughout the house. If I turn around, I practically run into her."
- "She can't sleep in her own bed at night. She has to get in bed with us, or we find her on the floor next to our bed."
- "He won't go to sleep until my husband, who works second shift, gets home from work. He has to know we are both in the house before he will go to bed."
- "She can't go to a sleepover."
- "She has to be with us at church. She won't stay in the Sunday school class."
- "She interrupts when any of my other children try to talk with me."
- "If I am trying to help one of the other kids, he'll create such a disturbance that I have to tend to him."

A second type of ambivalent attachment is seen in the child who appears to "push and pull": "I want you." "I don't want you." These children had birthparents or caregivers who exhibited inconsistency in responding to the child's needs; sometimes they were unavailable or unresponsive, and at other times they were intrusive. The care giver misread the child's signals. Thus, internally, this child is uncertain as to his own needs and emotional state. This is a child who may not soothe easily, even when the parent is providing exactly what is necessary to aid in calming the child.

A parent of this type of ambivalently attached child may state:

- "She asks for help with her homework, and when I come to help her she tells me I am doing it wrong. 'That isn't what the teacher said.'"
- "When I have bananas, he doesn't want one. If I don't have a banana, look out, there will be a huge fit."
- "Getting dressed for school is so difficult. We pick out an outfit and a few minutes later it isn't right. He is screaming and shouting that he can't possibly wear the red shirt! It is so hard to help my son and daughter get ready for school with all his chaos."
- "She asks for a hug and when I give it to her, she pinches me or hugs so tight I have to ask her to let go because she is hurting me."
- "We have a great time making brownies, and then she won't eat any with us."

Disorganized Attachment

Disorganized attachment is a mix of the attachment styles discussed above. These children lacked the ability to be soothed by their birthparents because these early care givers were a source of fear—abuse. These children must cope with the loss of their birth parents on top of resolving the terrifying events that most likely led to the separation from the birth parents. Children with disorganized attachment have been found to be the most difficult later in life, with emotional, social and cognitive impairments (Siegel, 1999).

These parents report many of the themes as pointed out in the ambivalent and avoidant attachment descriptions. Yet, these parents also report, "He can do something that just incenses me or his brother. There is a big fight. Then, five minutes later he asks me what we are having for dinner. It's like nothing happened! He can't figure out why we are still angry!" Or, "When one of us is infuriated with him, he smiles. We all struggle to control ourselves! Many abused children utilized smiling or hugging the past perpetrator as a defense against further abuse. They thought, "If my abuser is happy with me, maybe he won't hit me today." When triggered, this coping mechanism appears again in the adoptive family.

Recognizing an Insecure Attachment: Does Your Child Act Like You?

I get lots of calls from folks all around the country. Often, the conversation starts with the mom or dad saying, "We're sure our daughter is attached. She's always giving us hugs." I'm always happy for families when their adopted youngster can give and receive affection. Reciprocal affection is one skill I look at when deciding whether our services are warranted. Yet there are many facets of the child's and family's life that point to an attachment problem.

How Did You Come to Live with Your Family?

Each assessment includes spending a portion of time with the child and the parents together. I want to know how the youngster, tween or teen views his trauma narrative. I want to get a sense of the internal working model. If the child is older than an infant or young toddler, I ask questions like, "How did you come to live in this family?" "Where did you live before this family?" "Why don't you live with your birth family?"

> **Lydia** is 4 years old. She was placed with her aunt and uncle when she was 18 months old due to neglect. Lydia visited her birth mother, at the social services agency, each week for two years! Sometimes her birth mother was present for the visits. Sometimes not. As this is a kinship placement, Lydia sporadically sees her birth mother at family gatherings. Lydia was a bundle of anxiety and sadness! I spent a few minutes getting acquainted with Lydia. Then, I asked her, "Why don't you live with Andrea?"—her

birth mom. She was quick to reply, "I just waiting for her to come back."
Her aunt and uncle were stunned! They had no idea she had thoughts
about Andrea! Empathically, we explained to Lydia that she wasn't going
to live with her birth mom again. She would be living with Mom and Dad
(her aunt and uncle) who had adopted her. Lydia sobbed in Mom's arms
for a long period of time."

It made sense that Lydia thought she would see her birth mother again.
After all, she had been seeing her at visits and family events for two years.
Andrea does keep coming back. Lydia's thoughts about her abandonment
interfere with her attachment to her adoptive family. She needs help
accepting that she can't live with birth mom Andrea again.

Jed was 14 years old when I met with him and his adoptive parents. His
birth mother abandoned him at birth. He resided in an orphanage for
about fourteen months. He was then adopted. When he was age 5, with
little explanation, his adoptive family legally terminated their parental
rights and Jed was adopted for the second time by Dave and Sally. When
I asked Jed, what happened to his first adoptive family he said, "I just
don't know! One day we went on a boat ride and the next day I moved.
Everything seemed so peachy!" He sincerely asked me, "Do you know?"
Nine years had passed since Jed's adoption by Dave and Sally and he
still hadn't processed his earlier experiences. Socially, emotionally and
cognitively, Jed resembled a 5-year-old. If was as if he had barely moved
past this time. Abrupt moves often overwhelm children.

Jed's first family "rehomed" Jed because they felt his behavior was intol-
erable. But Jed had many memories of fun family outings. This mismatch
made it difficult for Jed to resolve this loss. So, he struggled to connect
with Dave and Sally.

We'll be learning more about the trauma narrative in an upcoming
chapter. Here I would like to say that our attachment-adoption-trauma
competent therapy does start at the assessment. Our child clients have a
hard time forming relationships. We don't spend time establishing a trusting relationship with the child client. We want to cultivate an attachment

between mom, dad and their child. We certainly work at a pace we feel the child can manage. Parents are in the room to comfort their child. Children deal with their trauma and grief in the arms of the folks most needed to help them through it—their forever mom and dad.

Is Your Child on "Red Alert"?

I'm interested in the stress response system which we learned about earlier in the book.

Eric was 9 months old when I first met him. He was placed with a foster family upon discharge from the hospital. Circumstances in this foster home led to his second foster home placement at 3 months of age. Eric couldn't settle! If he was on Mom's lap, within minutes he was arching his back and screaming. If he was on Dad's lap, in minutes, he physically started pushing him away. The family spent their time passing Eric back and forth. Toys held no interest! He pushed them around. He didn't inspect them or taste them or have a desire to see what the toy was all about. In fact, the only object that held Eric's interest was the iPad. He could sit and watch a program for about 20 minutes while the family took a breath. Eric had a lot of anxiety about relationships! He couldn't tolerate intimacy or engagement. It was anxiety producing!

Abbie was 18 months old. She arrived in her adoptive family when she was 6-weeks-old. From the start she only wanted Mom. This was initially endearing. As time went on, Abbie continued this pattern. If Dad or Grandma held her, she screamed. If they kept holding her, she became totally enraged and wet with sweat. She gasped for breath. She would bite, slap and kick. If Mom went to the bathroom, she stood outside the bathroom door; she pounded on the door yelling, "Mama!" During the assessment at my office, Mom went to use the restroom. Abbie quickly jumped up and shut my office door. She stood in front of the door blocking Mom from leaving the room. Mom was becoming a captive! Abbie had an ambivalent attachment and an overreactive stress response system.

What is a Typical Day Like?

I like to spend time talking with parents about the child's daily routine, the skills exhibited, the level of compliance, the impact of this child on the family dynamics and the behaviors exhibited. We do have behavioral symptom checklists on our website (see Resources) for children over 5 and under 5. Symptom checklists are one part of a thorough evaluation. If the family is or has been involved with other professionals, I study these reports. In-depth conversation with the parents best helps me get a handle on the age at which the child functions in comparison to the chronological age. I glean how things are going in all environments of the child's life. I get a good picture of how the adoption has impacted the parents, brothers and sisters. Common questions include:

- How are relationships at home? At school? In the community?
- Does the child have genuine friends?
- Does the child play?
- Does the child have interests or hobbies?
- Can he generate solutions to day-to-day problems?
- Can he set a goal and carry out the steps necessary to achieve the goal?
- Is the child lacking motivation or initiative?
- Does the child accept responsibility for his actions?
- Is the child reciprocal? Or, is there little give-and-take?
- Does the child learn from mistakes?
- How does the child sleep?
- What are the eating patterns?
- Is the child able to go on outings with the family successfully?
- Is the child able to participate adequately in family time at home like watching a movie, playing a board game or holiday celebrations?

If assessing an infant or toddler, the questions are tailored to the development tasks of the age group the little one belongs to. In this chapter, I am presenting charts on how empathy and cause-and-effect thinking progress from birth to age 3–5. I'd be looking for whether the baby or toddler is meeting the milestones of development. *I'm using the same charts for preschoolers on up through high school-age kids. The trauma was early.* Other charts yet to come are emotional development/emotional regulation and social skills.

Too often, children are viewed as behavior problems. Too often, parents are blamed for the son's or daughter's poor actions. Behavioral interventions dominate treatment planning. Charts and reward systems are put in place. The view at our office is through a broader lens. Certainly, we want to cease undesirable behaviors. We believe conduct problems stem from the immature development caused by the early trauma. Treatment must advance all aspects of development. We must help children construct an accurate narrative. Revising the youngster's internal working model is critical to the child navigating relationships—and life—successfully. We design and implement therapeutic interventions and parenting tools tailored to lessen the effects of the early traumatic experiences. We help kids determine that compliance works better than defiance. We foster the acceptance of nurture. We encourage fun! Academic learning improves as the process unfolds. The adoptee "grows up." Life for each member of the family improves.

That being said, let's turn our focus to empathy and values. I am very interested in whether the adoptee acts like the parents. I frequently say to parents, "If you aren't lying, stealing, swearing, destroying property or shirking responsibilities, then your child shouldn't be either." Securely attached sons and daughters mirror the values of their parents. They display empathy. They act like their mom and dad. Do you remember a time when you thought to yourself, "My mom would kill me if I did that?" Usually this occurs at some point in our grade-school years. A friend wants us to engage in a behavior that isn't the "right" thing to do. We hear our mom's voice in our head guiding us to make the decent choice. We have internalized the moral code of our parents and we use it as a lifelong guide. I'm 58 years old and I still hear my mother's voice! I'm sure many readers do too.

Empathy: Many Ingredients Necessary!

Insecurely attached children present with delayed moral development. Boy, does this ever upset the equilibrium of the family! Parents want to extend trust to their children. Brothers and sisters expect honest family relations as well. The casual way in which the traumatized adoptee walks into her sister's bedroom and takes her cell phone—and then denies it—can raise a parent's (and sister's) ire in a heartbeat! The daily barrage of such behaviors eventually alters the emotional climate of the home. Trust erodes into suspicion, skepticism and disappointment.

Each time a crying infant is picked up, he learns that his actions produce a reaction—a cause-and-effect. Babies and toddlers are privy to thousands of cause-and-effect experiences! Slapping water makes a splash. Getting soap in the eyes stings! Smiling at mom gets a smile in return. Pushing a ball makes it roll. Dropping a spoon causes an adult to pick it up—repeatedly! Falling down is an "ouchy!"

Trauma reduces the number of cause-and-effect experiences. For example, the infant laying in an orphanage crib is fed on a schedule, not when he is necessarily hungry. There is no connection between food and hunger. Children constrained to car seats or carriers for long periods of time aren't learning that stacking one too many blocks tips them over. Or that shaking a rattle makes a sound. They also don't learn that adults are comforting. These infants inaccurately connect to their bottle as the source of comfort. Many very young and older kids who arrive in families don't play. They flit from toy to toy or scatter play items all about. They never learn that turning the handle makes Jack pop up, or that pushing the orange button makes the lion roar.

Cause-and-effect thinking is necessary to develop problem-solving skills (covered in a subsequent chapter) and to realize that our actions affect others. Learning that our actions affect our mom, dad, siblings and friends, we begin to understand that we can hurt a person's feelings. We experience guilt—regret over a wrongdoing. We can also share another's feelings, and we can provide comfort when a family member or friend is feeling distress. We develop empathy. Today, we encourage kids to put themselves "in someone else's shoes." Linking with others via feelings strengthens our connection to them. Empathy leads to prosocial behavior. Helping, sharing, and comforting or showing concern for others are prosocial behaviors that reflect empathy.

Guilt is different than shame. When a person experiences shame, they feel totally exposed, inferior and degraded.[4] Shame is painful! A person who feels shame is less likely to repair the transgression. Moms, dads, brothers and sisters frequently exclaim, "He never even says he's sorry unless we make him!" The focus is more on the self and that, "I'm not being the person I should be." Guilt is a separation of the individual from the behavior. "I'm a good person. I made a mistake. I need to make reparation." I noted earlier that traumatized boys and girls feel "bad," dumb," "stupid," or "defective." These kids are full of shame! My clinical experience shows that shortly after acts of negative behavior, traumatized adoptees are apt to act like nothing even happened. The family is still stewing over the latest rule infraction and the adopted child is asking, "What's for dinner?" They disconnect from the rule-breaking to avoid the shame. Or, there is misplaced blame:

> **Shanah**, age 15, entered her sister's bedroom—again! This time she took her make-up. When confronted, she stated, "If she didn't leave it on her dresser, I wouldn't have taken it!"

Children who exhibit intense emotional reactions are shown to be low in sympathy and empathy.[5] This makes sense. There is less logic and reasoning in heightened emotional states. This diminishes the capacity to take in and think about information about others—cognitive perspective taking.

It is also important to point out that children with age-appropriate attentional skills demonstrate social competence and prosocial behavior.[6] Vice versa, concentration problems are associated with lower level moral judgement as children grow to teens.[7]

Developmentally, many ingredients need to blend together for a youngster to mature into a moral being. The fixings include cause-and-effect thinking, problem-solving skills, a healthy heaping of guilt and attention, and focus. Saying "I'm sorry. What can I do to make this up to you?" is an intricate recipe when a child arrives with a history of complex trauma. Reflecting the family will take parenting and therapeutic interventions.

Following are the two charts (Table 5.1 and Table 5.2) that go along with the content of this chapter: cause-and-effect thinking and empathy. Both develop early in life. Complex trauma interrupts the progression of these skills. Look over the charts. Ask yourself, has my child accomplished these early developmental milestones? Remember, we want to get an idea of how "young" your adoptee is.

Table 5.1: The development of empathy from birth to age 5

By age 1	By age 2	By ages 3–5
At around 7–8 months of age, children begin to respond to other people's expressions of emotion and appear joyful often.[8] For example: • Establishing a secure, strong, loving attachment to parents leads to the baby feeling accepted and understood. This helps the growing child learn how to accept and understand others as he grows.[9] • One baby cries when another baby is crying. Or, a baby stops playing to observe another child crying. Many moms and dads refer to this as "sympathy crying." It's interesting the number of families who participate in our services who comment that their child continues to exhibit this sympathy crying—well into the teen years. • Beginning to use social referencing, at about 6 months old. This is when a baby will look to a parent to gauge their reaction to a person or situation. For example, a 7-month-old looks carefully at her father as he greets a visitor to their home to see if this new person is good and safe. The parent's response to the visitor influences how the baby responds. Social referencing, or being sensitive to a parent's reaction in new situations, helps the babies understand the world and the people around them.[10]	This is the beginning of taking the perspective of another and recognizing feelings of another. This demonstrates that the child, himself, can express a wide range of emotions.[11] For example: • Many of us have observed a child leading his mother to a crying playmate. He wants to offer his mother to help the playmate feel better. • Many of us have the experience of being patted by an older toddler. This is an effort to make us feel better when the toddler thinks we are sad or upset. • The child may give a special toy that comforts him to his mom if she is sad or upset. • The ability to express guilt increases from 14 to 24 months,[12] and remorse increases from 14 to 18 months and 30 to 40 months.[13] • By age 2, pretend play begins to take off. This type of play is interactive, requiring playing with others. It includes scenarios. One child is the patient and the other the doctor. The doctor says, "How do you feel?" This leads to social skills and greater understanding of the thoughts and feelings of others.	Children age 3 are still learning to be sensitive to the feelings of others. A classic example is noticing that someone has a large nose. The child says this out loud, much to the parent's dismay. But, at times, there is also observing feelings correctly. One child is smiling petting a dog, and another child says, "She is happy petting the dog." For example: • Discomfort about wrongdoing, apologizing, compliance with standards of conduct and concern about other's wrongdoing increase from 21 to 33 months and 34 to 46 months.[14] • The child may want to kiss a boo-boo for a parent, sibling or friend. A friend says he has a stomach ache and the child pats the stomach. Or, the child may punch the stomach much to the dismay of adults.[15] Again, kids are still learning to make logical connections at this age, and still learning the feelings of others. • The child has words now and may say things like, "It's okay." The child may say, "Bobby is sad because Jimmy took his snack." • Kids also recognize the feelings of characters in books, and they like to point the feelings out. • Kids will take the initiative to come and get an adult when a child has fallen or has injured himself.

cont.

By age 1	By age 2	By ages 3–5
		• By age 4, the child makes connections by watching parental actions and reactions. Dad helps elderly neighbor with her lawn. The child thinks, "I need to be helpful to older folks." There is emergence of empathy, conscience, and social skills.[16] • Will work with Mom to pull out toys for a play date. Learning that he must think about others' needs and feelings to get along.[17]

Table 5.2: The development of cause-and-effect thinking from birth to age 5

By age 1	By age 2	By ages 3–5
Between 4 and 7 months-old, infants often stumble upon cause-and-effect by accident. They may be kicking their mattress and notice that the crib is shaking or realize that their rattle makes a noise when they hit or wave it. Once children understand that they can cause reactions, they'll continue to experiment with other ways to make things happen.[18] For example: • Each time your baby cries, they learn that a parent comes. This is the beginning of cause-and-effect and sequencing. Sequencing and patterns are important for learning math. • Notices that hitting water makes it splash.	Children learn that their actions manipulate the world and the people around them. Children firmly realize that their actions bring about a predictable response. For example: • By 15 months they are winding the toy up themselves.[19] • Banging on the piano makes noise. This is a great way to get Mom or Dad to come see what the child is doing too! Opening and closing cupboard doors. Taking objects out of the cupboard to play with. Putting things in and out of a box.	At around 36 months of age, children demonstrate an understanding of cause and effect by making predictions about what could happen and reflect upon what caused something to happen.[20] For example: • A child may attempt to build a house. They construct four walls, try to put the roof on, and must adjust the walls for the roof to fit. Here they're learning about cause-and-effect but also about space. One skill leads to development of another.[21] • "Why?" questions appear. Many of these questions appear. Many of these questions are opportunities to help the child determine cause-and-effect.[22]

- Pulls on mobile and learns that it plays music.
- Bangs a spoon on the table, notices the loud sound, and do it again.[23]
- Begins to shake things like keys, lids, plastic cups to discover the interesting sounds such objects make.[24]
- Drops an item on the floor—over and over—to see parent pick the item up.[25] Learns that different objects make different sounds when dropped.
- They may cry deliberately to see if a parent will come.[26]
- Pushing a truck to see the wheels turn.[27]
- By 9 months, they will watch an adult wind up a toy. Playing with the toy until it winds down. The child will look at the toy. They know you did something to make it move or play a song. They'll hand it back to you to wind it again.[28]
- Smile, clap, initiate peek-a-boo or hide to engage the parent to play.[29]
- Put a blanket on their head and pull it off to see if parent acts surprised.
- Infants learn to anticipate cause-and-effect events. If they roll a ball and it makes a family member laugh, they will do this again, anticipating the same reaction. Memory is developing.

- By age 2, makes a room out of blocks and puts a person figure inside. Another person knocks, and the child opens the door—a block—to let the second person figure in.[30]
- Stacks blocks over and over. It will take time to realize that blocks stack best when larger blocks are on the bottom. We have large cardboard blocks in our waiting room at Adoption & Attachment Therapy Partners—they are the most played with toy by kids of all ages!
- Drop different objects from various heights to see how they fall and to hear the noise they make when they land.[31]

- Intense desire to try things out for themself emerges. Kids want to know how everything works.[32]
- Ages 3 to 4 bring a "magical" cause-and-effect. Child sees a person with a broken leg and thinks they can catch this as if it's contagious. Connections are made but aren't always accurate.[33] This is also making a prediction about something that could happen. Parents often facilitate the skill of prediction; for example, when reading to a child Mom asks, "What do you think will happen next?"
- Greater thought about the feelings of others. A 3- to 4-year-old realizes the need to be quiet when the baby is sleeping.
- By ages 4 to 5, pride occurs when children realize they made a good choice—self-esteem is bolstered.[34]
- Begin to accept discipline—better sense of right and wrong. "I'm getting a time-out because I did something wrong."

Chapter Summary

- Forming a secure attachment requires completion of the cycle of needs. Thousands of repetitions of this serve and return occur just in the first two years of the infant's and toddler's life. A secure attachment facilitates healthy physical, cognitive, social, emotional and brain development. Loving, nurturing care givers instill a positive internal working model of relationships as trustworthy and of self as worthwhile. A secure attachment leads to success in relationships—and life—across the life-span.

- The adopted child may struggle to form a secure attachment to his parents and siblings. His past relational model is skewed. He may present with an insecure attachment that is avoidant, ambivalent or disorganized. He fears re-experiencing the pain that comes with the loss of past care givers, birth parents, previous brothers and sisters, orphanage mates, classmates and so on. The family built by adoption won't forge strong connections upon first sight! Navigating satisfying relationships with parents and between brothers and sisters will take time.

- Recognizing an insecure attachment style requires a thorough evaluation. This assessment needs to look at the stress response system, the trauma narrative, the abilities the child exhibits via daily life in all environments, the family dynamics post-adoption and whether the child mirrors mom's and dad's values. A treatment plan tailored to the child's unique developmental needs follows the first meeting. The treatment plan should result in closer connections among all family members and the "growing up" of the adopted child. Quality of life for the parents, siblings and the child who arrived after trauma improves.

- Moral development unfolds over the primary years of life. These skills require many ingredients to come to fruition: cause-and-effect thinking, problem-solving skills, a serving of guilt, and attention and focus. Therapeutic interventions and parenting tools with a broad trauma lens mature the child. The result is a scrumptious mirroring of mom's and dad's values.

Endnotes

1   Center on Developing Child at Harvard University & National Scientific Council on the Developing Child. (2011, September 29). *Three Core Concepts in Early Development: Serve & Return Interaction Shapes Brain Circuitry* [Video file]. https://developingchild.harvard.edu/resources/serve-return-interaction-shapes-brain-circuitry/

2   Schore, A. N. (1994). *Affect Regulation And The Origin Of The Self: The Neurobiology Of Emotional Development*. Hillsdale, NJ: L. Erlbaum, p.97.

3   *Ibid.*

4   Eisenberg, N. (2000). Emotion, regulation, and moral development. *Annual Review of Psychology, 51*(1). doi: 10.1146/annurev.psych.51.1.665, p.667.

5   *Ibid.*, p.678.

6   Ladd, G. W., & Profilet, S. M. (1996). The child behavior scale: A teacher-report measure of young children's aggressive, withdrawn, and prosocial behaviors. *Developmental Psychology, 32*(6), pp.1008–1024, doi:10.1037/0012-1649.32.6.1008, p.1018; Eisenberg, N., Guthrie, I.K., Fabes, R.A., Shepard, S., Losoya, S., Murphy, B., . . . Reiser, M. (2000). Prediction of elementary school children's externalizing problem behaviors from attentional and behavioral regulation and negative emotionality. *Child Development, 71*(5), pp.1367-1382, doi:10.1111/1467-8624.00233, p.1379.

7   Hart, D., Keller, M., Edelstein, W., & Hofmann, V. (1998). Childhood personality influences on social-cognitive development: A longitudinal study. *Journal of Personality and Social Psychology, 74*(5), pp.1278–1289, doi:10.1037/0022-3514.74.5.1278, p.1283.

8   Shelov, S.P., Altmann, T.R., Hannemann, R.E., & Trubo, R. (2014). *Caring for your Baby and Young Child: Birth to Age 5*. New York: Bantam books, p.241.

9   Lerner, C., & Parlakin, R. (2016.) How to help your child develop empathy. *Zero to Three.* https://www.zerotothree.org/resources/5-how-to-help-your-child-develop-empathy

10   *Ibid.*

11   Solms, M. (1997). Book review: affect regulation and the origin of the self: The neurobiology of emotional development. *Journal of the American Psychoanalytic Association, 45*(3). doi:10.1177/00030651970450030302, p.351.

12   Eisenberg, N. (2000). Emotion, regulation, and moral development. *Annual Review of Psychology, 51*(1). doi: 10.1146/annurev.psych.51.1.665, p.679.

13   Stipek, D.J., Gralinski, J.H., & Kopp, C.B. (1990). Self-concept development in the toddler years. *Developmental Psychology, 26*(6), pp.972–977, doi:10.1037//0012-1649.26.6.972, p.974. Eisenberg, N. (2000). Emotion, regulation, and moral development. *Annual Review of Psychology, 51*(1). doi: 10.1146/annurev.psych.51.1.665, p.679.

14   *Ibid.*

15   Kutner, L. (2016). How children develop empathy. *Psych Central.* Retrieved on August 11, 2018, from https://psychcentral.com/lib/how-children-develop-empathy/

16   *Ibid*, p.153.

17   *Ibid.*

18   Shelov, S.P., Altmann, T.R., Hannemann, R.E., & Trubo, R. (2014). *Caring for your Baby and Young Child: Birth to Age 5*. New York: Bantam books, p.236

19   Brazelton, T.B. (2006). *Touchpoints, Birth to 3: Your Child's Emotional and Behavioral Development*. Cambridge, MA: Perseus Books Group, p.158.

20   California Infant/Toddler Learning & Development Foundations. (2018, February 14). Foundation: cause-and-effect. https://www.cde.ca.gov/sp/cd/re/itf09cogdevfdcae.asp

21   Healy, J.M. (2004). *Your Child's Growing Mind: Brain Development and Learning from Birth to Adolescence*. New York: Random House, p.67.

22   Brazelton, T.B., & Sparrow, J.A. (2001). *Touchpoints: Three to Six*. Reading, MA: Perseus Books, p.19.

23   *Ibid.*, p.237.
24   *Ibid.*, pp.236–237.
25   *Ibid.*, p.237.
26   Brazelton, T.B. (2006). *Touchpoints, Birth to 3: Your Child's Emotional and Behavioral Development.* Cambridge, MA: Perseus Books Group, p.92.
27   *Ibid.*, p.127.
28   *Ibid.*, p.144.
29   *Ibid.*, p.126.
30   *Ibid.*, p.181.
31   Ginsburg, H.P., & Opper, S. (1988). *Piaget's Theory of Intellectual Development (3rd edition).* Englewood Cliffs (N.J.): Prentice-Hall, p.56.
32   *Ibid.*, p.20.
33   *Ibid.*, p.129.
34   *Ibid.*

CHAPTER 6

Breaking Out of the Collective

If you are a *Star Trek*, *Next Generation* or *Voyager* fan, you are already familiar with the Borg. The Borg are an alien group of drones linked together in a hive mind known as the Collective. They co-opt the knowledge of other species into the Collective. It's as if they function using one brain. I feel like some adoptive families become like the Borg. There is a chronic use of the parents' brains by the child who arrives after complex trauma.

I believe one of the most important ways to form attachments with children with histories of abuse, abandonment and neglect is to get them to "think, think, think" as Winnie the Pooh says. When kids can think on their own, they are responsible and enjoyable. Thinking kids are pleasant to be around! Thinking kids reflect the family's values.

This requires some more "growing up" of the child whose development is at discord with their chronological age. We don't just want to manage the undesirable behaviors. We want the child to acquire the brain growth and the cognitive, social, emotional and physical development needed to engage in close, connected relationships and to inhibit negative behaviors. We want to help boys and girls mature. We particularly want to influence the sequence of development below. We want to get from cause-and-effect thinking to moral development, see Figure 6.1.

The tips provided in this chapter are designed to help parents reflect on changing their son's or daughter's behavior. Many are top-down interventions. There are many strategies that can be implemented quickly. I am putting forth tools that I think reflect the real world. That is, as teens and young adults enter work, college and marriage, these parenting strategies prepare them for the realities of these endeavors. I would like to reiterate; the parenting tools require parents to make changes long-term. That is, they aren't just an intervention to use two or three times. These are new approaches that you'll use through the healing process. You might like them so much that you keep them permanently!

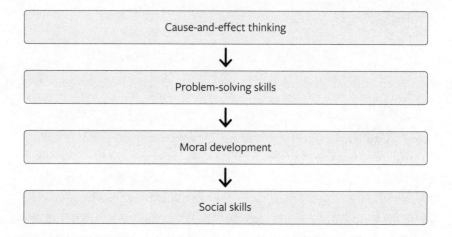

Figure 6.1: A developmental progression of critical skills from cause-and-effect thinking to social skills.

We'll start with some information about what doesn't typically work. Then, we'll move right into new tools. Every parent I meet has made significant effort to improve the behavior of their adopted child. Yet, these moms and dads and their arrival from foster care or a foreign country often wind up locked in patterns of interaction that are frustrating, and that aren't leading to improving behavior or the mood in the home. Parents blame themselves. Parents feel like poor parents or failures. This is not the case. Trauma renders many "normal" parenting techniques ineffective. Parents will need new ways of working with these boys and girls, the same as a child with juvenile diabetes needs a new diet.

What Doesn't Work

No Brain Sharing!
Reminders, warnings, lecture, threats and bribes fall under a category I refer

to as "brain sharing." Parents are doing the thinking for their youngster, and the child is happily allowing this scenario to continue! Right now, take out a piece of paper and a pen. For the next week, jot down the situations in which you caught yourself "brain sharing." Over time, work to help your youngster use his own brain in these instances! Take a "no brain sharing" approach!

Reminders

Reminding the child to carry out his daily chores, daily hygiene routine and homework goes on every day! Mom or dad gets the child through the day. "Brush your teeth!" "Eat your breakfast." "Get your shoes." "Don't forget your back pack." "Get your coat. It's cold." "You don't need long sleeves! It's hot!" "Did you feed the cat?" "Do you have your homework?" "Are you working on your science project?" "Where's your trumpet?" The list is endless! Children developing in an age-appropriate manner, respond to the reminders. Three- and 4-year-old children begin carrying out their own routines with minimal prompts. They also learn that the mailman comes everyday at 11:00am or that Dad arrives home just as Mom is setting the dinner table. They internalize the routines of others in addition to their own schedules. The adoptee simply will not when reminders are provided. Years pass, and Mom and Dad are still saying, "Bring in the garbage cans!" Living in a world of reminders generates anger and frustration for each member of the family. It's difficult to form attachments amid this circumstance.

Lecture

"If I've told him once, I've told him 1000 times...!" Likely, 1001 won't matter either. Children who have experienced trauma have difficulty paying attention. A couple of minutes into a lecture, you've lost her! She's tuned you out! Like Charlie Brown all she's hearing is "wah wa wah wa." Infants, toddlers and preschool-age kids learn about cause-and-effect via experiencing it. There is no action involved—for children—when they're being lectured. There is no experiential learning. Besides, who wants to attach to someone who is lecturing them all the time?

Warnings

Warnings—"The next time you forget your math book, I'm not driving it to the school." What would be wrong with not driving it this time? Parents deliver warnings—chronically! Usually, little action is taken. The child perceives that his parents don't mean what they say. Why would he make changes? Warning puts the onus on the parent. You need to remember what you told your child. Life is stressful and chaotic when a child arrives via adoption. Don't make it harder on yourself. Overall, words with no follow through have no meaning.

Threats

Kenny is 10 years old. He was adopted as an infant. He's been a particularly challenging adoptee. His not getting in the car when the family needs to go someplace and be on time is particularly taxing. Kenny's mother said, "I've told you seven hundred times that I won't drive you to soccer practice if you won't start getting in and out of the car. What aren't you getting?" What Kenny was "getting" was that his mom made a lot of threats that she didn't carry out. He didn't feel like he needed to listen to her. She'd blow off some smoke. He'd get to soccer practice.

Bribes

"If you do a good therapy session today, we'll stop at Chipotle on the way home." This is a common occurrence at our office. Life can't be one bribe after the other. I don't bribe the therapists or the administrative assistants to come to work. No one bribes me to run the office. Bribing usually encourages working for some material reward—a privilege, food, money. I think it robs kids of the intrinsic joy that comes from carrying out daily responsibilities. Besides, many younger and older traumatized children are obsessed with material possessions, sugar and carbohydrates! They don't need more of these things. They need to learn to do things out of a desire to be reciprocal. Putting your plate in the dishwasher makes Mom and Dad happy. When Mom and Dad are glad, good things come your way naturally—not in a contrived way. I would like to see kids work with the end goal being enhanced relationships!

Reward Systems

Once we're past potty training, I'd like to see a decrease in the use of reward systems. I think we reward for lots of things that should simply be expected.

> **Christy**, age 12, was placed in an alternative classroom due to her behaviors of talking out in class, swearing at the teachers, loitering in the hallways and failure to complete assignments. The alternative classroom used a reward system. If Christy managed to decrease her behaviors by 70 percent overall each week, she would earn a trip to Burger King® each Friday.

Would you have a job if you swore at your boss 30 percent of your work week? Why would Burger King® be considered a way to reward any child? How about a nice salad if we think we need to provide a reward? What about all the tweens in the middle school who always talk respectfully to their teachers? These kids don't get a reward at the end of the week.

Certainly, there are times when a company does well and the employer provides a bonus. On a routine basis, folks perform their work tasks and get a paycheck. This is expected. Children do chores and homework because these things are expected. The rewards are happy parents. The rewards are the good feelings that come along with contributing to our family and our home.

Often, boys and girls who suffer trauma make a choice of the reward system. If the prize for good behavior is something they desire, they may work the system for the time required. Yet, upon completion, they most often revert to the undesired behavior. Others blow the reward before it is earned:

> **Candy** is an 8-year-old adoptee. Her dad promised a trip to the zoo if she "behaved" all week. Friday evening, Candy lost it! She threw her dinner plate, had a big fit and hit her mom. The trip to the zoo was cancelled.

I think sometimes the anxiety of holding it together for a week or longer is too great for these children. I think others who are riddled with shame don't believe they deserve good things. So, they find a way to wreck the reward.

The only time I use reward systems is for the moms and dads. I encourage them to make a chart for themselves. Each time they avoid "brain sharing," they get to put a sticker on the chart. If they earn 15 stickers in a month, they get to send themselves a prize. When it arrives in the mail, they can announce, to all their children, that their prize for being such wonderful parents arrived! Give this a try! Have some fun with it!

Removal of Privileges

> **Paul and Barb** parent 13-year-old Peter. Peter was adopted as an infant. Over time he has displayed a wide array of negative behaviors—lying, stealing, ripping holes in his clothing, spitting around the house, rummaging through his classmates' lunches for snacks and always walking around the house with his hoodie up over his head and face. One day, Peter's dad had it! He removed everything from Peter's bedroom except a mattress and dresser. Three months later Peter had made no effort to "earn" his possessions back. Paul and Barb were at a loss. How would they get Peter to "straighten up?"

Many traumatized arrivals feel like they already lost everything important to them—their birth mother, their birth siblings, orphanage mates, a special care giver or foster parent. You can literally take away everything, as in the case of Peter, and there is no motivation to make behavioral change. Please also refer to what we learned about the limbic system. When the limbic system dominates, motivation isn't operational.

> **Renee**, age 14, continued to text peers inappropriately. She was either flirtatious or making rude remarks. Mom removed the cell phone for a week. Then, Mom removed the cell phone for two weeks. Then, Mom removed the cell phone for a month. Renee continued to text in ways that were unsafe or unkind.

Renee lacks cause-and-effect thinking and moral development. She doesn't learn from her mistakes in such short periods of time. Going back to our cause-and-effect development chart, children are about 3 years old before they being to question, "What will happen if I take this action?" Renee doesn't make any predictions about the consequences of her actions. She's too "little" to reflect the values her mom and dad cherish.

If you take an item away, please consider not returning it until your child is developmentally old enough to use it wisely. Some kids are "too young" for the privileges they are given.

Time-Out

Time-out is a way to help toddlers, preschool-age children and young grade-school age children calm down and think about their negative actions. Time-out doesn't always go as planned with adopted little ones. They won't usually sit on the step. They may yell louder once they're anywhere near the step. Mom or Dad start to add minutes. "Okay. That's four minutes now. Do you want five?" "Okay. Five it is." "Okay. Now it's six minutes." Pretty soon, the time-out has been extended to an unreasonable amount of time. The youngster still isn't sitting on the step. I mentioned previously that a child exposed to abuse, abandonment or neglect hasn't learned emotional regulation. So, asking a child to sit down and calm down is not something they may be able to accomplish.

Traumatized children have often been isolated or alone for long periods of time. Time-out is familiar to them. They need to learn how to time-in with a loving mom and dad.

I do strongly encourage time-out for a mom or dad who is on their last nerve. If you are this angry, separate yourself from your child until you are calmer. Then, get back together with your youngster to reconnect, repair and go forward.

Extending Trust and Responsibilities: Maybe Not Such a Good Idea

Parents want to trust their children:

> **Kevin** is 9 years old. He was adopted as a toddler. He is rarely compliant without a lot of prompting and arguing. He lies all the time! This morning, his mom asked him to run down to the basement freezer and get some sausage. Upon his return, Mom asked if he shut the freezer door. He immediately replied "Yes, Mom." Later, Mom went down to the basement to take care of the laundry. There sat the freezer with the door wide open! Mom was livid! Kevin had lied—again. Kevin was irresponsible—again.

Certainly, a freezer full of meat thawing would make any parent angry! Kevin does need to make amends for this situation. Yet, in this case, parents need to be mad at themselves too. If you live with a liar, don't accept their responses as truth. If you live with a thief, don't accept their cry of, "I didn't take it! You always blame me!" Let's go—ourselves—to see if the freezer door is shut, until sons and daughters learn to be honest, trustworthy family members.

> **Nancy** is 12 years old. She was placed with Mike and Jane as an infant. Nancy never cleaned her room on her own. She regularly "forgot" to put her laundry away, to shower and to eat with her mouth closed. The family recently opted to get two kittens to help teach Nancy responsibility. Mike and Jane explained to Nancy that the new pets would be a way for her to demonstrate that she could be responsible. "This is a way for you to show us that you can be trusted. If you take care of the kittens, then we can talk about the cell phone and some of the other things you want", said Mike and Jane. Yet, each day, Nancy required a reminder to feed the kittens and clean the litter box. Mike and Jane found themselves providing more care to the kittens than Jane. Jane seemed not to mind the pets' cries for food and fresh water.

Responsibility is built by completing simple chores and working up to complex tasks. Go ahead and get a pet if you want this addition to your family. A dog, cat, rabbit or bird need care. When youngsters haven't mastered small responsibilities, they most likely won't carry out higher-level duties. Setting them up to be responsible may result in letdown.

The parenting tools above don't work well with children with early histories of trauma because they don't have the developmental underpinnings—the logic, reasoning, cause-and-effect thinking, internalized values—to make the strategy effective. Or, the tool keeps the thinking on the parent, rather than on the child. Nothing happens that leads to learning causality or problem-solving. Some ideas are rendered unworkable because of the child's self-esteem or the fact the child has had exponential losses—"stuff" has no meaning. In other cases, "stuff" has too much meaning! Stuff is more important than people. Trauma—in one way or another—limits the usefulness of traditional disciplinary methods moms and dads make use of to teach kids to function in moral and successful ways.

What Does Work

Keep Expectations in Check

Every day I drive to the office making a mental note that I really can't control the behavior of any of the kids coming to the office. I get my expectations in check. We don't expect a blind person to see. We can't expect a child without cause-and-effect thinking to just "get it." We can't expect a young child, tween or teen with no moral development to say "I'm sorry" in a genuinely remorseful manner any more than a deaf child will hear. Yet, I do know that I have choices about how I respond. Moms and dads have options too! In this section we'll look at some of these alternatives. Please, make expectation checks a part of your daily routine too.

Closing the Divide!

Often, the child with a history of complex trauma creates conflict between her parents. She is kind and respectful to one parent—usually the father (sometimes the mother). The mother experiences a child who is disrespectful and uncooperative. Dad begins to say things to Mom like, "You are too hard on her." "Why don't you lighten up?" "If you would just leave her alone more, she'd be better." Things go downhill from here! This "splitting" leads to serious marital tension!

Splitting can occur because the adopted child feels very let down and hurt by her birth mother. She was supposed to be her "forever mom." She was supposed to protect her and keep her safe." The emotions are vented onto the mother who is present—the adoptive mother.

In therapy, we often need to help Dad understand that Mom is not the problem. If the child had an attachment to Dad, then this child would reflect Dad's values. She would be nice to Mom because Dad would want this. Dad's style of parenting isn't better than Mom's. Dad's relationship with the child isn't better than Mom's. Splitting is the culprit!

If splitting is occurring in your home, please work to repair it. In a two-parent home, it takes both parents working together to attain post-traumatic growth. Marital quality impacts the quality of parent–child relationships. Marital conflict has been associated with the quality of parenting practices and parent–child attachment.[1] This applies to all the parent–child relationships in the family—birth and adoptive, whether having arrived at birth or at an older age! Marital relations can be a source of support for, or can undermine, the parenting role.[2]

It's not uncommon for splitting to occur in places like school too:

> **Eli**, a ninth grader, went from lunch table to lunch table soliciting students for food. Teachers and cafeteria aids noticed this several weeks into the new school year. Many asked Eli why he was asking for food. He replied that he "don't have any." Eventually, the teachers involved the principal. The principal opted to call social services. A social worker made a visit to the home. The cupboards and fridge were full. The investigation went no further. In this case, Eli knew he had plenty to eat at home. He had lived in his adoptive home for ten years. There had never been a food shortage. Eli frequently liked to make people feel he wasn't being cared for. Eli really wanted to go back to his country of origin. He had a strong desire to be reunited with his birth mom. He thought that if he could make his adoptive family look "bad", he might get sent back "home" to Guatemala.

Certainly, relations between this family and the school were strained and remained so for a long time to come.

Post-adoption it's devastating when the splitting causes rifts between the adoptive family and the extended family. It's shocking to moms and dads when they lose the support of their parents and siblings.

> **Daniel and Kate** and their son and daughter, Kyle and Kimberly, went to a water park for a four-day weekend. Kyle and Kimberly are ages 5 and 6 respectively. Extended family came too. In attendance were several aunts and uncles, and Daniel's parents. Kyle enjoyed the water slides very much! Kimberly struggled. She had "meltdowns" each day. This caused a lot of stares from onlookers. Daniel or Kate would take Kimberly back to their room to help her regulate. By day three, Daniel's two sisters said to him, "Why don't you just give her back? Every time we try to have fun she ruins it." Daniel and Kate were upset! Kimberly is their daughter!

> **Dylan and Chelsea** parent 11-year-old Allison plus two teens by birth. If they mention any of Allison's undesirable behaviors, their parents and

siblings immediately start giving advice! "Maybe you should lighten up!" "Maybe you should be tougher!" "All kids do that!" Recently, "Chelsea's sister said, "I think you treat her differently. I don't think she feels as loved as your other girls." Chelsea burst into tears. How could her own sister think this?

Jessica, age 16, visited her grandparents for a few hours. Later that evening, Grandpa called and said that Grandma had misplaced her iPhone. They had been looking all over for it. When Dad hung up, he went straight to Jessica's room and began searching. He found it in her closet stuffed into a coat pocket. Dad drove Jessica to her grandparent's house to return the phone and apologize. Jessica's grandparents have since decided that Jessica isn't welcome at their home. This includes family events that take place at their house.

Certainly, some of our clients maintain the support of family and friends. Yet, these folks are the minority. Many learn to spend time with their relatives in ways that don't cause conflict for themselves. Yet, the emotional pain caused by the family rifts doesn't go away. Trauma is an "invisible" disability. Those who see the child being charming, don't get it. Adoptive moms and dads often wind up isolated. If you find yourself in this situation, please find an online or in-person support group. People who "get it" can be a great asset on this adoption journey.

Six Tips for Extended Family

If you are a relative reading this book:

- Educate yourself to the impact of trauma on children. Reading this book is a great start. Check out the Resources at the end too. Understand that boys or girls with insecure attachment put forth their most extensive array of behavior in the most intimate relationships—those with mom and dad. Relationships are scary. These kids use their behaviors to protect their heart.
- Believe your son, son-in-law, daughter, daughter-in-law, cousin, brother, brother-in-law, sister or sister-in-law. If you never see the behaviors described—believe them! Provide empathy, not advice. You've known these folks a long time! You've seen their

competence and honesty. Show that you know they are good parents!

- Acknowledge that parenting a child with a history of trauma is hard. It's heartbreaking when your child can't do things other kids his age can do. It's painful to be rejected by your own child—every day! Lend an ear. Be a shoulder to cry on.

- Offer a casserole or a few hours of baby-sitting. Gift cards for a house cleaning or lawn mowing service, gas or restaurants that deliver come in handy. Post-adoption, there are a lot of appointments—speech therapy, physical therapy, mental health counseling, psychiatric visits, meetings with teachers and more. Help your sister, brother, daughter or son free up some much-needed time.

- Ask what types of gifts are appropriate for birthdays and Christmas. The child with a history of trauma is "younger" than his age.

- The traumatized adoptee is overwhelmed and overstimulated by holiday shopping and holiday preparation. If you are hosting the holiday celebration, ask if there are any accommodations that can help the youngster manage to get through the event calmly.

- Ask! "What can I do to help you?"

They Have a Ph.D. We Have a Bachelor's Degree

We really aren't ever going to "out control" these kids. They have an advanced degree in control, a Ph.D. We are undergraduates! Their control comes from a need to survive their early life circumstances. There is an underlying anxiety about being re-abandoned, being hungry, being beaten or sexually abused.

Bill lived in an orphanage for the first ten months of his life. He was malnourished when he met his forever family. He's struggled with food issues ever since—he's 15 years old now. His parents have tried everything to keep Bill from gorging. They put the snacks in high cupboards when he was young. He climbed onto the counter and opened the cupboards. They put an alarm on his door at night to keep him from eating while they were sleeping. Bill figured out how to disarm it. They put keypads on the refrigerator and freezer. Bill always found a way to get the combination. Recently, the family created a pantry with a padlock. Bill worked at the lock with various tools until he was able to break the lock.

Sometimes, the more intense we get, the more intense they get. The battle ramps up! More doesn't always lead to less behavior.

Joining In: Let's have Some Fun!
I like to encourage moms and dads to think about having some fun with the barrage of negative behaviors that comes their way more days than not. Yes! Fun! Joining in leads to chuckles. It really makes kids think. Laughter leads to attachment.

Doug, age 8, hates to ask for anything! Rather than ask, he comes and stands in front of his mom and stares at her. What he wants is for her to start asking him what he needs or wants. Instead, she handed him a kumquat, and went about her business. Doug stood there inquisitively. It was obvious he was wondering why on earth his mom had handed him a kumquat? He sat the kumquat back on the kitchen counter and went back to the living room. Mom giggled! This was much better than guessing if he needed a pencil, a snack or help with his homework. A couple of days later, Doug again came and looked at his mom intently. Mom replied, "I do think I look very pretty today. Thanks for noticing." Doug stomped off to the living room! Yet, after another two days, Doug came and said, "Mom could I have some pretzels please?" Bingo! Success! Doug figured out what he needed to do if he wanted something from Mom. He needed to use his words! Mom is becoming a "no brain sharing" mom!

Isabella, age 11, mumbles all the time! No one in her family can understand a word she says! They must keep asking her to repeat herself. One night at dinner, Isabella's parents and four siblings all mumbled throughout the meal. By dinner's end, everyone was laughing—including Isabella.

I noticed one day how many children clients were writing on the waiting room walls. The secretary and I covered one wall with large blank sheets of paper. We put out a bucket of markers. Shortly, we had an entire wall of art work, much of it quite imaginative. The kids have contained their creativity to this wall with paper since. Less scrubbing is nice!

> **Lisa**, age 11, was adopted from the foster care system at age 3. She was removed from her birth parents because of severe neglect. She has always "collected" household items. As a preschooler, this included shoe boxes, little pieces of string and bottle caps. Once she entered Kindergarten, pencils became her object of choice. She would arrive home with five, six or more pencils. Fellow students were always looking for their pencils! This has continued through each grade. Her fifth-grade teacher, Mrs. Baily, a wise woman, purchased an array of pencils after a consultation with Lisa's mom. Each day she gave Lisa several pencils. The pencils were different colors, some were fat, some were skinny, some had animal shaped erasers, and some had messages on them like, "great job." Lisa loved these pencils. She looked forward to getting to school to see what pencils she would receive from Mrs. Baily. This very economical solution ended the disappearance of classmates' pencils. After several months, Lisa, on her own, said, "No thanks, Mrs. Baily. I think I have enough pencils now."

Joining in can be a powerful way to get kids thinking and it's fun! The key to joining in is to be quick about it. Take the action. Move on. The goal is having some fun. Please don't feel the need to interject, "See, how do you like it when we mumble?" "If you would have asked, I would have given you a cookie, not the kumquat." These statements detract from the outcome.

Paradoxical Interventions

These children do like to do the opposite of what you ask! So, go ahead and tell them to do what you know they are going to do anyway. "Please take out the trash. Make sure to have a big fit about it." The facial expression of the child is priceless. There is a pause and then a facial contortion while they think through this. "What? Wait. Did Mom just tell me to have a fit?" Most often, there is no temper tantrum. Paradoxical strategies require the child to hear the request, hear the choices you provided and pick an option. This is a lot of nice thinking! When a good selection is made—win-win.

The rubbish is taken care of quickly and quietly. If a temper outburst does happen, Mom can reply, "Good listening. I did give you that as an option." Win-win again.

Natural and Logical Consequences
Natural and logical consequences have been a staple of the attachment community since the development of attachment-oriented therapy. Natural and logical consequences are the heart of developing cause-and-effect thinking. Yet, they are underutilized. I think there are many reasons why we don't make the most of this valuable parenting tool:

- Many parents comment that, "I can't think of them in the moment." This is true. Natural and logical consequences take practice before they become habit.
- Many others say, "I don't think he would ever figure it out!" Not at first. He won't figure "it" out the first or second time. It may take a hundred or a thousand experiences with causality. It will be worth it. When kids can think about consequences *before* they take an action, lots of behavioral problems melt away. Remember, it takes from birth to age 3 or 4 to lay the foundation for cause-and-effect thinking. These first three years are replete with cause-and-effect experiences. Repairing this skill is going to take time too.
- One dad recently said to me, "If he doesn't have everything he needs for his school day, then I feel like I've failed." I suggested that this man give some thought to this. The job of the parent is to provide the school supplies. The job of the child is to take the supplies to school. The job of the parent is to give their child a toothbrush and toothpaste. The youngster must choose to use these items. In the meantime, apples are nature's toothbrush. Hand your child an apple and say, "I'll be helping you take care of your teeth until you decide to brush regularly."
- Many parents have told me that they just hate the idea of their child "failing." Here we can quote Colin Powell, former Secretary of State, "There are no secrets to success. It's the result of preparation, hard work and learning from failure." I think we've all locked our keys in our car—one time! Mistakes, like this, are good teachers!

I would love to see us view natural and logical consequences positively. I see them as a helpful path to healing. Letting kids experience the consequences of their actions when they are little offsets the consequences that will come with their actions when they are adolescents:

> **Danny** arrived for services at age 16. This was a referral from the juvenile court. Danny had a long history of aggression. As a toddler, he threw things at his mother when he was angry. He never grew out of this pattern of behavior. As he aged, the behavior intensified. He's kicked the doors off the kitchen cupboards, flipped over furniture and he'd shake his fists at his mom. All the while he screamed obscenities and "I hate you!" One day, he did hit his mom and injured her. She called the police. Danny was arrested for domestic violence. Danny had received few consequences for his behavior. Mom and Dad both admitted that they were often afraid of "setting Danny off." Once he calmed down, they let things go. The family "walked on egg shells" around Danny. Via services, the family found the support to hold Danny accountable. He had a decent balance in his bank account. Birthday and Christmas money had added up. Danny and Dad started going to the bank to withdraw the funds needed for the court costs and the gas for trips to therapy. Each time Danny broke something, Danny and Dad went to the bank to withdraw the funds to replace the item. Each time he raised his fist to Mom, life stopped! No rides. No special snacks. No privileges! Within a year, Danny was finding new ways to deal with anger. Eventually, he worked his way out of court involvement.

Many families dealing with violent children follow the path of this family, "walking on eggshells." Instead, we want to implement natural and logical consequences early on. If you are immobilized by this type of behavior, I encourage you to seek professional services. There is help! Most aggressive children can learn to live peacefully in the home. You do not have to live like Danny's family.

I think natural and logical consequences lead to intrinsic good feelings:

> **Elanor** was leaving the office. She forgot to take a book she had brought along—a library book. Her mom emailed me about the book and asked

if I would drop it in the mail as their next appointment was in two weeks. I emailed back that Elanor, age 11, could give me a call and arrange with me how to get the book back. Later that evening Elanor and I had a conversation. She decided that her options were to ask me to mail the book back to her which would cost her an envelope and postage—likely $6 or $7. It was a good size book. Or, she could pick up the book in two weeks and pay the library fine—a nickel a day. She did the math herself and realized it would be cheaper to pay the overdue fine. I was insistent that she let the library know that she would be returning the book late. At the next appointment, Elanor again arrived with another library book. Leaving the office, she, made sure to ask for the left behind book. She also made sure to take the book she brought to this appointment. She smiled at me and proudly said, "I remembered it this time!" Success is nice!

Cumulative small accomplishments lead to being responsible and feeling competent. When you get the hang of natural and logical consequences, I think you'll find them a relief. Mostly, you can sit back and let them occur. They are easy on your brain!

Before I end this segment on natural and logical consequences, I feel I should provide an example for stealing as I know it is one of the most common behaviors. It creates a lot of chaos in the family! Intermixed in this vignette are several natural and logical consequences to help kids stop having "sticky fingers,"

Zoe is 11 years old. She came to live with her forever family just before her second birthday. Zoe's parents and four older sisters fell in love with her instantly. When she was little, they thought it was cute that she took their make-up or jewelry. As she grew, she stole coins off their dressers or money from their purses. She also stole from their friends' wallets. She'd take their devices. She'd take their clothes. She'd hide these things! Chronically, they'd have to look for things. Some items were never located! Fights among the sisters were chronic! Zoe's mom and dad started making Zoe pay for her stealing in various ways. Zoe had the option of doing their chores. After all, her sisters were tired! All that searching for stolen items was exhausting! Zoe had the option of giving them the monetary value of the missing item. Zoe could give them gift cards she received on special occasions.

Sometimes, at the store, Mom would say, "I'd like to buy you that outfit. I think we'll give the money to your sister instead. You owe her for a bracelet." Zoe ordered less expensive menu items. She always ordered water, rather than pop when the family dined out. That saving went to her sisters too. One day, Zoe said to her mom, "I think I want to stop taking things. I don't get to have much fun. I'm always doing chores!" Cha-ching! Zoe was finally making the connection between her behavior and the natural and logical consequences. Indeed, Zoe did cease her stealing.

Natural and logical consequences come from Love and Logic. I've included them in the Resource section of this book. They have books, DVDs and CDs. You can listen to them while you're driving to work or the grocery store. Their speakers are informative and funny! They'll have you cackling! You'll learn the natural and logical consequence for just about any behavior. Jot a few down. Set a goal for implementation. Remember to give yourself a sticker for being a "no brain sharing" parent!

All I'm Askin': Respect!

Respect is a key component to forming and keeping relationships. Truly, children with histories of trauma frequently tend to be very disrespectful! The tone of voice, the insinuation that mom or dad is not very intelligent—goodness! I'm not always certain how there can be a parent–child attachment if the child is consistently rude. I think it happens so much that parents become immune to it. There is so much going on when you have one or more adopted child or a combination of birth, adopted, foster and/or step children. Yet, I want to remind parents that you have the car keys and the money. Gaining respect is important. How about making some statements and following through, "I'll be driving respectful kids to dance class." "All the respectful family members are getting dessert." "I'm only buying snacks for respectful children."

Ignore as Much as You Can

There are many instances in which we can ignore undesirable behavior.

Jeff, age 7, loved to take handfuls of dirt out of his mom's houseplants. Several times per week, little piles of potting soil appeared by each pot.

Mom said nothing. The dabs of dirt got a little bigger. Mom said nothing. She acted like she really didn't even see them. She'd vacuum them up while Jeff was at school. The piles continued to get even bigger. Finally, after about two months, Jeff stopped.

Some kids seek angry reactions. We'll talk more about this in a later chapter. If you can manage not to react to various behaviors, these behaviors fade away. Give this a try. Expect, as in the case of Jeff, that the piles get bigger for a bit of time. Most likely, if you don't say anything, the piles will go away.

"I am working on..."

We must always remember that kids need to know what they're working on. Too often, we only tell them what not to be, rather than what we want them to attain. They need to know, "I am working on being a truth teller." "I am working on being honest." "I am working on being respectful." "I am working on being a peaceful member of the family." These statements reflect the value or quality we want them to develop and display in their interactions with others.

Denise is a very creative mom. Her son, Troy, age 8 is learning to be a peaceful member of the family. Since Troy arrived, the family has lost peace and quiet! Troy loves to play music while watching TV while playing with a toy that makes noise! Troy can't stand silence. In a family of six, no one can relax! Watching a family movie doesn't happen anymore! Troy chatters the whole time! Denise purchased felt peace signs with adhesive backing from the craft store. She displayed them throughout the house. Every room Troy walks through, he is reminded to be peaceful.

Immediate? Not Necessarily

If you're opting to use a consequence, don't stress. It doesn't have to be doled out right now! These kids make life chaotic! You can take the time to wait for you and your youngster to settle. I think when parents pause, there is less chance of a consequence that isn't feasible like, "You're grounded for a month!" You can even say, "I'm going to think about this and get back to you." I often say things out loud to remind myself—mostly—about what

I'm doing. Later today, tomorrow or the day after, you can assign a chore or not. It's my experience that the first task for a mom or dad is getting a grip on their own emotional state. Then, decide about the discipline.

If you do assign a consequence that you wished you didn't, go ahead and change your mind. You are the parent. It's your prerogative! "I've decided that instead of a grounding, I'd rather you help your Mom with the laundry."

Consistent? Not Necessarily Either

Families have mostly consistent routines. Each family member gets up at a set time, eats breakfast, gets dressed and goes off to school or work. As folks arrive back home, chores and school work are completed, dinner is made, clean-up occurs. Kids get to sports. Then, comes the bedtime routine. Grocery shopping, banking, bill paying, repairs, doctor visits, dentist visits—everything gets worked into family calendar. This type of consistency is great.

Consistency in your parenting strategies isn't necessary. Reiterating a point from above, boys and girls with histories of complex trauma see many situations as choices. The child knows if he takes a cookie, Mom will be mad. He views the anger as a small price to pay for a sugary delight. When you mix things up, you interrupt these types of patterns.

So, go ahead, join in today. Put a note in the cookie jar that says, "Take two. Enjoy! Love, Mom and Dad." Ignore tomorrow. Use a natural and logical consequences this morning, and a paradox this afternoon. Inconsistency generates thinking! Kids begin to wonder, "If I take this cookie, what will Mom or Dad do?" You've got a child using his brain—not yours! You've also got a glimmer of moral development! This child is showing concern about you and your reaction!

Congratulations! You're moving at warp speed out of the Collective! Wonderful!

Chapter Summary

- Cultivating closer attachments with adopted sons and daughters means moving away from the Collective to a "no brain sharing" parenting approach. Kids who can "think, think, think" are responsible, enjoyable and reflect the family's values.

- Traditional parenting tools often prove ineffective when a child arrives with a history of abuse, neglect and/or abandonment. Time-out, reminders, warnings, bribes, lecture, threats, removal of privileges and reward systems are no match for trauma residue. Moms and dads are encouraged to let go of feelings of failure and guilt. Your child will heal as you utilize parenting strategies designed to "grow up" the social, emotional, cognitive and brain development.

- Adults can't always make children "behave." Yet, moms and dads can decide how they respond to undesirable behaviors. Recognizing the tools at your disposal increases feelings of competency. Keeping expectations in check helps parents stay focused on their options. Review and revise expectations frequently.

- Splitting occurs between martial partners, school personnel and extended family. Spouses are encouraged to work out their differences, obtaining professional counseling if need be. Parent–child attachment is enhanced when couples parent as a united front. Support is recommended when the adoptive family finds themselves isolated. Online parent groups and in-person groups can be a lifesaver on the adoption journey. People who "get it" offer invaluable insight and validation.

- We must be clear with kids about the values and qualities that we want them to internalize and make use of. Verbal statements such as, "I am working on taking care of my teeth" make clear and concise goals. Visual aides like a picture of a sparkling smile reinforce the objective.

Endnotes

1   Davies, P., & Cummings, E. (1994). Marital conflict and child adjustment: An emotional security hypothesis. *Psychological Bulletin.* 116, p.402. doi: 10.1037/0033-2909.116.3.387.

2   Cowan, C.P., Cowan, P.A., Heming, G., Garrett, E., Coysh, W.S., Curtis-Boles, H. & Boles, A.J. (1985). Transitions to parenthood: His, hers and theirs. *Journal of Family Issues* 6(4). p.476.

CHAPTER 7

Tips to Create Connects

A baby cries. The baby's primary care giver, attends to the baby—a bottle, a clean diaper, comfort, a pacifier and so on. The baby calms. During this process of going from fussy to feeling safe and secure, there is eye contact. There is talking, "You are such a good baby." "What a beautiful girl you are!"

And there is warmth—babies get warm when we hold or swaddle them. Feeding and fragrance are also a part of this very sensory cycle—perhaps we put lotion on the baby. Movement occurs—rocking or bouncing the baby on our knees. Touch is involved every step of the way!

So, when we talk about increasing nurture—forming secure attachments—we are really talking about ways to increase the components of the cycle of needs through the child's senses: eye contact, food, smells, movement, talking and touch. We want to find ways to create "connects"—moments of attachment—with these kids!

The ideas in this chapter are designed to help parents nurture their wounded adoptee. A lack of nurture or the child's inability to accept affection in cases of prenatal substance abuse, for example, contributed to your child's problems. Helping the child accept your hugs, kisses and caresses is an essential key to healing your traumatized child.

Of course, nurturing a traumatized child is no small task. Adoptive parents are being asked to embrace and stroke kids who are quite like porcupines! Their quills—behaviors—rise up, shoot out and penetrate—reject the parents and the siblings—frequently! Yet, nurture is an entitlement.

The types of changes that parents want—and that the family needs to be happier—are likely not going to occur until the adoptee's void of cuddles, tickles and nuzzles is filled! Remember, the child who experienced trauma was robbed of thousands of repetitions of the cycle of needs!

The tips in this chapter are ways to cycle to connects!

Massage, Dance, Singing and More!

> **Evelyn**, age 8, arrived for therapy—brooding! The family didn't stop at McDonald's® before therapy. She was mad! I decided this was a situation for the "ugly remover." Once at a gift shop, I purchased a ceramic lotion jar that is inscribed with "ugly remover." I escorted Evelyn to her mom's lap. Mom and I told her that the ugly remover was very special! It had the power to change her mood—if she was willing. It's a very special prescription that a doctor makes just for kids who come to our office. Intrigued, Evelyn agreed. Mom spread some of the unique lotion on her arm. A small grin appeared. Mom rubbed some on her tummy. Then, decided maybe her toes needed some too. Soon, the grin broadened, and giggles could be heard. The "ugly remover" had worked. Evelyn was happy and connected to her mom!

Earlier in the book, we learned about the brainstem. Bruce Perry, nationally recognized trauma expert, blogged (I'm paraphrasing):

> The brainstem contains powerful associations to rhythmic somatosensory activity created *in utero* and reinforced early in life—like maternal heartbeat. These rhythms equate to a sense of safety. When the child becomes dysregulated, the symptoms first appear in the brainstem. Massage, dancing, singing, running, walking and meditative breathing is rhythmic. They contribute to calming, to connecting and to accessing the frontal brain reasoning and logical functions.[1]

The ugly remover worked because it included Mom's loving, massaging touch. The lotion has a lovely sensory smell and its texture feels good to the skin. A little dab of lotion became a bottom-up brain technique to help Evelyn's stress response system settle. The best part was we created a "connect," rather than a "disconnect." Evelyn and Mom enjoyed a nice moment of being attached.

> **Jackson and James**, 15-year-old twins, were socially and emotionally more like 3-year-olds. They had been a challenge to parent. One day, Mom was genuinely sad about all the little fun things she had missed over the years. Neither of the boys connected to her often. Mostly, they treated Mom like a maid. "Get me a snack." "I need a ride." "Where's my blue shirt?"
>
> She said, "I used to sing nursery rhymes. They never sang along." With that, we looked up "Old Macdonald Had a Farm" on my cell phone. I brought Jackson and James into the room and announced we'd be starting with a song. They moaned and groaned. We persisted. It was a complete disaster. They were unable to get the beat. They couldn't follow the sequence. For the next eight months, we started each therapy session with "Old Macdonald." Finally, we were successful! They sang along nicely. They remembered the animals in order. They tapped their feet rhythmically! They both hugged Mom! Mom was immeasurably happy to have a childhood moment with her boys! They were proud of this accomplishment. Frankly, so was I! Subsequently, the family made it a ritual to sing nursery rhymes on the trip into the office.

Traumatized kids are never too old to experience the simple pleasures of childhood! Often, these small things we take for granted allow for some of the best "connects." Besides, "Old Macdonald" helps with sequencing and memory—two skills that lag in our clients. Rhythm calms the brain. Who knew that a nursery rhyme had so many benefits!

"Music Soothes the Soul"

Piggy-backing from above, isn't this heading true? There is simply nothing like music to connect people to one another, or to raise a down mood. Who doesn't tap a beat on the steering wheel when driving a long distance? Or start singing along with the current top hit or a favorite oldie? Your wedding was accompanied by a special love song. You sing your child to sleep with a favorite lullaby. Even picking up toys is done to the Barney "Clean-Up" song. The iPod rage is another indicator of the pleasure millions of Americans receive from music. PBS has a lovely music education link on their website. They point out that:

- Music helps develop brain areas involved in language and reasoning. Language competence contributes to social skills.
- Children involved in music have larger growth of neural activity than people not in music training.
- There is a link between music and spatial intelligence—the ability to visually and mentally picture things. This is a type of intelligence used in math, engineering, art and architecture.
- Students in elementary schools with superior music education programs scored around 22 percent higher in English and 20 percent higher in math scores on standardized tests, compared to schools with low-quality music programs, regardless of socioeconomic disparities among the schools or school districts.
- Music provides a means of self-expression.
- Performing to an audience in a concert or chorus helps kids conquer fears. They learn that anxiety can be overcome.
- Most importantly music contributes to being disciplined, learning a skill, being part of a group—a chorus or band—and being part of something you can be proud of![2]

This list could go on to fill volumes!

In therapy, I find that even the most difficult children will settle down and gaze intently into their parents' eyes during songs about family and adoption. Some of my clients' favorites are from the CDs: *Do You have a Little Love to Share, Adoption … The Songs You Love, The Spirit of Adoption* and *Same/Same: Songs for Adoptive Families* (see Resources). Steven Curtis Chapman songs such as "When Love Takes You In" are also popular.

On a very bad day, order a pizza and put on some music. The aroma of the pizza wafting through the house, the texture of cheese and sauce and the beat of the music are sure to turn the "disconnect" into a "connect."

Let music bring your whole family closer together!

Direct or Indirect? Quelling Even the Prickliest Porcupine

There are sons and daughters who pull away at even a pat on the shoulder. "Ouch! You're hurting me!" they exclaim! These instances may require *indirect* nurture initially, with the goal being that the child, tween or teen will gradually accept more and more love and affection over time. These strategies still use components of the cycle, yet they can be delivered without the proximity that sends kids into a tailspin!

Indirect nurture can be as simple as:

- A Hershey's Kiss placed on the bed pillow.
- A love note in a lunch box.
- "I love you" written with soap on a mirror.
- Painting fingernails.
- Sprinkling chocolate chips on pancakes.
- Baking cookies.
- Warming mittens in the dryer on a cold school day morning.

These are all indirect ways to begin to increase nurture.

> **Nicole**, age 11, had a habit of writing apology notes and tucking them under her parent's bedroom door. When they awoke, the letter would say "sorry" for the previous day's misdeeds. Mom started writing back. Sometimes Mom commented back on behavior. Sometimes Mom described a reason why she loved Nicole. Other times, Mom congratulated her on an accomplishment like a good grade. In therapy, we pieced all the notes together in a scrap book. When Nicole viewed it with Mom, she said, "Wow! I'm not such a bad kid after all!" She hugged Mom. After this, there was a distinct increase in cuddles and snuggles. An indirect means of nurture fostered a budding attachment.

If you want about a hundred more nurture suggestions, direct and indirect, then look in *Parenting the Hurt Child: Helping Adoptive Families Heal and Grow* by Gregory C. Keck and Regina Kupecky (see Resources). This book provides list after list of ways to nurture children, and they are applicable to *all* children. I'm sure your typically developing sons or daughters would enjoy some extra love!

Theraplay®

The developers of this form of therapy define it as a structured play therapy for children and their parents. Its goal is to enhance attachment, self-esteem, trust in others and joyful engagement. Because of its focus on attachment and relationship development, Theraplay® has been used successfully for many years with adoptive families.[3]

> **Avery**, age 6, was adopted when two years old. He was aggressive. He urinated in the heat registers. He ripped holes in his clothes and mattress. He mumbled. He hated to change his clothes or take a bath. Avery needed to form an attachment to his adoptive parents! Using a finger puppet that looked like a bumble bee, Mom and Dad taught Avery to push away the "bad bees" and let in the "good bees." Mom would say, "Here comes the kicking Mom bee. Should we let him in?" Avery would gently push this bee away. "Here comes the being clean bee. Should we let him in?" Avery would let this bee tickle his neck. He giggled! In this kind, fun manner, Avery was learning which behaviors to embrace and which needed to cease. Avery was having fun with Mom and Dad.
>
> Avery was a little one who would overstimulate easily. So, after six or seven different behaviors, Mom and Dad gave Avery a peck on the cheek. The game ended on a positive note.

> **Sean** was 15 years old. He was adopted at age 3 by Wilma and Andy. He had presented various challenges for 12 years! He especially liked to dismantle things. Anything he could get his hands on was immediately taken apart, because he wanted to "see how it worked." Unfortunately, he lost pieces of items, and so many of his learning projects were ruined. He loved to take batteries. It was difficult to keep a flashlight, the remote control, the other kids' toys and so on operational.
>
> He displayed symptoms of an ambivalent attachment. He hated it

when Mom was out of the house or out of sight. He called her on her cell phone constantly. Even if she didn't answer, he kept calling and leaving messages. When she was home, he followed her everywhere. She had had a shadow for 12 years!

Theraplay was selected as one intervention because Sean so resembled a 3-year-old socially and emotionally. He eagerly participated in the activities. He especially enjoyed a cookie game. He laid across his mom's lap and looked into her eyes. She held an animal cracker, and she provided directions. "I want you to bite off the back feet. Good! Now, bite off the head! Great, you are listening so well!" He giggled and giggled and asked for another cookie and another cookie and yet another cookie!

Children, little to big—sometimes very big—love Theraplay®! Give it a try. Make sure to stock up on the cookies—the other kids will want a turn!

Hugs Shouldn't Hurt Your Body!

Opel, age 9, hugged Mom too hard! She squeezed Mom until it was painful. She'd sometimes put her arms around Mom's neck and placed her body so she was hanging on Mom. Mom had to brace herself or the two would topple over.

Ian would greet his dad by running at him and throwing his arms around him. I do mean throwing! Dad commented, "Before I come in the door, I put my brief case down. I basically have to catch him or he knocks the wind out of me."

Affection isn't supposed to hurt. Parents often say that they don't want to do anything that the child may take as rejection. So, they tolerate hugs and cuddles that are hard on the body. I never accommodate the irrational thinking of the kids. Rather, we want to alter their thoughts to those more "normal."

So, it is okay to stop these types of advances. You can reposition their arms around your neck and say, "I prefer to be hugged this way." We recommend "hug practice" or in the case of Ian, "greeting practice." A few minutes each day, the child practices these skills with their mom and dad. We say to the kids, "You practice baseball. Now, you're practicing greeting your dad. Practice makes perfect!"

Like Drops in Bucket: Connects Add Up!

Vacations, weekend get-aways and day outings are wonderful ways to enjoy quality family time. Yet, the "little things" that parents can do day-to-day add up. Like drops in a bucket, connects accumulate! Soon, the bucket is overflowing with growing fond feelings—attachment is blossoming. I was reminded of this recently when a lengthy power outage occurred in my neighborhood on a day that was sweltering hot. As dusk turned to darkness, a father and son emerged from their house with a jar. Off they went to a field across the street to catch lightening bugs. Soon, about a half dozen families were out searching for the cherished insects! The group was laughing. So much fun was happening! Returning home, one young boy endearingly said to his dad, "This was the best! I love you Dad! When can we do this again?" Don't wait for a power outage. Turn off the game system, put down your phone—take a few minutes to make a connect! Let simple pleasures build bonding in your family!

Chapter Summary

- Nurture is a key element to creating relationships and thriving development. It is acknowledged that the child with a history of trauma rejects parents often—daily in some cases. Yet, love, snuggles and cuddles are an entitlement. Moms and dads are encouraged to find ways to repeat the cycle of needs via its elements of touch, smell, taste, warmth and movement.
- Activities parents have carried out with kids for generations prove to be calming and connecting. Singing songs, a backrub, dancing (plenty of options on YouTube) or taking a stroll all soothe the brainstem. From bottom-up, you can settle your child, turn on logic and reasoning, and make a connect!
- The prickliest porcupines require creativity. Indirect nurture

is suggested. Heart-shaped pancakes or sandwiches, love notes or heart-shaped Post-it® notes strewn about the house, baking or cooking together, pursuing a hobby—all lead to building an attachment. Over time, you'll work up to helping your child accept your hugs and kisses.

- Connects are like drops in a bucket. Drips trickle and soon there is a full stream! Attachment is flowing!

Endnotes

1   Perry, B. (January 31, 2014). Music makes your case. https://attachmentdisorderhealing. com/Music-Perry-1/; Perry, B.D. (April 11, 2014). Rhythm regulates the brain. https:// attachmentdisorderhealing.com/developmental-trauma-3/

2   Brown, L. (n.d.). The benefits of music education. www.pbs.org/parents/education/ music-arts/the-benefits-of-music-education/

3   The Theraplay Institute. (2017). What is theraplay? https://theraplay.org/index.php/ what-is-theraplay-3

CHAPTER 8

Emotional Development: Life with Icebergs

This realm of development includes the ability to identify, express and regulate feelings. This domain also includes learning to delay gratification and developing the capacity to understand the feelings of others. These skills allow us to have successful relationships. Earlier, we looked at the brain from bottom to top. Let's look now from right to left. Trauma renders the left and right sides, or hemispheres, of the brain unable to work in a cooperative manner. This makes life akin to living with an iceberg.

To recap, each time a parent picks up a baby who is wet, hungry or craving attention, the youngster calms. Repetition of this dance—cycle of needs—helps the brain learn the skill of regulating emotions. As kids grow from infants to toddlers to preschoolers and into grade school age, they can express and manage their own feelings. The skill of emotional regulation has transferred from mom and dad to child.

Children with histories of trauma lacked a nurturing adult to lead the dance or to be in *attunement* with them. The orphanage setting, stressful womb life or chaotic birth home wasn't soothing the crying infant with the consistency needed to develop emotional regulatory capacities. In fact, the stress of living in a chaotic and/or neglectful environment creates a brain more vulnerable to stress. The girl or boy arrives in the adoptive family with an overactive stress response system. This is because brain growth is experience dependent. Experience shapes which neural networks get strengthened.[1] If you work out at the gym, the muscles you use most become the strongest and most well-shaped. Early social experiences play a pivotal role in determining which brain structures, behaviors and skills are strengthened over time.[2]

Social experiences during the infant and toddler years will continue to influence the way the brain responds well into the later school years and perhaps beyond. The arrival of an adoptee with a history of maltreatment will require time and effort to help heal and grow. The content of this chapter and the subsequent two chapters of tips are a key piece of the healing of the adopted child. When children can develop emotionally and learn to settle their feelings, they can then implement the rich skills of the pre-frontal cortex described in an earlier chapter.

Without further ado, let's learn what icebergs have to do with traumatized kids and how you can avoid wreckage!

Right Brain, Left Brain: We Need to Talk!

The brain's right and left hemispheres perform differing, yet intertwined, functions. The table shows some of the functions of each side:

Table 8.1: Basic functions of the brain's left and right hemispheres

LEFT	RIGHT
• Generally described as logical, language and linear.	• Generally described as emotional, autobiographical, non-verbal and experiential.
• Puts details in order.	• Processes emotions.
• Linguistic. It puts experiences into words. It expresses logic with words.	• Processes autobiographical memory which is the information you have about yourself. Processes general knowledge of facts about the world.
• Makes sense of feelings and recollections.	
• Wants to know the cause-and-effect relationship.	• It's intuitive. "Gut feelings." "Gut reactions."
• It's linear. It puts things in a sequence.	• It's non-verbal. It responds to facial expressions, eye contact, tone of voice, body postures, gestures
• Analytic—Breaking something down into its part. The IT director is concerned with his department and his role.	• Holistic—"Big picture" thinking. A CEO recognizes how IT contributes to the overall business.
• Mathematics.	• Arts.
• Comes online from 18 to 30 months.	• Dominant from birth to age 3.

The left and right sides of the brain are connected by the corpus callosum. The corpus callosum facilitates the communication between the right and left sides. This ability of the right and left to talk to each other is what allows us to put words—left, with our feelings—right. The logical left side allows us to get perspective—"get a handle on"—right-side emotions. The linear left helps us put an event in order. Step by step, we can recall what happened. We can make sense of the event. Once we have the facts, we can deal with the emotions of the situation. Children who experience abuse and neglect have reduced size of the corpus callosum.[3] Left–right communication is decreased.

Putting top, bottom, left and right together, we have situations in which the stress response system and the right hemisphere dominate interactions. The left hemisphere and the frontal brain regions can't carry out their logical and linear functions. The brain is hijacked! A temper outburst happens. Doors get slammed. Objects get hurled. Arguments ensue! Or, the opposite. Kids shut down. Parents say, "She looks at me like a deer caught in the headlights." "He just sits and stares. He won't respond to me!" The emotions are denied. We call this *emotional dysregulation*. Flight, fight and freeze are descriptors of emotional dysregulation. We refer to this scenario as a lack of integration in the brain.[4] All the brain parts can't come online and work together to help your youngster, tween or teen "calm down," "settle down," "just stop," "get a hold of yourself," or "get a grip."

Getting to the Bottom of Things: Explicit and Implicit Memory

Memory really isn't a filing cabinet. Rather, memory is all about associations.[5] The brain processes something in the present moment and links that experience with similar experiences from the past.[6] My relatives were all dairy farmers. When I see cows or smell manure, I recall very fond memories of spending time at my grandpa's house making homemade ice cream, playing with my cousins and watching black and white TV. For many of us, a song coming on the radio takes us back to a high school dance and a first love. We have *triggers*—smells, tastes, sights, sounds, the way something feels—our senses lend to memories. One definition of a trigger is an *identifiable* event that can give us feelings.

One type of memory is *explicit*. This is the type of memory likely most of us think of when we think about memory and memories. These are events we can recall—our drive to work, a vacation, the birth of a child, a conversation with our spouse, a holiday, a trip to the grocery store, or a meeting with a teacher. Recall isn't exact. There are likely to be some distortions although you believe you are being accurate. Two people can share an experience and each recall it differently.[7]

Implicit memory is the memory that helps us ride a bike. We can get on a bike and start peddling—even if we haven't been on a bike for weeks, months or years. We just know how to do this. We don't have to think about it. Implicit memory leads to a baby recognizing voices when he is born. He's heard them in the womb. Implicit memory starts before we are even born and is used exclusively through age 18 months.[8] Implicit memories don't just help us ride a bike, they shape our perceptions and expectations about the world and relationships. I am always reminded of the movie, *Inside Out*, when I think of implicit memory. Riley, the main character, was born to two loving parents. Her core—implicit—memories are the color, gold, which is joy. Her implicit memories are of being well-cared for. Her implicit memory anticipates that the future will continue to provide consistent, predictable and loving caregiving. Relationships are safe and filled with happy feelings. Riley's implicit memory system helped her form a positive internal working model.

Children who were abandoned, abused, exposed to neglect or domestic violence would have core—implicit—memories that could be red, blue and/or purple—respectively anger, sadness and/or fear. For these kids, relationships were scary or lonely or rageful. Their expectations of the world and relationships are that they aren't predictable. They may be frightening! There could be distance rather than proximity. Life may have been loud and chaotic or isolating. The implicit memory system contributed to a negative internal working model.

The hippocampus is designed to integrate implicit and explicit memories.[9] Highly emotional events—trauma—disconnect brain areas like the hippocampus from other brain areas that are necessary for the storage and integration of information.[10] Traumatic memories are not organized as coherent logical narratives, but in fragmented sensory and emotional traces, images, sounds and physical sensations.[11] When these elements remain in implicit-only form, when they haven't been integrated by the hippocampus, they exist in isolation from one another as a jumbled mess in our brain.[12] We can't construct the story of who we are. *The unremembered memory*[13] *affects who we are and how we interact with others—and we aren't even aware of it!* Many parents believe their child will "forget" their past. "He's got us now." "He'll learn that we love him. He'll be happy with us." Just as we don't forget how to ride a bike, so the unremembered memory isn't going anywhere on its own.

While we can't recall implicit memories, they can be triggered.[14] So, a second definition of a trigger is an *unidentifiable* event that can give us feelings. I think this is why implicit memory is akin to an iceberg. Under the surface of a traumatized child is a large mass of feelings, smells, sounds, images and physical sensations. Intense feelings surface when a day-to-day happening triggers these unremembered memories. Let's look at four examples, that play out in adoptive families frequently,

Emma is 11 years old. She was adopted when she was 16-months-old. She was abandoned at birth. She then resided in an orphanage until her adoptive mom and dad arrived. While institutionalized, Emma was noted to have had many "respiratory problems." She went back and forth from the orphanage to a hospital several times.

Today, Emma arrived home from school like a bear! She was ranting and raving—and pacing! To Mom, "You never do anything for me! The lunch you packed was terrible! Why'd you let me go to school dressed like this? You are the worst mom ever!" Dad arrived home from work and got the same treatment! Neither, Mom nor Dad had any idea why Emma was so upset! The family texted that they'd likely be a bit later for therapy as they were having difficulty getting Emma in the car. They did arrive, and Emma was still dysregulated. She slammed the car door and the office door! She started in me. "You're the worst therapist ever! You're a big poopy-head! No wonder I'm not better!" This continued for another hour. Finally, Emma blurted out, "everyone leaves me." She started crying. Mom took her in her arms. Emma said that she had learned four kids in her class were leaving the school. Two were moving. Two were changing schools. She said, "Everyone just leaves me. My whole life, no one stays." Emma's brain associated the implicit memory of her abandonment with the present event of classmates' departures. Emma was triggered about her abandonment. Her implicit belief about relationships, "everyone will leave me" surfaced and havoc reigned until we were able to get to the bottom of what was going on.

Scott is age 5. He was removed from his birth home at 8 months old due to failure to thrive. He was life-flighted to a local hospital. Three weeks later he arrived in a relative placement. The birth mother was put on a Family Service Plan with the goal being family reunification. Scott was transported to visits with his birth mother every Wednesday. Nine months passed, and Scott was returned to his birth mother's care. The great aunt was assigned the task of driving Scott to the birth mom's apartment and handing Scott and his belongings over to the birth mom. The great aunt tried to make this transition as positive as possible. Within a few days, the birth mother called the great aunt to come take Scott for the day as she "wasn't feeling well." The "day" soon became a pattern—the great aunt had Scott many days and some weekends. The great aunt provided this child care as she was afraid the birth mother would leave Scott alone if she didn't. Ultimately, Scott was again removed from his birth mom as her drug addiction had resumed. Scott went back to his great aunt who subsequently became his adoptive mother.

To this day, the car presents various problems. Scott won't stay buckled in. He screams and cries in his car seat. He throws objects if he can. He kicks the back of the driver or passenger seats. The entire family struggles to go places. Riding in the car is no fun when Scott's on board!

Scott's implicit memory translated his early experiences as "no one wants me." "My good mom keeps giving me back to the mom who doesn't take care of me. Neither of these moms seem to want me. There must be something wrong with me." The car triggers his shame and his anger.

Patty arrived in her adoptive family at age 2. She was exposed to drugs in utero. She experienced neglect and domestic violence. Patty's temper tantrums were intense even as a toddler. The length and the loudness of the fits grew along with Patty. It was common for Patty to sit on the floor screaming and flailing for two hours at a time. Yet Patty never had an outburst at church, school, shopping or when extended family gathered. Patty's adoptive parents, Maria and Travis, wondered why Patty only threw fits at home. "If she can manage this in other places, why not for us?" In therapy, I asked Patty this very question. She was quite quick to reply, "That'd be embarrassing! I'd never holler at school!" Patty's internal working model was that "families fight." She had internalized this pattern while living with her birth parents. It took quite some time to help Patty change this internal working model.

Deanna joined her adoptive family when she was 11 months old. Deanna was adopted internationally, and her adoption was trans-cultural. Already present in the family were three older siblings. As Deanna grew into a preschooler and a school-age child her robust competitive streak emerged. She'd race to the car to be the first one in! She'd push family members to get to the dinner table first! If she saw a sibling headed to the bathroom, she'd charge in ahead! The entire family became frustrated with Deanna!

Deanna always felt "different" from the rest of the family because she didn't "look like them." If she couldn't be first, she wasn't "good enough." If she thought anyone in the family was "getting ahead" she became triggered. She sprinted into action.

Neither Emma, nor Scott, nor Patty nor Deanna has development that matches their chronological age. When triggered, the behavior deteriorates further. Skills they display when less stressed seem to vanish. This is *regression*. Regression is part of the healing process. Development goes back and forth. However, when kids take steps forward—new skills should present. The development matures. The cracked foundation is stabilizing. Eventually, the better periods get longer. Undesired behaviors are less intense, less frequent and of shorter duration. Vice versa, the dysregulated times get less extreme. This is genuine progress. If your family is stuck on a roller coaster of ups and downs—seek help.

The implicit memory system confounds parents. Many parents report, "He can behave when he wants to!" The child with emotional dysregulation doesn't get a free pass when it comes to discipline. Scott spends time with his dad cleaning the car on Saturday mornings. Emma and Patty have received various natural and logical consequences for taking up so much of Mom's and Dad's time with their temper outbursts. Yet, the notion that these emotional displays are always purposeful is thinking that needs to be shed. The brain has hijacked your adoptee temporarily. They will return—and can recover more quickly when we implement parenting and therapeutic interventions that help us avoid the wreckage icebergs can cause. Fortunately, due to advances in neuroscience, we have the tools that allow us to diminish or cease the impact of the implicit memory system on day-to-day life for the adoptee, mom, dad, brothers and sisters. The following two chapters cover these tips.

Table 8.2 contains a chart highlighting the developmental milestones that lead to emotional maturity. Notice the overlap of emotional, social and cognitive skills. Child development should be akin to a set of gears. The developmental domains—gears—work together to churn development forward. One realm of development influences others. Trauma causes missing cogs. Deficits occur as the gears can't rotate smoothly. Depending on the age at which trauma happened, it unfortunately can adversely affect a vast array of skills.

Again, ask yourself, "has my child accomplished these early developmental milestones?" Remember, we want to get an idea how "young" your adoptee is. This helps us select the best tools to get the gears turning!

Table 8.2: The development of emotional skills and emotional regulation from birth to age 3

By 8 months	By 18 months	By 36 months
• Babies spend much of the day watching and listening to people around them. They'll experiment with grins. If the parent smiles back, baby will feel good.[15] • Babies spend much time gazing. They will look away to avoid overstimulation.[16] They may also fall asleep. • Babies begin to imitate faces quickly. Imitation is important for empathy development. "Social smiling" begins at 5–8 weeks. The baby starts smiling in response to something specific—their mother's face, or Dad's gaze. In turn, the parent enjoys this and playfully provokes this. This elicits joy in parent and child.[17] • Reaching for objects, tracking objects, and manipulating objects with his hands—this playing is the beginning of learning to self-soothe. The baby can entertain himself a bit.[18] "Protoconversation" arrives. The baby is cooing. The parent responds with surprise, and the parent imitates. This is an emotional exchange.[19] • Babies begin to really feel their feelings at about 6 months, and can relate these feelings to those around them.[20] The baby responds to others' feelings and genuinely seems happy.[21]	• By 12 months, children are sensitive to the emotional cues of others, especially in uncertain or threatening situations. This is social referencing.[22] • Mood fluctuates from openly affectionate to clingy and anxious (around unfamiliar people and objects) at 8–12 months.[23] • Stranger anxiety peaks at 10–18 months. It subsides at 24–30 months.[24] • Temper tantrums may start at about 12 months.[25] • Expresses a wide array of emotions.[26] • Children can now use words and gestures to communicate needs and wants. This alleviates feelings of frustration, for example. This occurs at about 15–18 months.[27]	• By age 2, children can be helped to use words to express emotions.[28] • By age 2, children begin to show spontaneous affection for familiar playmates, family members, others who are familiar like siblings.[29] • By age 2, children understand that people have inner experiences of thinking, feeling and desiring. (This leads to theory of mind—developing a framework for inferring what other people want, think, feel, intend and then making predictions about how they will behave.) They know that people feel good if they get something and bad if they don't.[30] • Children become capable of anticipating, talking about and using their awareness of self and others to manage everyday emotional experiences.[31] • Emotional repertoire has expanded and now includes pride, shame, guilt and embarrassment. This reflects self-understanding and self-awareness.[32] • Preschoolers are beginning to anticipate other's emotions and adjust accordingly. • At age 2 to 3, children start referring to themselves as "I" and can label feelings. "I sad." Spilling a drink on themselves feels uncomfortable and embarrassing. Self-conscious emotions initiate self-regulation. Others can see me and react emotionally to my behavior. Reactions can be positive or negative. In part, emotional regulation depends on development of self-concept.[33]

cont.

By 8 months	By 18 months	By 36 months
• Attachment begins to emerge and with it comes separation anxiety. • Babies respond to other people's expressions of emotion.[34] • Babies, by 8–9 months can read faces for emotions.[35] • Temperament begins to appear.[36]		• By age 3, children can separate easily from their mom and dad.[37] • Mood may still change drastically from one moment to the next, but they are more likely to talk about being angry or sad rather than having a meltdown.[38] • May still get upset about changes in routine/transitions.[39]
For example, the child may: • Begin to accept the nurturing response of a parent. Stops crying when a parent picks him up. • Hold a parent's gaze longer and longer.[40] • Cry not only when hungry or uncomfortable but also when they want a toy or to change activities.[41] • Smile accompanied by lifting hands and feet and moving in rhythm with your voice. This helps the brain form a foundation for conversation.[42] • Develop a favorite toy. • Enjoy playing with other people like siblings. Will be upset when the play stops.[43] • Know the difference between a familiar face and a stranger. May react with fear or wariness.[44] • Vocalize to get a parent's attention.[45] • Cry if he crawls too far out of sight of a parent.[46] • Bump head and cry to seek comfort from parent. • Cry inconsolably less often than in the early months.[47]	**For example, the child may:** • Clutch parent when they are going someplace without the child. • With adult help use a strategy, like cuddling a teddy bear to help calm down. • Look at parent's face for encouragement to try something new. • Begin to label feelings they have. • Express anger at having a toy taken away for example. May use aggression to show anger.[48] • Smile directly at other children when interacting with them.[49] • Exclaim, "That hurt," if they get a hit or a bite from a peer.[50] • Also take toys from playmates when angry.[51]	**For example, the child may:** • Hug family members and friends spontaneously. • Use self-talk to manage emotions by age 2. They are developing strategies to be emotionally regulated. This makes compliance easier, as well as promoting better interactions and promotes feelings of happiness.[52] • Express pride, "I'm dry at night!" May express shame by hanging head or hiding face. Overall, extends the use of language to express feelings. • Have fewer tantrums because of language growth. Tantrums will still occur from time to time. • By age 3, looks to adults for comfort when there is a conflict. When a child takes a toy, may seek a hug from the preschool teacher or parent. With the help of the adult, one child will talk to the other to work this problem out. A wider array of coping skills develops. • Express concern for a friend who is upset/crying.[53] • Recognize the feelings of other. When they see Daddy after work, they may exclaim, "Daddy is happy!"

Chapter Summary

- Emotional maturity means having the capacity to identify, express and regulate feelings. It also includes understanding the feelings of others and being able to wait to obtain privileges or to reach goals. Attunement experiences—early in life—cultivate emotional regulation. These social interactions influence the way the brain responds in later years. Children with histories of trauma lacked a nurturing parent leading the dance of attunement. The experience-dependent brain was deprived of the rich psychological care needed to grow the skill of emotional regulation. Rather, emotional dysregulation is its norm.

- Brain integration is essential to calming the brain that wants to loop through flight, fight or freeze regularly. Left and right hemisphere communication is needed to put words to feelings. We can "get a handle on" or "get a grip on" life events when the left brain provides a linear and logical perspective. Facts allow emotional release. Calming occurs.

- Implicit memory or unremembered memories are like icebergs. They're under the surface and often unknown to us. Yet, they contain our internal working model of relationships. They affect how we relate with others and we don't even know it! Explicit memory includes the events we can recall. Memory is about associations. Memory is really a linking of experiences over time. Once triggered, implicit and explicit memory set in motion a chain reaction. The feelings for unresolved traumatic events surface. Wreckage tips family interactions upside down! Fortunately, today we have the tools to decrease the iceberg's impact. The family is put on an even keel and smoother sailing becomes prevalent.

- Regression is part of the healing process. It's certainly disappointing to see a son's or daughter's skills seem to evaporate. Once calm, skills return and new abilities emerge. Over time, the child's developmental foundation stabilizes. Cogs are repaired. Gears smoothly churn genuine progress.

Endnotes

1   Garner, A.S. & Saul, R.A. (2018). *Thinking developmentally: Nurturing wellness in childhood to promote lifelong health*. American Academy of Pediatrics, Itasca, IL, pp.40-41

2   *Ibid.*, p.40; National Scientific Council on the Developing Child. (2015). Supportive relationships and active skill-building strengthen the foundations of resilience: Working paper 13. https://46y5eh11fhgw3ve3ytpwxt9r-wpengine.netdna-ssl.com/wp-content/uploads/2015/05/The-Science-of-Resilience2.pdf, p.2; Center on the Developing Child Harvard University. (n.d.). Brain architecture. https://developingchild.harvard.edu/science/key-concepts/brain-architecture/

3   McCrory, E., DeBrito, S.A., & Viding, E. (2011.) The impact of childhood maltreatment: A review of neurobiological and genetic factors. *Psychiatry 28* (July). https://doi.org/10.3389/fpsyt.2011.00048, pp.3–4.

4   Siegel, D.J. & Payne Bronson, T. (2011). *The Whole Brain Child: 12 Revolutionary Strategies To Nurture Your Child's Developing Mind*. New York: Bantam Books, pp.5-15.

5   *Ibid.*, p.67.

6   *Ibid.*, p.68.

7   *Ibid.*, pp.69–70.

8   *Ibid.*, p.71.

9   *Ibid.*, p.77.

10 van der Kolk, B.A. (2014). *The Body Keeps the Score. Brain, Mind and Body in the Healing of Trauma*. New York: Penguin Group, p.176.

11 *Ibid.*

12 Siegel, D.J., & Payne Bronson, T. (2011). *The Whole Brain Child: 12 Revolutionary Strategies To Nurture Your Child's Developing Mind*. New York: Bantam Books, p.77.

13 Fisher, S.F. (2014). *Neurofeedback In The Treatment Of Developmental Trauma: Calming The Fear-Driven Brain*. New York: W.W. Norton & Company, p.62.

14 Briere, J., & Scott, C. (2006). *Principles of Trauma Therapy: A Guide to Symptoms, Evaluation and Treatment*. Thousand Oaks, CA: Sage Publications, p.154.

15 Shelov, S.P., Altmann, T.R., Hannemann, R.E., & Trubo, R. (2014). *Caring for Your Baby and Young Child: Birth to Age 5*. New York: Bantam Books, p.210.

16 *Ibid.*, p.20.

17 *Ibid.*, p.220; Eliot, L. (1999). *What's Going on in There: How the Brain and Mind Develop in the First Five Years of Life*. New York: Bantam Books, p.301.

18 Shelov, S.P., Altmann, T.R., Hannemann, R.E., & Trubo, R. (2014). *Caring for Your Baby and Young Child: Birth to Age 5*. New York: Bantam Books, p.212.

19 Eliot, L. (1999). *What's Going on in There: How the Brain and Mind Develop in the First Five Years of Life*. New York: Bantam Books, p.302.

20 *Ibid.*, p.303.

21 Centers for Disease Control and Prevention. (June 6, 2018). Important milestones: Your baby by six months. www.cdc.gov/ncbddd/actearly/milestones/milestones-6mo

22 National Research Council and Institute of Medicine, Committee on Integrating the Science of Early Childhood Development, Shonkoff, J. P., Phillips, D. A., & Board on Children, Youth, and Families, Commission on Behavioral and Social Sciences and Education. (2000). *From Neurons to Neighborhoods: The Science of Early Childhood Development*. Washington, D.C.: National Academy Press, p.107.

23 Shelov, S.P., Altmann, T.R., Hannemann, R.E., & Trubo, R. (2014). *Caring for Your Baby and Young Child: Birth to Age 5*. New York: Bantam Books, p.274.

24 *Ibid.*, pp.274–275.

25 *Ibid.*, p.326.

26 *Ibid.*, p.346.

27 National Research Council and Institute of Medicine, Committee on Integrating the
    Science of Early Childhood Development, Shonkoff, J.P., Phillips, D.A., & Board on
    Children, Youth, and Families, Commission on Behavioral and Social Sciences and
    Education. (2000). *From Neurons to Neighborhoods: The Science of Early Childhood
    Development.* Washington, D.C.: National Academy Press, p.112.

28 Shelov, S.P., Altmann, T.R., Hannemann, R.E., & Trubo, R. (2014). *Caring for Your Baby
    and Young Child: Birth to Age 5.* New York: Bantam Books, p.366.

29 Centers for Disease Control and Prevention. (2018, June 19). Important milestones: Your
    child by eighteen months. https://www.cdc.gov/ncbddd/actearly/milestones/milestones-
    18mo.html; Centers for Disease Control and Prevention. (2018, June 19). Important
    milestones: Your child by two years. https://www.cdc.gov/ncbddd/actearly/milestones/
    milestones-2yr.html

30 National Research Council and Institute of Medicine, Committee on Integrating the
    Science of Early Childhood Development, Shonkoff, J.P., Phillips, D.A., & Board on
    Children, Youth, and Families, Commission on Behavioral and Social Sciences and
    Education. (2000). *From Neurons to Neighborhoods: The Science of Early Childhood
    Development.* Washington, D.C.: National Academy Press, p.110.

31 California Infant/Toddler Learning & Development Foundations. (2018, February 14).
    Foundation: Emotional regulation. https://www.cde.ca.gov/sp/cd/re/itf09300ccmodcv.
    asp#emoreg

32 National Research Council and Institute of Medicine, Committee on Integrating the
    Science of Early Childhood Development, Shonkoff, J.P., Phillips, D.A., & Board on
    Children, Youth, and Families, Commission on Behavioral and Social Sciences and
    Education. (2000). *From Neurons to Neighborhoods: The Science of Early Childhood
    Development.* Washington, D.C.: National Academy Press, p.110.

33 *Ibid.*, p.112.

34 Shelov, S.P., Altmann, T.R., Hannemann, R.E., & Trubo, R. (2014). *Caring for Your Baby
    and Young Child: Birth to Age 5.* New York: Bantam Books, p.241.

35 *Ibid.*, p.273.

36 *Ibid.*, p.238.

37 Centers for Disease Control and Prevention. (2018, June 19). Important milestones: Your
    child by three years. https://www.cdc.gov/ncbddd/actearly/milestones/milestones-3yr.html

38 Benaroch, R. (2016, October 19). Preschooler emotional development. https://www.
    webmd.com/parenting/preschooler-emotional-development#1

39 Centers for Disease Control and Prevention. (2018, June 19). Important milestones: Your
    child by three years. https://www.cdc.gov/ncbddd/actearly/milestones/milestones-3yr.html

40 Shelov, S.P., Altmann, T.R., Hannemann, R.E., & Trubo, R. (2014). *Caring for Your Baby
    and Young Child: Birth to Age 5.* New York: Bantam Books, p.210.

41 *Ibid.*, p.228.

42 Klaus, M., Klaus, P., Keefe, M., & Fox, N. (Producers). (2011). *Amazing Talents of the
    Newborn* [Motion picture on DVD]. United States: Johnson & Johnson Pediatric Institute
    LLC

43 Centers for Disease Control and Prevention. (2018, June 19). Important milestones: Your
    baby by four months. https://www.cdc.gov/ncbddd/actearly/milestones/milestones-4mo.
    html

44 Shelov, S.P., Altmann, T.R., Hannemann, R.E., & Trubo, R. (2014). *Caring For Your Baby
    And Young Child: Birth To Age 5.* New York: Bantam Books, p.228. Centers for Disease
    Control and Prevention. (June 6, 2018). Important milestones: Your baby by six months.
    https://www.cdc.gov/ncbddd/actearly/milestones/milestones-6mo.html

45 Shelov, S.P., Altmann, T.R., Hannemann, R.E., & Trubo, R. (2014). *Caring For Your Baby
    And Young Child: Birth To Age 5.* New York: Bantam Books, p.238.

46 *Ibid.*, p.239.

47   Eliot, L. (1999). *What's Going On In There: How The Brain And Mind Develop In The First Five Years Of Life*. New York: Bantam Books, p.303.

48   Shelov, S.P., Altmann, T.R., Hannemann, R.E., & Trubo, R. (2014). *Caring For Your Baby And Young Child: Birth To Age 5*. New York: Bantam Books, p.308.

49   Brazelton, T.B. (2006). *Touchpoints, Birth To 3: Your Child's Emotional And Behavioral Development*. Cambridge, MA: Perseus Books Group, p.172.

50   *Ibid.*, p.173.

51   *Ibid.*, p.172.

52   National Research Council and Institute of Medicine, Committee on Integrating the Science of Early Childhood Development, Shonkoff, J.P., Phillips, D.A., & Board on Children, Youth, and Families, Commission on Behavioral and Social Sciences and Education. (2000). *From Neurons to Neighborhoods: The Science of Early Childhood Development*. Washington, D.C.: National Academy Press, p.112.

53   Centers for Disease Control and Prevention. (2018, June 19). Important milestones: Your child by three years. https://www.cdc.gov/ncbddd/actearly/milestones/milestones-3yr.html

CHAPTER 9

Let's Get Regulated: Avoiding Wreckage!

The tips in this chapter are geared to help moms and dads parent to the emotional state of the brain. Parents want to move away from the icebergs, avoiding wreckage. Learning to react calmly when your child is triggered and emotionally dysregulated helps the brain settle itself. Let's go back to this graphic from earlier in the book. I've added the iceberg—the implicit memories—now.

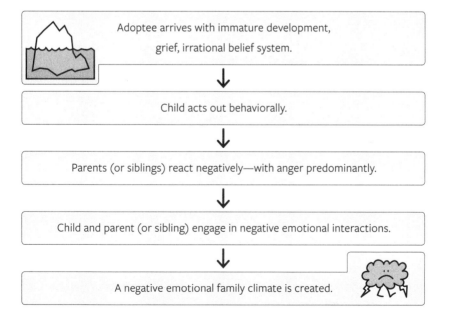

Adoptee arrives with immature development, grief, irrational belief system.

↓

Child acts out behaviorally.

↓

Parents (or siblings) react negatively—with anger predominantly.

↓

Child and parent (or sibling) engage in negative emotional interactions.

↓

A negative emotional family climate is created.

Figure 9.1: The arrival of a child with a history of trauma can create a negative emotional climate in the family—especially due to the implicit memory system.

This scenario in the graphic repeats and repeats and repeats. The emotional dysregulation is reinforced. It becomes ingrained. I'm asking parents to step out of the pattern. When parents make changes, kids change too! I'm asking moms and dads to go first. It's certainly hard to respond calmly when you're being lied to or stolen from or you're being told you're a "dummy(or worse)" for the umpteenth time! I'm suggesting that reducing heated interactions is a key to cultivating the performance of your adoptee's brain. Besides, toddlers and children exposed to trauma—especially physical abuse—allocate more attention to angry faces and require more attentional resources to disengage from such faces.[1] The emotional dysregulation is extended!

If you can change your response even 50 percent of the time—you're halfway there! When moms and dads can regulate themselves, the child's brain will model the parents' brain. Infants are taught emotional regulation by their parents as we learned in the chapter about attachment. Grade-school, middle-school and high-school-age kids can learn this skill, at their older ages, from their mom and dad too! We are "growing up" the adoptee by repeating the cycle of needs. We are re-doing what should have happened in the first place. We pacify a fussy baby with nurture and composure. If we want tranquil home interactions, we need to soothe our fussy school-age child, tween or teen similarly. The result will be a brain that will settle faster. Flare ups will be less intense and less often! The tips that follow are ways to help parents achieve this goal! Each member of the adoption-built family benefits when the emotional climate of the family is set for smooth sailing.

Let the Fizz Settle: Waiting on the Brain

This Strategy is Applicable to Older Kids

When the brain is hijacked by implicit or explicit memories—there's nothing to do but wait. The logical centers of your child's brain are offline. It's like a bottle of pop that's been dropped on the floor. We don't twist the cap off until the fizz settles. I encourage family members to go on as best as they can around the temper outburst, the yelling or the being "tuned out." Sometimes, I grab a snack and sit patiently until the coast is clear. I keep a watchful eye to make certain safety is maintained for everyone who's at the office. Other than that, I wait. Once settled, we have our therapy session. We make certain to have some type of nurture. We complete the cycle of needs (see attachment chapters). Reiterating, the beautiful dance that occurs between parent and infant creates emotional regulation. The baby cries. The parent tends to the need. The baby calms. We wouldn't argue with a crying baby! We want to quarrel less with our "little" older kids! Then, reconnect when possible—even if this is hard. I don't think anyone ever said that parenting would be easy! Reconnecting can be as simple as "Hey, come on back and watch TV with us." "Join us for snack." "I'm going to the store. Hop in the car."

This Strategy is Applicable to Younger Kids
Toddlers and preschoolers, I pick up and lay on the parent's lap. We hold them through their dysregulation. We talk once they have regulated. If it seems like this could become a restraint, I keep them in proximity to parents. Once emotionally stable, I put them on their mom's or dad's lap. We listen to a song or use Theraplay® to make a connection.

Create a Code Word

It's helpful to have teamwork when carrying out the goal of reducing negative interactions with your child. Spouses—and other children in the family—can work together. A code word—broccoli—or whatever you like can be spoken out when ire is rising. This signal means that a parent needs to disengage. Walk away. This battle doesn't need to wage, unless there is a safety issue and you need to remain in the vicinity of your child. There can't be a war if two sides don't show up to fight. You can give a consequence later, tomorrow or not at all. You're the parent. This is your call. Just do it when you and your traumatized adoptee are both calm.

Don't Ask "Why?"

Austin, age 15, cut the top off his sister's large, hollow chocolate Easter egg. He filled the egg with urine. He meticulously replaced the top. Louise,

9 years old was excited when Mom said she could have a piece of her Easter egg as an afternoon snack. When she picked the egg up, the top tilted. She lost hold of the egg. It fell to the floor. Urine splashed everywhere! Louise burst into tears! Her beautiful Easter egg was ruined!

Austin's mom fumed! She called Austin down to the living room. "Why? Why would you do this?" From this point, an argument ensued. Austin denied that he peed in his sister's Easter egg. Austin's mom became incensed that he kept lying!

Even if Austin answered why he urinated in his sister's Easter egg—how would this be helpful information? Would any response resolve this? Would Louise be less disappointed?

"Why?" usually leads to a downward spiral—wreckage. The child lies. The parent gets angrier. The child lies again. The parent gets even more irate. Work to rid "why" from your interactions with your traumatized adoptee. Deciding, "what" you want to do about the problem behavior is the issue.

Below I'm listing some of the reasons "why" undesired behaviors occur. Many are rooted in the original trauma. Reiterating, therapeutically reducing the impact of the abuse, neglect and abandonment, is what will eventually lead to improved conduct. The parenting tips in this book will be helpful too. In the meantime, these explanations can alleviate the need for asking "Why?"

- As earlier chapters made clear, many behaviors result because the child is "young."
- Implicit memories get triggered.
- The adoptee's traumatic experiences often occur when they have had little or no language development. Their traumas are extensive. It is difficult for them to find words to describe their sufferings. Overall, there is an inability to verbalize the events and the emotions. These kids show us how they feel via behavior. Boys and girls who lose things feel "lost." Youngsters who steal things often feel "stolen." Kids who pee about the house are "pissed off!" Children who poop feel like "crap." Listening to the behavior can tell us a lot about what the traumatized child thinks and feels.

Betty, adopted internationally, called her country of origin on her play phone daily! This happened for years. She would ask to speak to her birth mom. Apparently, she was told, by the pretend voice from her country of origin, that her birth mom wasn't available. She would respond, "Tell her to call me. I want her to know I'm here. She can come for me." Betty felt that her adoption occurred because her birth mother "lost" her. Betty loses everything—permission slips for class trips, homework assignments, jewelry, winter coats and mittens, pens and pencils. You name it. Betty can't find it.

- Insecure attachment styles cause sons and daughters to create distance in relationships. This push-pull is brutal! One minute the family is having fun. The next, the child is overflowing the toilet. Mom and dad are puzzled. "What happened?" Anger creates distance. The child "pushes buttons" to get ire. It makes him feel safe. He thinks, "When you are angry, we aren't so close."
- Thoughts drive behavior. If you feel ashamed of yourself or you feel unlovable, then your actions are designed to reinforce the way you think. Simply put, kids act poorly to validate their shameful thoughts about themselves.
- Misery loves company is an apt expression. Children who have experienced abuse, neglect or abandonment arrive in the family with a ton of feelings! They'll say in therapy, "I want them to feel as bad as me." Again, its hard for them to talk about what happened. Instead, they transfer their feelings to their family members— mostly parents. This is referred to as inducement, a term coined by Maris Blechner, Family Focus Adoption Services. If you as a mom or dad feel angrier than you ever imagined or have become anxious or depressed since your child arrived, you may be experiencing inducement. Kids learn how to deal with their feelings by watching adults. So, they pass their feelings to you! It's a good idea for adoptive parents to take stock of the ways they express their emotions. Do you go along for a while and then blow up? Do you stuff your feelings? Do you avoid your feelings? Do you eat? Do you brood? Do you threaten? Do you go off to do something by yourself? Are

you able to articulate your emotions? Do you call someone and vent? Do you laugh things off? Do you change the subject? Moms and dads are encouraged to reflect on their style of expressing their feelings. Is it the way you want your sons and daughters to deal with their emotions?

- Sometimes, the child's history has been withheld. The child arrives knowing that she has a lot of feelings. Yet, she doesn't know why. She assumes the anger, sadness or fear is for something happening today, like her mom or dad asking her to vacuum. She doesn't associate it with a past circumstance.

> **Skye**, now age 9, was vaginally penetrated, by her birth father, when she was an infant—9 months old. She had to have surgery to repair the tearing. To date, she masturbates—frequently. Her adoptive parents have re-directed this behavior to her bedroom. Now Skye has friends and she has become aware that other girls her age don't masturbate. Skye spoke with her mom. Subsequently, Mom and Dad decided to seek help telling Skye about her sexual abuse. Certainly, learning about her sexual abuse was upsetting! Yet, Skye said, "At least I know I'm not just some weird kid! There's a reason I masturbate!"

We'll talk about the "when" and "how" of sensitively telling children their whole story in the upcoming chapter on the trauma narrative. We'll also talk about how we can create a narrative when the family received little to no history prior to adoption.

- The youngster's world may be riddled with cognitive dissonance. They look around and feel out-of-sync. For example, the international adoptee arrives at the airport. Grandparents, aunts, uncles and siblings are holding signs and balloons. They are excited, smiling and crying tears of joy. The adoptee, on the other hand, is scared, sad and lonely. He is thinking; "Where am I? Who are these people? They don't smell or sound familiar. What happened to all the other babies or kids I was living with? What is this place called America? What is this place called home?" His experience does not match with those around him. As he ages, he realizes that his life in the orphanage was a different beginning from that of the other children in his neighborhood, his preschool, Kindergarten and so on. Feelings continue to develop. Inadvertently, adoption is frequently portrayed in a positive light. "Your birth mother was so poor, she couldn't keep you. She wanted you to be adopted because she loved you so much." The adoptee is again in a situation that may be inconsistent with his thoughts and emotions. He feels sad and angry that he was "given away," no matter what the circumstances. He feels the loss of the life that was supposed to be. Yet, he is not sure how to convey these feelings, because those around him are not demonstrating that they understand his perspective, which seems to be so different from theirs.

Going back to Louise and her Easter egg, I would believe that Austin destroyed the egg to get an angry reaction. The family had had a lovely Easter holiday. He was feeling too closely connected. He needed to push the family away. He always worried about being re-abandoned. Over time, Austin worked through his anxieties. Today, he is a college graduate and he is engaged. He, Mom, Dad and Louise get along well!

Now you know all the "whys" that I know. You can work on calming yourself and moving on.

Traumaversaries and Triggers: Offsetting the Impact

Previously, I defined a trigger. Triggers that occur annually can be referred to as traumaversaries. Anniversaries, "returning yearly," are associated with happy occasions for many of us—birthdays, wedding days, holidays and so on! Yet, returning yearly can also lead to a downward spiral—behaviorally and emotionally—for children (or adults) who have experienced losses associated with moving, abuse, abandonment, etc. These annual traumaversaries can affect children adopted at all ages—infant to adolescent.

There are some steps moms and dads can take to offset the impact of triggers.

Common Triggers and Traumaversaries
- Mother's/Father's Day.
- Birthdays.
- Holidays.
- Gotcha Day.
- Family dinner.
- Anniversary of removal from birth family and/or separation from siblings.
- Anniversaries of moves to foster homes or orphanages.
- Illness or death of adoptive parent.
- Divorce.
- Airplane rides.
- Visits with birth siblings.
- Birth or adoption of a child.
- Kindergarten or first grade.
- Beginning and end of each school year.
- Puberty.
- School classes like Biology and Genetics.
- School-related projects and classes.
- Questions/comments from strangers.
- Adoptive parents drinking alcohol.

Identify Traumaversaries to the Best of Your Ability

In a date book, record your adopted son's or daughter's date of abandonment (if different than their birthday), move to your home, move from one orphanage or foster home to another, termination of parental rights, separation from siblings, adoption finalization, "Gotcha Day," etc.—record as many important dates as you know. Also, record all family members' birthdays. Keep in mind, the adoptee's anniversaries and/or a month full of family occasions can contribute to the adoptee experiencing a traumaversary. For example, one family I know has four kids' birthdays in September. This amount of focus on family time and special celebrations triggers their adopted daughter's memories of the birth siblings from whom she is separated. Overwhelmed with grief, her negative behaviors escalate. Review your date book frequently. "Seeing" these potential triggers is easier than trying to remember them for the busy adoptive parent.

Review your date book every few weeks so you can prepare for the approaching traumaversary.

Expect Regression

Triggers are causing the child to remember painful, frightening events— implicit or explicit. This is stressful. In reiteration, when kids are stressed, they often return to "younger" developmental stages.

> **Mitch**, age 12, had been dry at night for several months. So, his mom was surprised to find urine-soaked sheets stuffed in the hamper. She took a few minutes to think. Mitch was working on a family tree project at school. This project was hard for Mitch. It dredged up memories of the three birth sisters that Mitch gets to visit only sporadically. Mitch was regressing under the stress of the class project.

Regression can be a return to the social and emotional age at which the trauma occurred. Thus, in the example of Mitch above, he moved to his adoptive home when he was 3½. This is the age when kids are mostly dry at night. An occasional accident still occurs.

Rather than discourage the behaviors of the regressed child, parents are encouraged to step back and recognize the source. There is no harm, to the child, in allowing "little" behavior. In fact, regression can be a wonderful source of healing. If we nurture this "young" child in the same manner that we would a child at this "actual young chronological age," we repair the broken cog. We solidify the adoptee's development. Over time, this lessens the impact of the trigger or traumaversary.

You can also plan for the regression's potential impact on planned celebrations. One family whose son's birthday was still a few weeks away was experiencing such a regression that they surprised him with what the mom called an "unbirthday." She picked up a cake and a gift and decided that the upcoming Tuesday would be his birthday this year. This surprise early birthday did the trick. He was back on track in no time. The family enjoyed this so much that each member of the family has now celebrated an "unbirthday."

Other parents make plans to simplify special evets by reducing sensory stimulation, shortening the timeframe or deciding for one parent and the adopted child to leave early or take breaks. Do what makes sense for you and all your children. Sometimes, just knowing and anticipating potential behavioral decline can make things go more smoothly because our expectations are in check.

The best ideas for handling adoption-related school projects come from *Adoptive Families Magazine* (see Resources). This online resource has nice printable resources for teachers and parents. Or, you can email your son's or daughter's school staff links to topics such as *Re-thinking the family tree and other tough assignments*, *The great back-to-school kit*, *Should we tell our son's teacher that he was adopted?*, and *Bringing up adoption at school*. In any event, I encourage moms and dads to do their best to keep current with school topics and course work. A landmine of potential triggers awaits in the classroom.

The Ripple Effect

About two weeks before the identified potential or known traumaversary, parents, can use the ripple effect—an idea is put forth as to what the problem may be and eventually the child realizes the idea is a safe topic. Thus, conversation occurs.

Brianna was placed with her adoptive family over the Christmas holiday at age 5. Brianna was also removed from her birth family shortly before Christmas when age 2. Christmas is a traumaversary for Brianna. Brianna becomes very sad and sullen. Sometimes she sits with tears streaming down her face. She withdraws to her room. She picks at her food and is lackluster in conversation at family dinner. Clearly, Brianna spends the holiday depressed. She longs to know how her birth mom is doing. She becomes consumed with thoughts of her birth mother. Brianna can't enjoy the Christmas festivities. Her mood dampens the cherished family event for all members of her family.

In Brianna's case, her mom or dad could state:

> Christmas is almost here. I think about your birth mom around the holidays. If it weren't for her, I wouldn't be your dad. I know she hurt you and I am sad about that. I am also happy to have you for a daughter. I notice that your mood gets worse around Christmas. You get so sad. I wonder if this is because you are thinking about her too. I'm sure that when you think about her it causes you to have a lot of feelings. We can talk about them.

The parent has established that the birth mom is a safe topic. He has acknowledged that there is hurt. He has identified a potential feeling, and he has expressed feelings of his own. He modeled talking about feelings. Kids do learn from their parents! In fact, merely assigning a name or label to feelings literally calms down the emotional circuitry in the right hemisphere.[2]

Keep in mind, you may have to put forth a few ripples before your child becomes willing to participate in a conversation. However, the sooner you give this a try, the sooner you are on your way to reducing the swells of emotional backlash involved in these yearly occurrences.

Rituals

Trigger management may also include rituals. Many adoptive families create rituals, symbolic ways to remember and reflect. Adoption has been steeped in rituals for celebrations, such as "Gotcha Day," as well as in rituals to acknowledge loss. A candle may be lit, or a helium balloon released to acknowledge the birth mother on Mother's Day. A small box can be decorated and called a birth mother, birth brother or birth sister box. At times when birth family members are missed, the adopted child can draw a picture or write a letter which is added to the contents of the box. School pictures or other favorite pictures can be added as well. These actions also label and name feelings, calming the right brain. The left brain can come online and use words to process the child's thoughts, sadness, anger or fears. The trigger's or traumaversary's impact subsides. The child has had the opportunity to share with their mom or dad.

Praise and "No" Can be Icebergs Too!

Most parents tell their kids "no" from time to time, and most parents want to praise their child for a job well done! Both seem innocuous. Yet, adoptive parents know from experience that both can sink the emotional climate of the home.

Praise: Accurate and Reflective of the Job Completed

A moment of praising, complimenting or "patting the adoptee on the back" can cause a sudden downward behavioral spiral! As soon as Mom or Dad says, "Wow, you have been good all week!" or "You've been getting along so well with your sister," things go downhill—quickly! Praise can be a trigger for the shame children feel. Once told that they did well, the thoughts of how "bad" they are set in. They plummet.

There is another group of adoptees who strive to be perfect to compensate for the poor self-image. These kids excel at everything! Praise increases their anxiety. Once performance is commended, they feel the need to raise the bar even higher for themselves. This pressure causes stress, and then emotional dysregulation happens.

In doling out kind words, keep in mind:

- When adoptees alter their internal working model, they can move on to accept themselves as worthy individuals, and as deserving your kudos. They won't feel the need to act "bad" or "perfect."
- Consider "specific" rather than "global" praise. State, "You did a great job cleaning your room today." "Your history report is wonderful." "I'm happy with the way you acted at the store today." This type of praise is like giving a "slice" of praise. Many children can handle such a "slice" rather than a "whole" chunk.
- "Indirect" kudos is often successful as well. Many children love to

get mail. Consider sending a note to your adopted child. Receiving a short note or a card doesn't require accepting the compliment directly. Of course, lunchbox notes are always wonderful.[3] On one side is a preprinted compliment. On the flip side is a trivia question. The latter makes for an after-school conversation starter. Homemade love notes are special too! Indirect praise can also be delivered by calling a friend, grandma or even the weather—when your adopted child is within earshot—and state, "Wow, you will never believe what Billy accomplished today! He weeded the flower beds all by himself!" Billy gets a direct message in a more diffused manner.

- Parents can "teach" the child to accept an accolade. Mom or Dad could say, "Sallie, I know when I compliment you, you often feel the need to act up. But, I'm going to tell you anyway how much I appreciate you helping with dinner today. I hope someday you can learn that parents like to praise their children for a good job. In the meantime, if you feel the need to give me some behavior, I'm ready for it." This is a version of the paradoxical intervention we learned about in an earlier chapter.

- Think carefully about the accuracy of the pat on the back articulated. Today, we do offer children lots of acclamation. We praise for tasks that we could really expect. Sitting in your seat at school is expected. Eating with your mouth closed is expected. I'm not always sure praise is warranted when these routine responsibilities are performed. Research findings are mixed. Yet, there is evidence that praise is best when it closely reflects a child's actual performance, and it is delivered in a way that the youngster perceives is accurate.[4] Receiving compliments is one component of self-concept. Self-concept is one facet of a youngster's make up. Balance, rather than overdoing, is something to give thought to. We'll talk about helping kids piece together a positive image of themselves as we move on to the trauma narrative chapter. We'll talk about how to help kids see their qualities and accomplishments, two vital components that help youngsters, tweens and teens put together a picture of self as worthwhile.

The "Yes" Choice

Moms and dads know that "no," "now" and "don't" can lead to an argument! Kids tell me that "no" triggers rejection:

> **Sherry**, now 16, has lived with her adoptive parents for 15 years. She hates the word, "no." Instantly she begins to bargain—relentlessly! "Please Mom!" "I'll do the dishes for a week. Just let me go to the mall." This line of badgering continues—on and on. Sometimes its hours before she finally backs down. Sherry's mom said she felt like she was "living with Monty Hall!"
>
> Once in a therapy session, I asked Sherry about "no." She said, "I automatically hear my birth mom saying 'no' you can't stay with me." Her feelings about her abandonment swell up.

Sherry's parents started using a "yes" choice more often. "Yes, you can go to the mall when all your homework is done." "Yes, I'll be happy to drive you to your friend's house, when your room is clean." Sherry heard "yes" more than "no." Sherry's parents were happy to stop the "let's make a deal" lifestyle. Over time, as Sherry came to resolve her abandonment, "no" was readily accepted.

Parallel Healing Process

Becoming a parent, by any means, causes a life review. Becoming a parent to a child who has experienced maltreatment intensifies thoughts and feelings about childhood experiences, and the type of parenting received while growing up. Many adoptive moms and dads will find they must rework their own earlier life circumstances while simultaneously assisting their adopted child in resolving their trauma. This is referred to as the parallel healing process—healing your child and yourself at the same time.

> **Anna** and her husband fostered and subsequently adopted two drug-exposed infants. Both children had great difficulty regulating their emotions. This emotionality continued as the children grew into school-age youngsters.

Anna's husband traveled during the work week. He arrived home each weekend. Anna would spend all day Friday tidying the house, making a gourmet meal and encouraging the children to "behave when Daddy gets home."

Anna grew up in a home with an alcoholic father. Her mother was a "peacemaker." She acted as a buffer between Anna, her siblings and her father. This façade even stretched to extended family and the community. Anna assumed her mother's role. She felt it her job to "keep peace" or "to keep everyone happy."

Each Friday, as soon as Daddy came through the door, the kids— over-excited—decompensated. Anna would burst into tears. She felt like a failure. Friday was spent re-grouping, rather than having a wonderful family evening.

John and his wife adopted two children from foster care. The children were 5 and 7 years old. The kids had an extensive history of physical and sexual abuse. Over the years, John gradually drifted away from his family. He spent more and more time at the office. John's wife had to assume the bulk of the parenting responsibilities. This was no small task given that each child had an array of behavioral, emotional and academic problems.

Once in services, John discovered the extent of his depression. John grew up in a family that financially provided well for their children. There was no abuse. But, affection was rare. Relationships were distant, rather than connected.

Adopting two children unable to form loving attachment triggered John's past loneliness and disappointment with his family of origin.

There are times when we spend entire therapy appointments with the parents, helping them cope with their "icebergs." This is important work. The mental health of adoptive moms and dads is essential for their own sake as well as that of all their sons and daughters There are no benefits to any family member when parents are worn out, exhausted, frustrated, over-worked, stressed out, rushing from one place to the next, distraught or suffering recurring experiences.

Too many moms and dads, at our office, struggle with high blood pressure, gastro-intestinal conditions, depression, anxiety, poor quality sleep, thyroid problems and weight gain. Caring for a traumatized child creates a secondary trauma or compassion fatigue which is characterized by feelings of incompetence and emotional exhaustion.[5] Parents get burned out!

If you need assistance, consider networking with other adoptive parents or finding a therapist with whom you can develop rapport. Please make the time needed for yourself.

Chapter Summary

- Moms and dads must take the lead in helping the adoptee settle the fizz—the emotional dysregulation. Recognizing that the brain has been hijacked helps parents calm themselves. In turn, the child will regulate. Wreckage avoided! This is a repetition of the cycle of needs. Parents help babies and toddlers learn the skill of self-regulation. Moms and dads can help sons and daughters learn this skill at later ages.

- Parents can learn to anticipate and manage triggers and traumaversaries. Moms and dads can identify times and situations that present emotional challenges for the traumatized child. Parents can plan ways to acknowledge these occasions via rituals and the ripple effect. The act of labeling feelings helps the right brain circuitry calm. Left-side functions resume. Thoughts and feelings can be processed.

- Regression is part of the healing process. Triggers and traumaversaries can cause the child to temporarily slip back to earlier stages of development. Rather than lament, regression can be viewed as an opportunity. Nurturing this "young" child in the same manner that we would a child at this "actual young chronological age," helps repair the injured cog. Repairing the gears moves development forward. The child grows up.

- Moms and dads may find that they are healing themselves simultaneous to healing their child with a history of trauma—the parallel healing process. Compassion fatigue can undermine the parenting role as well. Parents are strongly encouraged to take care of themselves. Locate the support needed to ensure your own physical and emotional health. You are the most important people in the family! Your even keel is essential to the smooth flow of the family.

Endnotes

1   Pollak, S. & A Tolley-Schell, S. (2003). Selective attention to facial emotion in physically abused children. *Journal of Abnormal Psychology, 112*(3), pp.323-338. doi:10.1037/0021-843X.112.3.323, p..324

2   Siegel, D.J. & Payne Bronson, T. (2011). *The Whole Brain Child: 12 Revolutionary Strategies To Nurture Your Child's Developing Mind.* New York: Bantam Books, p.29.

3   I particularly like the Lunchbox love notes available on the website www.sayplease.com

4   Lee, H.I., Kim, Y.H., Kessebir, P., & Han, E.D. (2016.) Understanding when parental praise leads to optimal child outcome: Role of perceived praise accuracy. *Social Psychological and Personality Science* 8(6), pp.679–688. https://doi.org/10.1177/1948550616683020, p 685.

5   Craig, S.E. (2017). *Trauma-Sensitive Schools For The Adolescent Years: Promoting Resiliency And Healing, Grades 6–12.* New York: Teachers College Press, p.100.

CHAPTER 10

Tips to Tell the Story! Making the Implicit, Explicit

We can lessen the negative impact of implicit memories, and explicit too, by telling children their story. Children can sort out their trauma history when we work at their pace and when we provide the nurturing support—parents—needed through the process. I've been helping young children, tweens and teens piece their pre-adoptive experiences together for 23 years. I always have parents present to comfort their child through the hard facts and the grief.

Tell Me My Story and Reap the Healing!

The story makes the explicit accurate, and the implicit explicit. Narrative work allows the left hemisphere to put the remembered and unremembered memories in order and to label the feelings with words. The story helps the iceberg melt away. Tempers won't flare as often or as intensely. The narrative is another way to contribute to the emotional well-being of the child arriving with a trauma history.

The narrative contributes to healing in a host of other ways as well:

Hal came in for therapy at age 16. He was adopted when he was 4½ years old. He spent six months with his birth mother. She asked her neighbor to babysit Hal. She never returned. The neighbor took Hal to a social services agency when he was 7 months old. Hal was placed with a foster family, and he resided with this foster family until he was adopted.

Hal's behavior had been challenging over the years. Hal stood in the kitchen—salivating—while his mother made dinner. Hal gorged until he vomited. He made a mess when eating. He would wipe his hands on his shirt, make sure to drop food on the floor and to let food fall out of his mouth. He rubbed his penis at home and in stores. He lied. He stole. He yelled. He swore. He damaged all kinds of things around the house—lamps, doors, dishes, furniture, knick-knacks and pictures. Hal wouldn't ever join the family when they were hanging out watching a movie, playing a game or going out for dinner or dessert. Hal stayed in his room as much as he could.

In a therapy session, we were reviewing photos of Hal's parents arriving at the foster home to meet Hal. Hal intently studied a picture which included the foster parents, four foster brothers, and the members of his adoptive family-to-be—Mom, Dad and their son, Hal's brother-to-be. Hal said, "I wanted to tell you to 'go away.'" In fact, Hal had been telling the family to "go away" with his behavior since the day he had arrived.

Hal believed that his foster mother was his birth mother. Thus, Hal felt as if his adoptive parents had "stolen" him from his birth mom. He was angry with his adoptive family. He viewed them as a barrier between him and his birth mother.

Hal's distorted thought pattern, his feelings about being "stolen," his fantasy that his life would be wonderful if he had been allowed to stay with his birth mother, all combined to drive a pattern of undesirable behaviors.

As Hal learned his story, he came to realize why adoption became the choice for him. He grieved his many losses. He became more closely connected to his forever family. His behavior improved. He developed an identity. It's hard to decide "Who am I?" when you're misunderstanding the events of the first 4½ years of your life! He became able to discern past, present and future. Developmentally, Hal began to "grow up."

As for dinner with Hal, it has become much more enjoyable. When Hal arrived at his foster home, he was malnourished. In therapy, we helped Hal understand that he hadn't been fed enough as an infant. Hal was able to compare this situation to the fact that his adoptive family hadn't ever run out of food—in the 11 ½ years Hal had lived with them! There was no need to drool over the stove every day! There was no need to eat as if the food was about to disappear!

I believe the trauma narrative essential to healing children with early histories of trauma. Hal's parents adopted him when he was 4 ½. Hal was finally able to adopt his parents and his brother as his forever family when the explicit memories became evident and the implicit memories were made explicitly clear.

Earlier in the book the internal working model was presented. Two main beliefs fall out of traumatic experiences. Hal's main internal belief system was that relationships weren't safe places. Adults were not to be trusted.

The second primary belief is that, "I am bad, dumb, defective or unlovable."

Maggie and Noah were placed with relatives when they were ages 5 and 2 respectively. Their early history was chaotic. The birth mother moved from place to place, man to man. Substance abuse and domestic violence dominated the lifestyle. When Noah was born, the birth mother kept handing Maggie to various relatives to provide her care. She kept Noah with her. Over and over, Maggie spent days or weeks with aunts and uncles. Noah didn't.

To Maggie, this happened because her birth mother found Noah more desirable. She said, "Well she wanted him. She didn't like me."

The reality is that Noah was easier for the birth mother to take care of. As an infant, he could be left in his crib. Maggie, as a toddler, wanted to explore. She was walking and wanting to run around. The birth mother didn't have the patience to deal with an active toddler.

Once permanently placed with her relative parents, Maggie continued to play the role of the "bad" child. She wasn't cooperative at all. Getting dressed, brushing teeth, combing hair, eating breakfast—each task was a power struggle. Once dressed, she'd take her clothes off and run around the house naked. She'd scream when her mom picked her up and tried to dress her again. She'd spit her food at her mom. It was difficult to go anywhere or get anything done! It was difficult to spend any time with Noah, whose development was delayed due to the neglect he had experienced.

Over time, Maggie did come to understand that her early perceptions were inaccurate. She gradually changed her thinking. Her self-image improved. She no longer needed to be the "bad" child. She learned that she and her brother were both "good" kids. Her birth mother's dysfunction had been the problem.

Certainly, there are many instances when both negative beliefs are operating. There are variations to these two main beliefs as well. I've put some of the more recurring irrational thoughts in the box. It should be noted that this list is not exhaustive. Trauma affects each child uniquely. So, each youngster can present with distinctive thoughts.

Traumatized children think...

(This list is not exhaustive. It depicts recurring themes that emerge during therapeutic intervention.)

Prenatal Exposure to Drugs and Alcohol
- "Why didn't my birth mom give up her drugs for me?"
- "Why wasn't I more important than her drugs or drinking?"
- "I should have stopped my birth mom from doing drugs."
- "Will my birth parents go to jail for having drugs?"
- "Will my birth parents overdose and die?"

Abandonment
- "Why do 'strangers' want me? My own birth family didn't want me."
- "My birth family would have come back for me if my adoptive family didn't adopt me."
- "I got 'lost' from my birth parents. I'm sure they are looking for me!" Or, "I got stolen from my birth parents! I just need to be given back!"

Sexual Abuse
- "I should have been able to stop the abuse from happening to me." This belief may be intensified for boys due to the

socialization process which instills in males thoughts regarding their physical strength and capacity to take care of themselves.

- "I am damaged goods." "Who will want to date me?"
- "Who could possibly love me after what happened to me?"
- "I am so different than other kids my age."
- "Am I gay?" (This occurs frequently when the child's perpetrator was the same sex.)
- "If you love me, you'll have sex with me."

Physical Abuse, Domestic Violence and Emotional Abuse

- "What's happening to my birth mom now?" "Is she safe?"
- "I am older now. I can go back and take care of her."
- "I should have acted better. Then, they wouldn't have had to abuse me."
- "I could die or someone I love could die at any given moment."
- "If my birth mom had just left her boyfriend or my birth dad, we would still be together." "If she leaves him now, I can go back." Some children do not understand that the non-offending parent was supposed to stop all forms of abuse occurring in the birth home. The child believes he can return to the birth home if the perpetrating parent is no longer in residence.
- "I am bad, dumb and stupid. My birth parents told me so." Children believe they are what adults tell them they are.
- "She picked him (her boyfriend or the birth father) instead of me. I guess she loved him more than me." Other children realize that their birth mom could have removed herself and her children from a harmful situation. These children feel doubly rejected. They ask, "Not only didn't she pick me, she chose to stay with someone who was so mean to her. Why?"

Neglect

- "I need to take care of myself. You big people can't be counted on."
- "I must not be very good. My birth mom didn't pay any attention to me."

The "How To" of Telling the Story

Following are my ideas as to how and when to tell kids their story. I do believe that narrative work is best accomplished with a professional guide.

Start at the Beginning

The trauma narrative starts with "I got born..." We need to help the left hemisphere sequence the events of the youngster's life. Sequencing allows for comprehension. Sequencing leads to making the cause-and-effect connections that will aid in accepting the story.

Going back to Hal above, he commenced his narrative at the adoption. This blocked him from forming an attachment to his adoptive family. The actual start of his story was his abandonment. Helping Hal put his pre-adoptive experiences in chronological order led Hal to connect the dots *per se*—to make the cause-and-effect connections. He was able to shift the responsibility for the adoption to the birth mother. This is where the responsibility belonged.

Below is the basic narrative we created with Hal. Additional details were inserted into this framework. Within a relatively short period of time, Hal was provided with all the information his parents had been given at the time of the adoption.

- The abandonment led to placement in foster care.

  Your birth mom left you with a baby-sitter. She never returned. We don't know why. We do know that the social workers made many efforts to find her. She was never located.
- You moved to a foster family.

  The foster mom and dad were just that—a foster couple. This family wanted to take care of kids until an adoptive family was available.
- Mom and Dad wanted to adopt.

  Mom and Dad had one son. Mom and Dad decided they wanted another son. Mom and Dad learned about you from the social worker at their adoption agency. Mom and Dad wanted you to join their family.

Kids can't form attachments and mature when they view the adoptive parent as the source of the problem. Kids develop an array of implicit and explicit thoughts about their traumatic experiences. Narrative work helps kids revise their thinking. Kids become free to join the adoptive family and "grow up."

The "Whole" Truth

I think the "just the facts ma'am" approach from the old TV show *Dragnet* is best. I tell children, tweens and teens the "whole" truth with no "holes." If kids ask something that isn't known, then we need to say, "I don't know." We want to resist filling in the blanks with misinformation.

It is important for adoptive parents to know that you didn't cause the child's pain. Talking about the trauma history and letting the grief flow leads to healing. One reason moms and dads avoid telling the story is an innate desire to help their child avoid emotional strife. Please know that you didn't cause your son's or daughter's grief. Your child arrived with this pain—rooted deeply in their brain and heart. The story is a main pathway to healing.

"Fantasy flourishes where facts flounder" was a phrase given to the adoption community by Kenneth Watson, author and adoption professional. Clinical experience has validated just how true Mr. Watson's statement is. Once I was working with a young Russian adoptee. He kept talking about his birth mother living in a beautiful castle that people from all over the world came to see. When he could live with her again, he would get to live in this castle. He was referring to St. Basil's Cathedral. Adopted at 22 months, he and his new family did indeed see St. Basil's Cathedral prior to flying home to America. He came in for services at age 14. We used Google to help him realize that his birth mother didn't live in this landmark. His parents were sad with him as he began to realistically look at his abandonment. His St. Basil's Cathedral fantasy was a way to avoid dealing with the loss of his birth mother.

Parents, too, construct narratives for children that lack veracity. A common example is that your birth mom was "sick." We do classify drug addiction as a disease. Most children think sick is equal to a medical illness. A second common example is that of poverty. "Your birth mom was too poor to keep you." As kids enter the school setting, they meet many adults with illnesses who are still working and taking care of their children. Boys and girls come to realize that many poor people do raise their sons and daughters. These stories contain "holes." They often create more questions—long-term—than they answer.

The story is important in cases in which the birth mother planned for the newborn:

> **Mercy's** forever parents were present at her birth. They had been selected by the birth mom with the help of an adoption agency. The adoption was an open adoption. By the time Mercy entered grade school, her birth mother completed college, married and had two children.
>
> Mercy attended a Christmas party at her birth mom's home. On the way home, she screamed at her adoptive mom and dad, "Why do you always make me leave?" "Why won't you let me stay with her?"

> **Keenan** was adopted by his paternal grandmother. His birth mother had a drug addiction at the time he was born. She goes in and out of rehab. Keenan sees her when she is in recovery. Recently, she showed up for a visit with a new baby. Keenan is plagued with all kinds of thoughts, mostly he keeps asking, "Will she take care of this baby?" "Does the baby have enough food?" "Does she have a place to live?" "Where will the baby live if she starts using again?"

Open adoption and kinship adoption/legal guardianship have become popular types of permanency for children. Knowing your birth family growing up can offset the "Whys?" Kids can ask their birth mother what happened. They know who they look like and where their special talents come from. Yet, there will be times when the open adoption or relative adoption experience becomes complicated. Trauma narrative work can help these adoptees maintain a strong attachment to the permanent family, while simultaneously navigating the relationship with the birth family.

> **Janet's** birth mother also made a plan for her. Janet's adoptive parents drove through the night to meet their infant daughter. Several times each year, Janet's parents and the birth mom meet for lunch. Janet, now tween

age, Googled her birth mom and, much to her shock, learned that her birth mother had two children—older than Janet.

Janet angrily confronted her parents. It was true. Janet was her birth mother's third child. Her older brothers had lived with her birth mother all along. It was a long time before trust was restored between Janet, her birth mom and her mom and dad.

Truthful disclosures offset situations like Janet's. Withheld facts that come to light jeopardize trust. The question becomes, "What else haven't you told me?"

No matter what the circumstances surrounding the adoption, telling children the "whole" truth—starting as young as possible—works best in the long-run. The story facilitates attachment, identity and it helps grow the development up. The story helps the traumatized adoptee develop the emotional health and the self-confidence needed to function successfully in all spheres of life. Pro-actively searching for and obtaining information is essential now that technology makes the birth family or your child just a click away from that contact. Clearly, we can't prepare for everything. But, we can offset some possibilities.

Creating a Narrative When Facts are Sparse

Facts are scarce for some children. Yet, even with scant information we can construct a narrative. For example, many parents adopting internationally weren't privy to touring their child's orphanage. We put together a 20-minute video of different orphanages in various countries. These snippets came from clients who were free to explore their child's institutional setting. This gives youngsters a sense of what institutional life is like. We can say, "What would a baby living there think? "What would a baby living there feel?" "What would the baby want most?" "What would the infant think when Mom and Dad arrived?" The implicit memory system responds to this type of "cognitive feeding." This is a technique learned from Daniel Hughes, author and founder of Dyadic Developmental Psychotherapy.

Or, as a second example, the 13-minute video, *Removed*, which portrays a middle-school-age girl's removal from an abusive, alcoholic birth home through a series of foster homes. It is a well-done mini-movie—extremely realistic. It offers a way to help youngsters comprehend the safety issues in a substance abusing home. Using this video, kids can conclude that their removal from their birth parents was valid. Kids also understand why they have a pile of feelings inside.

There is also a video, *Wo Ai Ni Mommy*, which portrays a Chinese orphan, Fang Sui Yong, an 8–year-old, moving to America with her new family. Fang Sui Young's American name is Faith. Prior to being adopted she was abandoned and resided in an orphanage and with a foster family. The movie is poignant. It allows for lots of discussion whether your child was adopted as an infant or an older child, internationally or domestically. Children get a vivid look at what it is like to move, the types of things orphanage staff may say throughout the process, leaving the country of origin, adapting to a new home, adapting to a new country as a trans-cultural adoptee and much more.

Children who arrive with little detail must learn to live with many unanswered questions. However, options for search and reunion are becoming possible in many countries abroad and here at home. Technology has changed the face of adoption.

Subsequent vignettes will offer additional ways to augment storytelling whether there is minimal or much background information.

The Story is Developmentally Constructed

Studies of child development reveal that by age 3, narrative function emerges.[1] We have modified our storytelling to meet the needs of these littlest clients. We have worked with children even younger than age 3. We don't expect that they'll deeply understand their narrative. Yet, they can get a basic set of facts that'll they'll grow into over time—and that initiates posttraumatic growth now. Like soccer, piano lessons, building with LEGO® or playing a board game, the story will be one more facet of life. This is a wonderful case scenario. The story is out in the open early. A question arises. It's asked and answered. Craig's case offers a sample narrative delivered via language and interventions that Craig related to.

Craig was placed with his adoptive family-to-be upon discharge from the neonatal intensive care unit (NICU.) He was 34 days old. He was born exposed to opiates. His hospital stay was a detox period. He came in for services at 2½ years. Each time his mom or dad redirected him, Craig fell to the floor, face down saying "bad boy!" Craig's narrative included the children's book, *"The House that Crack Built."* This book has two pictures that show a pregnant woman smoking a crack pipe. Craig knew that sometimes he got a shot at the doctor's office. This was a "good" drug—it came from the doctor. There are also "bad" drugs that people aren't supposed to take. Craig's narrative included role-plays with Fisher-Price Little People. His birth mom's picture (which was a mug shot we obtained online) corresponded to a Little People figurine. There were also figurines that went along with the doctors and nurses that took care of him at the hospital, as well as the social worker who transported him to Mom and Dad's house. Craig would talk through his story. "I got born." "I was a good baby." "My birth mom did bad drugs." "She had the problem." "I had to stay in the hospital 34 days." "Miss Becky [social worker] drove me to Mommy's and Daddy's." "I'm staying with Mommy and Daddy until I'm a hundred years old!" One day, Craig was role-playing his story and he said, "I was a good baby!" It was as if a light bulb came on. He said again, "I was a good baby!" "My birth mom was 'wrong!'" (He substituted his own word for his birth mom's behavior. This is a good sign of internalizing the story.) He ran to his mom and said it again. Since then, Craig's parents have been able to redirect him without Craig hiding and saying, "bad boy!"

Craig's story presentation was also augmented with pictures of a NICU unit. He could see the tubes, needles, NICU-style cribs and all the machinery. He said things like, "That's not comfortable." "Those tubes in the nose must hurt." The pictures helped his brain make sense of his early experiences. Many clients have had various medical procedures as infants and toddlers. The images now available online make for great healing resources.

The little ones never cease to be amazing in therapy. They have an immense capacity to absorb facts—and to heal. They shatter the myth that we need to "wait until he's older" to tell the story! Children of all ages can participate in narrative work when we customize our language and our tools to meet each child' developmental level.

Language in Story Telling

Positive adoption language is a part of story-telling. For example, the birth mom is "birth Mom." The birth dad is "birth Dad." If I know the birth parents' first names, I use those names. Names are a helpful way for the child to discern who we are talking about, especially if the child has had multiple placements. In any event, the birth mom isn't the "real" mom. The adoptive parents are "Mom and Dad." If anybody is the "real" parent— it's Mom and Dad. Mom and Dad do the "real" parent things every day! An array of positive adoption language charts are available online should you like to provide this information to teachers or extended family.

Keep Values in Check

Too often we lavish praise on the birth mother, portraying her act of abandonment as a selfless act of love. It's a very painful event for the abandoned person. There is a mismatch. Sons and daughters can't resolve their grief in these contradictory situations. They think, "If she loved me so much, then I should love her." Inside, this isn't always what they feel. Sometimes they are livid. Sometimes sad. Sometimes they love the birth family. Sometimes not. Rather than apply our own values to the story, we can simply validate feelings as they crop up. "Yes. I'd be mad if I were you!" "I know. It's so sad that you don't get to know your birth mom. Let me give you a hug." "I don't know if your birth mom loved you. I didn't know her. What do you think?" "You can always love her if you want too." As kids grow, they'll integrate their thoughts and feelings. I find kids do a good job of this as long we offer ongoing support:

> **Molly** has been in and out of therapy since she was 7 years old. She has re-worked her story several times. Each developmental stage leads to new thoughts and questions about her pre-adoptive experiences of her birth parents' substance abuse, their domestic violence and their abandonment of Molly. She is coming to terms with drug addiction. She recognizes that overcoming addictions is a difficult process. She realizes

that domestic violence can result from the mind-altering high. She is integrating her story within a larger context of the social problems in society at large. She said, "I've decided to forgive my birth mother. I'll always be sad that she isn't the person I wish she could be. I'll always hold out hope that she'll change. I'll always love her. But, I've got a good family. In another year, I'll be off to college—getting on with life. I think I'm finally at peace."

Re-work and Repeat

Re-work and repeat are key to successful narrative work. Molly's story noted that Molly continued to expand her thoughts and feelings for her early trauma as she grew from a grade-school-age girl to an older adolescent. With each passing year comes new, expanded ways of thinking. Kids have new questions about their trauma. Updating the narrative at regular intervals leads to ongoing gains in all facets of your child's development. Kids love to hear their favorite story or watch their favorite movie—over and over! Parents of school-age children know that it takes repetition to learn math facts or vocabulary words. The trauma narrative is no different. Children will internalize their story as we review it—over and over!

"Heads Up!" for Questions

Telling kids their story generates lots of questions. Below are some of the common questions boys and girls ask. While we can't anticipate every question, having a "heads up" about those that frequently come up gives parents a chance to prepare some responses.

- "Why did my birth parents use drugs?"
- "Do you think my birth mom thinks about me?"
- "What do you think my birth mom is doing now?"
- "Do you think she's in jail?"
- "Does she have any more children?"
- "If they get better, can I go live with them again?"

- "Are my birth parents sorry for what they did?"
- "Why did I move so much in foster care?"
- "Why didn't anyone in my country want me?"
- "Why didn't the orphanage ladies take me home?"
- "Do you think my orphanage friends got adopted?"
- "Are my birth parents alive?"
- "Are my siblings safe?"
- "Do you think my siblings think about me?"
- "How did you find me?"
- "Why did you pick me?"
- "What would you have done if I had been your baby?"

Preparing Yourself...

Talking with children about trauma requires preparation for parents. Below are some "food for thought" questions to help you get ready to tell your child their story....

- How were losses handled in your family of origin?
- What is your experience of grief and loss?
- How do you respond to a loss?
- How do you include your children in the grieving process?
- How will you help your child grieve?
- What are your views on telling children the truth about their past?
- Can you picture yourself discussing abuse, neglect and abandonment?
- What potential losses may such discussions trigger for you?
- What will be the impact of such discussions on other children in your family?

Present Information Verbally and Visually

Making the story visual as well as verbal allows children the opportunity to be creative and to move around. Visuals accommodate concrete thinking which we'll learn about in our chapter on cognitive skills. Besides, we are working with kids. Whether they are young or older, they are all still "little." We must have playful approaches to the very hard work we're asking them to do. In addition to the tools described already, below are a few more techniques to help adoptees learn their story.

Timeline

The timeline requires graph paper, scissors, tape, crayons, a pen, clip art and stickers. We cut six to eight sheets of graph paper in half horizontally and tape them together. This helps the left brain organize content in a linear fashion. The length is to demonstrate the concept of "forever family." We say to children that they are staying with their parents until they are a hundred years old.

Each square, on the graph paper, equals one month. We plot each of the child's moves. The picture below is in black and white for the purposes of printing this book. When you are constructing a timeline, each placement would be a different color. Once completed, children can clearly see how many places they have lived, and the length of each placement. We use clip art to represent the birth mother and the types of trauma the child experienced. (I have used white out to conceal identifying information.)

Figure 10.1: The timeline described on the following page.

The timeline pictured was created with a boy, currently age 11. He resided with his birth parents until age 4. The home was replete with domestic violence and physical abuse. The birth father was arrested on numerous occasions for his violence. The birth mother was also arrested many times for drug trafficking. This youngster came into foster care when both birth parents were incarcerated simultaneously. He and his two older sisters were first placed with a relative. Shortly, the aunt and uncle asked for the removal of all of the children due to their behavioral issues. The children moved through two more foster homes after which they were separated. Each went to live with a different foster family. Subsequently, the boy moved through two more foster homes. Finally, at age 9, he found his forever family. Since arrival in his adoptive family, he has progressed in leaps and bounds!

As we work through the timeline, we'll add more pictures and stickers to represent the types of activities he experienced in each foster home and with his adoptive family. The latter end of the timeline is bright and colorful when completed. Adoptive families go on vacation, camping, celebrate holidays, cook, garden, ride horses, read, sing and play sports. It shows that life has improved. The child is safe and well taken care of. The child can move on.

Drawings

Drawing out scenes of traumatic experiences can help the brain put words with feelings. The drawings that follow will elicit feelings for the reader. The drawings make clear an internal working model of shame, embarrassment and not being loved.

Figures 10.2 and 10.3 were drawn by a teen who lived on the outskirts of life *per se*. He stayed in his bedroom for long periods of time. It took effort to get him to join the family for dinner, an outing or chores. He was withdrawn at school. He didn't join any extra-curricular activities or make friends. He felt too ashamed of himself. He couldn't comprehend anyone liking him. His internal working model did shift. Today, he is gainfully employed. He enjoys his relationships with Mom and Dad. He has made friends at his job.

Figure 10.2: The other children in the drawings are siblings from whom he was separated at the time of adoption.

Figure 10.3: This picture demonstrates how small he felt in comparison to his birth mother. It also captures how disempowered he felt.

Lifebook

The Lifebook is a chronological accounting of the youngster's, tween's or teen's life. I've seen many lovely Lifebooks created by moms who scrapbook. A three-ring binder will suffice as well. Children can draw scenes from their life. On sheets of copy paper lay out the captions that correspond to the experiences. For example, let's lay out the basic facts of the teen above. His story starts with, "I got born." "I lived with my birth mom." "I never met or lived with my birth dad." "My birth mom was abusive. She hit me and locked me in the closet." "She didn't always feed me and my brother and sister." "When I was 9 years old, she took me and my siblings to a 'friend' and left me there." "The 'friend' found my adoptive family at her church." "I moved to Mom and Dad's house." "I was adopted by Mom and Dad." Over time, we add the feelings that correspond to each scene.

As adoptees complete their art works, we talk about each drawing—restructuring the thoughts and facilitating the grief. The Lifebook is a project that is completed over a long period of time. Reiterating, working at the child's pace is critical.

All is organized into the binder along with any photos and paperwork the family may have received at the time of the adoption.

Please make a copy of the Lifebook:

> **Melinda**, now 15, was always reorganizing her Lifebook. Reports received at the time of her adoption were strewn everywhere as was the photocopy of the one picture Melinda had of her birth mother. The family had only received the photocopy, not the original. One evening, Melinda spilled pop on the photo. It did dry, but it was stained. It made it hard to recognize her birth mother.

Sometimes anger about the trauma swells up, children rip up their Lifebook. One of a kind photos and papers are destroyed. Any documents, photos or videos that you have are special. They are your child's life.

Please see the Resource section for additional information about constructing a Lifebook.

Self-Portrait: "I am a quality kid!"

Knowing who you are requires knowing where you've been. The story work helps builds a positive identity. Recognizing one's qualities and achievements is important to answering the question, "Who am I?" too.

Using a roll of paper obtained from a local printer, we have kids lay down and we trace their outline. They work to fill themselves in. They can list qualities, likes and dislikes, talents, accomplishments—anything that defines them. This is an ongoing project. It hangs in the home. Mom and Dad can add to it as well. "Seeing" the self-representation helps the child with a history of trauma internalize that, "I am a quality kid!" That's the name of the six-part group we run to kick off this part of services.

If you've felt "bad" or "shameful" for a long time, it's hard to decide who you are. This group provides the activities needed to help children of all ages get to know themselves. They can move to positive identity formation.

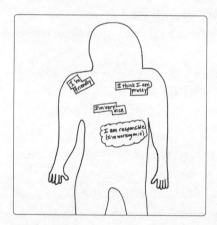

Figure 10.4: This teen girl recently entered services. Sadly, she can think of only a few qualities she possesses.

Figure 10.5: This tween told me that he felt like he was "half-way" there. He means that he is growing in his positive view of himself. Some of the statements on the drawing include, I love history, I know my Catholic faith, I am good at martial arts. He is proud of his accomplishments and qualities. It is wonderful to see him growing.

Role-plays

Role-plays give kids the opportunity to move around in therapy. Therapists and props allow playing out various scenarios from the child's life. We can go through moves, orphanage life, abandonment and arriving in the adoptive home. Most children like the opportunity to imagine they are talking to people from their past. Often, they set the record straight about their thoughts and feelings for what happened to them. Grief is often a part of role-plays. We're sure to end with a nice period of nurture in Mom's and Dad's arms. Role-plays can be very healing interventions.

Grief: Sit with It

Grief and loss are a part of adoption. Adoption is a relationship built on loss. No one particularly likes grief, yet expressing the feelings for past maltreatment and the loss of people loved frees the child up to move on psychologically.

Grief does enhance attachment. Think for a moment about when we mourn the passing of a friend or relative; throughout the viewing and funeral, we connect through story-telling and sharing feelings. Afterwards, we go and share a meal. We hug more and tell more stories about the deceased. We see folks we may not often see. We leave the event connected to those who are part of our life. We comfort one another via hugs. The same happens in therapy. Parents see a vulnerable child in need of their nurture. The child is viewed differently. No longer is she just a source of frustrating behavior. She is a wounded child in need of her mom and dad.

When grief flows, it is best to "sit with it." Instinctively, parents want to make their children feel happy. This is a natural reaction to a sad or scared child. "You have us now." "We have lots of happy times as a family." But, statements like these are at mismatch with the youngster. Moms and dads can sit quietly, dry the tears or accept the anger with statements like, "Yes. It is so sad that your birth mom left you." "You were so scared in the orphanage." "I'd be angry if I were you! It wasn't fair!" Reflecting the feelings helps to release the emotion. Healing arrives when the heart mends in this manner.

Chapter Summary

- Helping children create their trauma narrative at a careful pace makes the explicit memories accurate and the implicit memories explicit. The brain's left and right hemisphere can work together to put meaning to the experiences, and to facilitate the grief. The youngster's heart heals.

- The story leads to the child revising the internal working model. They learn that relationships are safe and loving. They come to view themselves as smart, capable and lovable. They are finally able to adopt their families, after having been adopted by the family perhaps years earlier.

- Truthful disclosures, the "whole" story, starting as young as possible allow the adoptee to grow up with his story. This builds identity development and strengthens the capacity to engage in healthy relationships. Developmentally appropriate and positive adoption language is utilized. Repetition of the story ensures understanding. Re-working the story at regular intervals accommodates the expanded thought processes of the growing child.

- The narrative is best absorbed when we present information visually and verbally. The timeline, Lifebook, drawings, role-plays, self-portraits, videos, Fisher Price Little People—many options exist to help kids see and hear the events of their early lives.

- Parents are encouraged to reflect on the impact of the story-telling on themselves prior to initiating trauma narrative work with their child. Food for thought questions provided in this chapter can assist with this process.

- Grief will flow during trauma narrative work. Moms and dads can help the child "sit with it." Empathically re-stating the feelings validates the youngster's emotional experience. Parent–child attachment is strengthened when feelings are shared.

- Trauma narrative work is best carried out with an experienced professional.

Endnote

1   Siegel, D.J. (1999). *The Developing Mind: How Relationships and the Brain Interact to Shape Who we Are*. New York: The Guilford Press. p, 322.

CHAPTER 11

Cognitive Development: The Traumatized Child Goes to School

A part of *intellectual* or *mental development*, cognitive activities include skills like thinking, perception, memory, reasoning, concept development, problem-solving ability and abstract thinking. Language, with its requirements of symbolism and memory, is one of the most important and complicated cognitive activities.

Cognitive skills are associated with school readiness and school performance. Academic success is valued as the means to secure a good future. It is concerning to parents when their child lags educationally. Cognitive skills become a priority.

Educating a child with an early history of trauma is often no small task. I'll qualify by saying that some children with early trauma histories do navigate their academics with minor assistance. Yet, for most, learning is a struggle.

There are many factors that contribute to educational outcomes for children with a history of maltreatment. I'd like to offer an overview of some of the critical factors supported by what I see clinically and in research.

Cognitive Skills Start with Secure Relationships

Babies and toddlers explore the environment from a secure base. A nurturing parent and an enriching environment allow the baby to safely examine and interact with all facets of her world. Cognitive skills, like other skills talked about in this book, start in infancy.

For example, right after birth vision is important as infants can't move much. Objects and faces are beginning ways of learning and interacting. Babies are particularly interested in patterns and faces. Infants like checkerboards or stripes at first. Then, they prefer circles and curves.[1] The human face is full of circles and curves. Patterns help children learn sequencing.[2] Patterns lend to making predictions, and they help establish order. Multiplication tables have patterns. Patterning skills are the basis of math, especially algebra. Babies are learning math skills within weeks and months of being born! Understanding weather patterns can save lives. The calendar is a pattern of days, weeks and months. We can make plans when we know our schedule. Recognizing and using patterns is an essential means to learning and to living life in an organized fashion.

Sequencing, like cause-and-effect thinking, can develop from the daily routine. The infant cries. Mom or dad arrives. This is a sequence. From this point, all types of sequences occur and are noticed by the infant and toddler. We use sequencing when we read or watch a movie—there is a beginning, a middle and an end. Recipes require a sequence of ingredients if you want a delectable outcome. We need to sequence sounds to make a word. We sequence when we give and follow directions, "Take off your coat. Hang it up. Come to the kitchen for a snack." School-age children follow increasingly complex directions as they mature to higher grades. Sequencing events is needed for reading comprehension and making conversation.

> **Taylor**, age 12, arrived for therapy. She has lived with her adoptive family since she was 19 months old. When asked, "What's new?", she replied, "Mom got mad." This is the middle of the story. The beginning of the story is that Taylor had lost her second winter coat. Mom learned this when the two got in the car to come to therapy. Taylor didn't have a coat. Taylor was ready to hop in the car—on a 20-degree day—wearing only a long-sleeve shirt and jeans. When Mom asked where the coat could be, Taylor replied, "I don't know."

This type of exchange is common at our office. It's hard to accept responsibility when there is no sequencing. Taylor was mad that Mom was angry.

Taylor wasn't upset that losing her coat created an expense—and perhaps a cold or the flu.

Or, trying to get the details of a field trip can result in the relaying of every minute detail or a story with no organization:

> In response to being asked how the field trip to a local farm park went, **Thomas**, age 9, responded, "We saw a cow. They went with them over there. Then there was milk. They got a hamburger. Then chickens were running around. They ate the hamburgers. Then they and me got back on the bus."

Overall, Thomas and his classmates got to milk a cow, feed the chickens and pet the baby colt. They learned much about growing vegetables too. Indeed, each child was provided a lunch of hamburgers, fries and cherry pie. It is hard to make passing grades and friends when rudimentary cognitive skills are at deficit.

Sorting helps children understand what is alike and different. This leads to comparing and contrasting. Sorting by color and shape is a precursor to distinguishing letters from numbers. We also use sorting every day when we do the laundry or grocery shop. Salad dressing is sorted into isle ten, while bread is in isle one. Sorting leads to order. Learning various shapes and then drawing shapes, helps kids eventually write the alphabet. Vocabulary is expanded when kids sort. We can say things like, "that's lime green or lemon yellow or sky blue." We add descriptive words.

The parent–child attachment puts in motion the child's ability to absorb every aspect of life around her. This exploration sets the stage for lifelong learning. The parent provides verbal praise and prompting as the child masters each step of growth. Simple things like stacking blocks or Dixie® cups get applause. Sorting blocks by color results in helping the toddler carry out a high-five. By age 2, every nook and cranny in the house has been explored. Pots and pans have been pulled out of the cupboard. A wooden spoon was the drum stick. Object permanency has been mastered. The little one knows that objects continue to exist, and they are located where he put them last. Hide and seek helps teach spatial relationships. Your child learns what size space he does or doesn't fit into. He's mastered push–pull toys, music boxes, rolling a ball and bath toys. She'll begin imitative play, riding a tricycle and using large crayons to scribble! Countless rounds of peek-a-boo set in motion working memory—a key element of executive function. The enriched environment that includes common household items (empty paper towel rolls, egg cartons, plastic containers, cardboard boxes, an unbreakable mirror, old magazines), simple toys (balls, blocks, cars, dolls, cardboard books, toy telephone) and family members fosters the skills for future scholastic success.

In the context above, the child trusts the parent and she wants to engage with her surroundings. She enjoys relating with her mom, dad, brothers and sisters. The insecurely attached child is anxious about relationships. She spends more time staying in proximity of the parent, than exploring. I have evaluated many young anxious children. They have very little sustained interest in toys or household objects. Normally, by age 8 months children can attend for two to three minutes, and by 12 months, many kids have an attention span of 15 minutes.[3]

Other insecurely attached children keep to themselves:

> **Ronnie** was described as a calm, quiet baby and toddler. In fact, the parents' concern was that he was too silent—and distant. They often had to go make sure Ronnie was in the living room playing. He never sought out Mom or Dad. This pattern of behavior continued into the preschool years. Ronnie's mom would go locate him several times during the day. She'd go to his bedroom and invite him down to the kitchen with her. Within a few minutes, he was off to another room. Mom started Ronnie in a play group. Ronnie was very possessive of the toys he selected to use. "Mine!" He pushed other kids away. Kindergarten arrived, and Ronnie still preferred a solo act. Ronnie wasn't interested in relationships at all. While he could play with toys, he was missing the rich skills that come from imitative play and pretend play. He was lacking in skills like turn-taking and sharing. Imagination and creativity were stifled.

Quality of the parent–child relationship cultivates the growth of cognitive skills. The enriching content—or lack of—is a factor too. Compare

Ronnie's story to what we have learned about the impact of neglect. Verbal interaction is sparse, as are furnishings and toys. Or, the infant in a home of domestic violence has learned to screen out human voices because they are loud and unpleasant. These kids have trouble later when they need to listen for information or make conversation.[4] Or, let's think about the baby detoxing after birth who can't read the mother's signals (or who may not get a foster or adoptive mother for several weeks or months.) Attachment is a two-way street. The mother learns to read the infant's cues. Vice versa, the baby learns to read the mother's signals. Prenatal substance abuse impairs this process. An insecure attachment can result.

The outcome is frequently that the "bright" or "smart" child or the child with a good level of intelligence as measured by an IQ test is a conundrum. We often equate intelligence with academic success. Parents and school professionals exclaim, "She's so smart! If she would just apply herself!" Application isn't always the issue. Motivation is inhibited when the stressresponse system is overactive. The culprit may be that the child lacks the foundational skills needed for academic success. Kids needs skills to go along with their IQ.

Cognitive skills can be re-built. Check in with your school psychologist or teacher to learn about games, workbooks, children's books and apps that can help rebuild sequencing, patterning and other early learning-based skills. Psychological or neuropsychological testing completed by a school district or a community-based professional can help identify your son's or daughter's specific gaps.

Self-regulation is Essential to Learning

Strong self-regulation relates to positive social and academic outcomes early on and throughout a child's life.[5] In contrast, children with poor self-regulation are more likely to struggle with building and maintaining positive relationships, paying attention and following directions—all of which affect school success and beyond.[6] Children with strong regulation by age 4, have nearly 50 percent greater odds than their peers of completing college by age 25.[7]

I use the term self-regulation to refer to emotional regulation. Others use it to describe cognitive regulation—attending to the task at hand. I think, often, the two go hand in hand. For example:

> Four years ago, we re-located our office. We didn't move far, just to the next town. We're on the same road. One evening shortly after we moved, **Randy**, a tween, couldn't get settled in the therapy session. He was looking all around and nervously fidgeting. He said, "What's that noise?" His mom and I listened. We didn't hear anything unusual to us. A minute went by and Randy said, "that noise coming from outside." Mom and I listened again. Other than some subtle traffic noises, we still didn't hear anything. We all sat quietly waiting for the sound to occur again. When it did, Randy said, "right there." The road in front of the office had a small bump. Indeed, trucks passing by made a slight thumping noise as they passed over the bump. Randy's mom said, "It's the way the truck sounds going over the bump." This explanation did calm Randy down. He was worried that someone was trying to get in a side entrance near the front of the building. He thought the sound was a person rattling a locked door. I never cease to be amazed by the hypervigilance that plagues traumatized adoptees. It interferes with their attention and emotional regulation.

Hypervigilance extends to the classroom. The child preoccupied with what's going on around him has a hard time hearing and following the teacher's directions. Chapters 3, 4, 8 and 9 focused on self-regulation because it's critical to learning and socializing.

Self-concept: "I can't" is the Mantra

Challenges become a major source of frustration and anxiety for the youngster, tween or teen with poor self-concept. They have a hard time finding solutions to problems and they are plagued with negative self-thoughts—"I am stupid," "I can't do anything right" or "I don't deserve a family." Faced with a new and immediate challenge, their immediate response is "I can't." They frequently become passive, withdrawn or depressed. Poor self-perceptions are also linked to teenage pregnancy, eating disorders, suicide attempts and suicidal thoughts.[8]

> **Kim**, age 10, had a hard time sitting down to do her homework. She put it off as long as she could—until her mother issued an ultimatum. Then, the tears came. She'd shove the book across the table and throw her pencil. Kim didn't believe that she could complete the assignments. She didn't feel "smart" enough. Kim had an early history of life in an orphanage. Care givers could only provide limited attention and kudos. Kim spent most days doing little more than laying or standing in her crib. She didn't get to learn and play.

Poor self-image is an iceberg as we learned in Chapter 8. It's a trigger and it leads to emotional dysregulation. Kim isn't going to start her homework until the "fizz"—emotions—settles. This scenario plays out in families built by adoption every day. Homework is a major stressor for families participating in our services.

> **Joseph**, age 13, arrived in his family at aged 18 months after abuse and neglect. Joseph did complete his homework each evening, yet he never turned his assignments in to his teacher. Every year he stuffed them in his locker or threw them out the bus window. I did enquire about this one evening in therapy when Joseph was particularly cooperative. He replied quickly that, "I don't always feel like my answers are okay. I don't want the teachers to be mad at me."
>
> Joseph's dad started faxing Joseph's homework to his teachers. He did this each day for one month. The teachers graded it and sent it back to Dad. Dad printed it and hung it on a wall near Joseph's bedroom. Joseph noticed that all the assignments had high grades. Joseph gained the confidence to hand in completed papers on his own.

Homework is one area that is affected by the child's internal working model of poor self-concept. Completing classroom work is a struggle as well. Many school-age children seem to do well in Kindergarten, first and second grade when they are learning to read. Then, they hit a wall—often third or fourth grade, later for some—when they need to read to learn. They aren't integrating information. As you are reading this book, you are adding the content and tips to your existing knowledge base. You're thinking about how you can apply the new ideas. You're deciding what you agree with and what doesn't suit you. You're evaluating the information. Your knowledge base grows. Many children we work with memorize well. Yet, when called upon to apply and evaluate the material in new ways, they simply don't have the ability. Comprehension is lacking. School work becomes overwhelming. Self-concept plummets further. Many tweens and teens will find ways to circumvent assignments. Parents must take an active role in advocating for services to bolster their son's or daughter's academic course of learning.

Getting along with others is a critical part of school life as well. We'll tackle how to help kids improve play and social skills in upcoming chapters.

Concrete and Abstract Thinking

Concrete thinkers are focused on facts and literal definitions:

> **Dean**, age 11, has been stealing since he was placed with Dan and Rita seven years ago. Dan stated, "Dean, you have sticky fingers and it needs to stop!" Dean, puzzled, began to feel his fingers. He replied, "Dad, I washed my hands a few minutes ago. My fingers aren't sticky." Dan, annoyed, said, "Dean, you know what I mean." Dean replied, "No, really, I washed my hands just a few minutes ago." Dan then stated, "Enough. I don't want to hear anymore."

Dean has no idea what his father was talking about. His immature thought processes only allow for literal interpretations. Because of this, arguments frequently occur due to the child's exacting manner. The rule, "no running in the house" is taken as fact. Kids like Dean exclude that implied in the rule about running are similar behaviors such as hopping, skipping and jumping across the living room. The concrete thinker sees the world as black or white, good or bad, mean or nice. Everything ranks as a 1 or 5—there is no 2, 3 or 4. There are no gray areas.

Children with histories of trauma move from concrete to abstract thinking along a continuum. In adolescence, we see youth with varying degrees of abstract thinking, rather than fully operational abstract thinking. Abstract thinking helps to devise plans and solve problems. We give thought to what we think and what others think—critical thinking. We can more easily have theory of mind as we can see other's feelings. We form opinions and principles. We can generalize and transfer knowledge from one content area to another. We understand metaphors and analogies. We can understand the relationship between verbal and non-verbal—symbols for instance—ideas. Higher-level math can be accomplished. We can picture things mentally and manipulate them. We see ourselves in the future.

Concept maps and graphic organizers can be utilized to help expand abstract thought. They can also be used to facilitate reading comprehension. Ask your school professionals about these tools if your kids aren't already using them. You can also visit the Reading Rockets website (see Resources) for examples of these tools.

Language and Literacy

Once children learn to talk, they can learn to read and write. Language leads to literacy. We don't often stop to think about all the things we do with language:

- Expressing feelings.
- Forming and stating opinions.
- Sharing fond memories of places, we've been and the people we've been with.
- Going over preparations that need to be made for the week or a special occasion.
- Coordinating the daily routines.
- Giving directions.
- Comforting a friend or family member.
- Correcting behavior.
- Passing on facts or news.
- Calling 911 for help.
- Seeking input.
- Completing a work project.

The list could go on! Everyday we use our words to talk about all kinds of things! We also use our body language to communicate via tone of voice, facial expressions, body posture, gestures. This is our non-verbal communication.

We start talking to babies before they're born! Once they arrive in the world, talking never stops! Recently I was in a clothing store. A mom was holding up two blouses for her young toddler to view. He was looking up at her from his stroller as she was asking, "Do you think Mommy would look better in the orange or the yellow blouse?" In another isle, there was a mom and a preschool-age child. This little one was screaming! Mom was saying, "I know you're mad. But, we don't always buy everything we want. Sometimes you get a toy. Sometimes you don't." She gave her a pat on the shoulder and continued pushing her cart. We converse all day about all kinds of things! We narrate thoughts, feelings, expectations, rules and so much more. Eventually our words become our kids' self-talk. With self-talk, kids can guide their own behavior.

Children with histories of trauma don't always get to be recipients of this verbal flow. They enter school with language deficits. This puts them at risk for literacy problems.

We've conducted about two hundred QEEGs (see Chapter 3)—brain maps—on children with early histories of trauma. Consistently we see underdeveloped, stressed language areas. An area known as Wernicke's area, is involved in the comprehension or understanding of written and spoken language. Another region, Broca area or Broca's area helps us put our thoughts into words. We can express ourselves. When the stress-response system perceives a threat and the child dysregulates emotionally, Broca area becomes stressed. When we confront boys and girls in this state, Broca area becomes more stressed. It follows then that the youngster, tween or teen becomes less verbal. We then view them as defiant because they aren't responding to us.

Together, these two brain areas contribute to our expressive and receptive language. They enable us to speak as well as interpret, process, and understand spoken and written language.

Many families we work with have invested resources into obtaining special education services, tutoring and speech therapy for their sons and daughters. The eventual result is a child with enhanced language skills. Talking and reading are essential for academic achievement—and life success. Visit Speech and Language Kids or The American Speech-Language-Hearing Association to learn more about advancing your son's or daughter's language and literacy.

Please know that it's never too early to start reading to your child.[9] Infants love the sound of your voice, whether you're talking to them or reading a story out loud. The more words kids hear, the more words they learn.[10] They enjoy your company very much! Select books they can chew on and pull on. The point is to give them a positive experience of books early on. They'll grow into a love of reading. If your child arrives at an older age, make reading a priority. His literacy depends on it.

Knowledge About Trauma: The Budding Trauma-Sensitive School Movement

The Adverse Childhood Experiences (ACE) study[11] has made clear that early experiences impact future violence, victimization, lifelong health and opportunity. The original ACE study was conducted by Kaiser-Permanente. The Centers for Disease Control and Prevention (CDC) continues ongoing surveillance of ACEs by assessing the medical status of the study participants via periodic updates of morbidity and mortality data.

The study consists of over 17,000 participants, 54 percent female, 46 percent male. The majority, 74 percent, are Caucasian. Seventy-five percent have obtained a college degree or undertaken advanced study. Ages 19–40 comprised 14.1 percent of participants, 18.6 percent were 40–49, 19.9 percent were 50–59 and 46.4 percent were over 60. Overall, the survey group is white, educated, middle-class folks. These individuals completed confidential surveys as part of routine physical exams at Health Maintenance Organizations in Southern California.

The study is eye-opening to say the least! It is worth taking a few minutes to visit the CDC website (see Resources) to view the study in-depth. Almost two-thirds of study participants reported at least one ACE, and more than one in five reported three or more ACEs.

All ACE questions refer to the respondent's first 18 years of life. The ACEs included responses to the following areas: abuse, neglect and household dysfunction. See Figure 10.6 for a graphic presentation of this information.

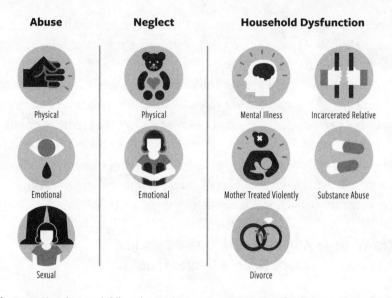

Figure 10.6: Adverse childhood experiences. Source: Centers for Disease Control and Prevention. Image credit: Robert Wood Johnson Foundation.

Abuse

- **Emotional abuse:** A parent, stepparent, or adult living in your home swore at you, insulted you, put you down, or acted in a way that made you afraid that you might be physically hurt.
- **Physical abuse:** A parent, stepparent, or adult living in your home pushed, grabbed, slapped, threw something at you, or hit you so hard that you had marks or were injured.
- **Sexual abuse:** An adult, relative, family friend, or stranger who was at least 5 years older than you touched or fondled your body in a sexual way, made you touch his/her body in a sexual way, attempted to have any type of sexual intercourse with you.

Household Dysfunction

- **Mother treated violently:** Your mother or stepmother was pushed, grabbed, slapped, had something thrown at her, was kicked, bitten, hit with a fist, hit with something hard, repeatedly hit for over at least a few minutes, or threatened or hurt by a knife or gun by your father (or stepfather) or mother's boyfriend.

- **Household substance abuse:** A household member was a problem drinker or alcoholic or a household member used street drugs.
- **Mental illness in household:** A household member was depressed or mentally ill or a household member attempted suicide.
- **Parental separation or divorce:** Your parents were separated or divorced.
- **Criminal household member:** A household member went to prison.

Neglect

- **Emotional neglect:** Someone in your family helped you feel important or special, you felt loved, people in your family looked out for each other and felt close to each other, and your family was a source of strength and support.
- **Physical neglect:** There was someone to take care of you, protect you, and take you to the doctor if you needed it, you didn't have enough to eat, your parents were too drunk or too high to take care of you, and you had to wear dirty clothes.

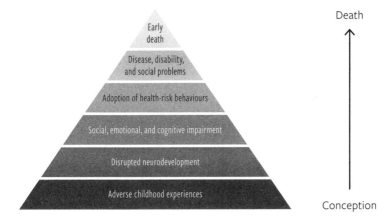

Figure 10.7: Mechanism by which adverse childhood experiences influence health and wellbeing throughout the lifespan. Source: Centers for Disease Control and Prevention.

As the number of ACEs increases so does the risk for the following:

- Alcoholism and alcohol abuse.
- Chronic obstructive pulmonary disease.
- Depression.
- Fetal death.
- Health-related quality of life.
- Illicit drug use.
- Ischemic heart disease.
- Liver disease.
- Poor work performance.
- Financial stress.
- Risk for intimate partner violence.
- Multiple sexual partners.
- Sexually transmitted diseases.
- Smoking.
- Suicide attempts.
- Unintended pregnancies.
- Early initiation of smoking.
- Early initiation of sexual activity.
- Adolescent pregnancy.
- Risk for sexual violence.
- Poor academic achievement.

The ACE study makes clear that early experiences are far more common than we ever knew, and that ACEs can have a lifelong impact on individuals.

This ACE study has increased awareness of how many school-age children are potentially experiencing ACEs. Slowly, a trauma-sensitive school movement is advancing. California, Pennsylvania, Massachusetts, Washington and Wisconsin are among the states leading the effort to highlight the prevalence of trauma among the school-age population.[12]

Clearly, the trauma-sensitive school movement is in its beginning stages. Yet, resources are being generated. This is good news for adoptive parents. Information is becoming readily available for you to pass onto your teachers, principals, superintendents, classroom aides, school board members and anyone else involved in the education of your child. (I know it gets tiring educating everyone in your child's life about trauma. We need to do it anyway!) Send the CDC link to your teacher today. It's a good way to introduce your child's special needs to school professionals.

Another wonderful resource is the website, Helping Traumatized Children Learn, Trauma and Learning Policy Initiative, a joint program with Harvard Law School and the Massachusetts Advocates for Children. At Helping Traumatized Children Learn there are two free downloads that help explain the impact of trauma on learning. This organization recently put five videos about trauma and learning on YouTube.

There are two books by Susan Craig, Ph.D. that are written for school professionals. Each explains the impact of trauma on learning. Each offers abundant classroom strategies for helping traumatized children learn. Please see the Resources for these titles. Many of Dr. Craig's ideas can easily be translated into 504 or IEP goals and interventions.

All these materials are in the Resources section of this book.

A Common Language

The trauma-sensitive school movement gives us a common language. Kids with traumatic beginnings get labeled with various mental health diagnoses: Attention-Deficit/ Hyperactivity Disorder, Oppositional Defiant Disorder, Conduct Disorder, Posttraumatic Stress Disorder or Disruptive Mood Dysregulation Disorder. Often, it takes several diagnoses to describe the youngster's symptoms. Your adoptee may meet the criteria for these diagnoses. He also has a history of complex trauma. The root problem is the poor beginning. Gaining a basic understanding of the trauma, we can all "talk trauma." When we all speak the same language, we'll more readily align on academic goals. Children will benefit from a shared understanding. Following are some talking points on my "wish list." These are suggestions, not criticism. If you are an educational professional reading this book, then you are seeking knowledge and this endeavor is commendable. If you are reading this book and have ideas to tweak this list, please feel free to email me.

- The child's behavior stems from the trauma. It is a manifestation of a larger underlying problem. It's invisible. We can't always "see" the trauma when we look at the child the same as we can "see" physical challenges, for example. It exists nonetheless.
- Emotional regulation is key to the traumatized child succeeding in the classroom. Calming is the daily goal. Behavioral consequences are secondary.
- One-size-fits-all behavioral modification and zero tolerance policies require re-thinking. Detention and suspension isolate students and interrupt learning for kids who already have academic challenges. Many tweens and teens begin to seek suspension,

Lyle, age 16, was suspended for chronic use of profanity and intimidating the teacher. He would get in the teacher's face and swear at her. Lyle had been suspended many times for other behaviors. Lyle wanted to get suspended. When life at school was too stressful, Lyle wanted to spend a few days at home. Lyle coped by avoiding and withdrawing. Once Lyle's school team understood this, they found ways to help Lyle take breaks within the school walls. Lyle was able to utilize this help. He stopped the cycle of suspensions.

- Certainly, there are kids who cause safety problems. Decisions do need to be made as to how to best manage these students based on the layout and resources of individual school buildings and classrooms. Even in these cases, return to classroom is a priority. Relationships buffer children from trauma's developmental disruption and help them develop resilience.[13] Reward systems aren't as rich with opportunities for developmental and personal growth as are techniques that foster accepting responsibility and making amends or restitution.
- The areas of language and literacy need ongoing assessment and services.
- Homework needs to be the child's responsibility. Often, they won't take parental help with their homework. Many are flat out defiant

about completing it. The adoptive home can't be a battleground each evening.

- Physical activity is important to brain functioning and classroom behavior. For example, reading scores improve after an active period.[14] Outlets for movement need to be provided.

Robbie, age 9, had a hard time on the playground. He was described as a "bully" by classmates. When an aide was available, Robbie was assisted, at recess, by the aide to play nicely with the other kids. When no aide was available, Robbie could go to the gym to participate in whatever class was in process. This teacher–parent-generated idea worked well for Robbie. Prior to this, Robbie had to sit in the classroom during recess. He didn't get the opportunity to exercise. His behavior deteriorated as the day progressed.

- Eligibility for extra-curricular activities shouldn't hinge on grades.

Age 14, **Marcus**, started thinking about his identity. His mood, behavior and school work declined. He became preoccupied with his birth family. He searched for them on the Internet, instead of doing his homework. His grades plummeted. Two semesters later, he was suspended from the soccer team due to his grade point average. This was a big blow to Marcus. After school, Marcus started hanging out in the local park. He fell in with the "wrong crowd." Drug use started. Marcus entered services. His recovery took time. Many adoptees experience a very difficult adolescence when the trauma narrative hasn't been dealt with. A "normal" developmental period was perceived as Marcus being delinquent.

Before we remove kids from supportive environments like athletics, let's be sure we really need to. Rules with case-by-case flexibility benefit children in temporary crisis.

- Interventions that are identified as effective should follow the student from one academic year to the next. Revisions can be made later.

204 THE SCIENCE OF PARENTING ADOPTED CHILDREN

Mia, age 10, had the capacity to become aggressive in the classroom. Her third-grade teacher noticed that there were signs when Mia was becoming emotionally dysregulated. Mia would shake her foot. Her facial expression changed to angry. Then, she'd start blurting out rude comments. When the teacher noticed the foot shaking, she'd ask Mia to take an envelope to the secretaries in the office. Mia loved this errand. It made her feel like a special helper. The envelope contained a blank piece of paper. This errand was pre-arranged with the secretaries. The secretaries always acted like the envelop was very important. This walk helped Mia calm down.

The next school year, Mom asked the fourth-grade teacher to consider this tool. This teacher responded that she preferred to develop her own plans. Within three weeks, Mia's mom received a phone call that Mia had tipped her desk over in the classroom. Other kids had been frightened. Subsequently, school staff agreed that Mia could run envelopes to the office.

Jack, age 12, a foster child moved to an adoptive home between 5th and 6th grade. His school records got lost in the transfer process. Jack's behavior plan, carefully crafted by his previous school, was finally obtained two months into the 6th grade school year. Jack had already made a poor impression on his new classmates, a reputation that didn't go away all year.

- Electronic device use requires input from the parents. School-issued devices and requests involving devices strain adoptive families.

Brianna, age 16, didn't have a cell phone due to her ongoing posting of sexually provocative selfies. One teacher wanted the students to take photos of instructions written on the blackboard. He felt he could cover more content in class, and he felt the kids had access to the specific workings of the math problems this way. The rationale made sense. When he realized that Brianna didn't have a cell phone, he told her she'd have to get other kids in the class to pass the information along to her. Brianna wasn't in the social loop at school due to her sexting. Brianna's parents had to meet with the teacher to resolve this matter.

Rides home from after-school activities often create the need for kids to be able to contact their parents. This puts pressure on the family to give their sons and daughters a privilege they'd rather not.

Sam's 9th grade teacher wanted to be able to Tweet her students their assignments. The last place Sam needed to be was on a social media platform. Sam's mom wound up creating an account to access the group. All year, she relayed information to Sam.

Then, there is the whole issue of iPads or computers assigned to students. Be it assigned to the adoptee or an adoptee's sibling, these devices wreak havoc. The adoptee exclaims, "I have to be on it. I have homework to do." Parents feel like they need to abide. The child escapes family tasks. Or, the other kids in the family are asking Mom, "Have you seen my school iPad?" If left unattended for a second, an adoptee who steals is waiting for the opportunity to try the device out.

Many are masters at getting around the safeguards. Recently, adopted brothers hacked into the school's computer system and changed student grades in exchange for payments. On the positive side, these guys may have good careers if we can facilitate their moral development! They have learned the ways of technology well!

The list of issues created by devices is very long. These are but a few examples. I am all in for technology. But, in the hands of kids socially and emotionally "little," the responsibility to use the device hasn't developed. Parents and teachers partnering together can brainstorm technology accommodations to suit the family, the academic goals and the safety of the child.

In discussions I have with parents about school, I do ask them to think about how hard it is for them to manage their child's actions. While we should be able to expect a friendly, supportive relationship with the school, we can't always expect that the academic setting is going to accomplish as much as we'd like. As we grow up the adopted child, academic learning does improve.

Executive Functions: The One-Track Brain

Executive functions were described in Chapter 3 as comprised of three parts: working memory, cognitive flexibility and inhibitory control. Solutions to improve attention and impulsivity were put forth in Chapter 4. Cause-and-effect thinking was discussed in Chapter 6. Causality underlies many executive functions. For example, planning, goal-setting and organizing all require an "If...then..." approach. "If I want to do well on my history test, then I should complete my math and science homework first. Then, I can spend the remainder of my time on my history." "If I'm going to play baseball, then I need to get the schedule. I'll need to work out rides with Mom and Dad. I'll need to see if practice and game times fit on the family calendar." Upcoming chapters will cover being social and playful. We'll see that "no batteries needed" play contributes greatly to executive function development.

I'd like to focus on cognitive flexibility now and in the tips chapter that follows. Daily, we must be able to prioritize and re-prioritize our tasks. We need to learn new perspectives and new ways to solve problems. We also need to be equipped to cope with challenges as they arise.

We learned earlier that toxic stress reinforces pathways in the brain. We used the example of the brain as a subway. Clinical experience has made clear to me that getting the brain to change tracks—to generate new solutions—is a long, hard venture. The brain loops to the same unworkable solutions over and over. The path is a rut! The brain that learned the skills to cope with survival is afraid to take a different train. Coaxing it to take a chance to act in a new way can take time and repetition.

Harry was adopted when he was age 4. For reasons unknown, his birth mother took Harry and his two brothers to the orphanage. Harry, age 2, stayed at the orphanage for younger children. His two brothers were moved to an orphanage for older children. One day Harry had a family. The next day he didn't.

Harry fears rejection. His entire internal working model is that he will be abandoned. He acts out in all environments. He moved from a regular education classroom, to a smaller classroom for children with emotional problems and then on to an alternative school. He moved to residential treatment for one year. He did well in this environment. There was little pressure to form connections. Kids came and went. Staff changed shifts every eight hours. Harry returned home. The pattern resumed. Harry had a one-track brain. Harry rejected everyone before they could reject him.

One solution to help Harry was trauma narrative work. Via this intervention, Harry came to understand that his adoptive family was keeping him. Yet, through this process, Harry needed tools to help him cope when his abandonment fears were triggered. Otherwise, at school, he would fall asleep at his desk. He'd swear at the teacher when she tried to wake him up. He stuffed up the toilets in the lavatories. He'd blurt out rude comments to classmates—during class. Sometimes, he'd get up and watch Kleenex® blow around the classroom when he held them over the heating/air conditioning unit. He loitered in the halls and was late for class. Harry came off as a "behavior problem." Really, Harry had an anxiety problem. In each school setting, a behavior modification system was put in place for Harry. None proved effective. The behavior was a symptom of the anxiety and fear of relationships.

I have learned over time the importance of initiating coping skills work in therapy at the first appointment. The sooner we get started, the sooner kids will learn, as we say at our office, to "make toast in the toaster, rather than the refrigerator." Yes. We use an analogy even with our concrete thinkers. Yes. We teach them to understand it—and to embrace it. We'll talk more about bread and kitchen appliances in the next chapter. Before moving to this information, it should be noted that there is a brain structure, the cingulate, which contributes to this one-track mentality.

The cingulate has as its primary function cognitive adaptability. It runs right down the center of the brain from front to back. It helps humans to be flexible in learning and processing new situations. We can recognize alternatives and determine the pros and cons. When the cingulate functions improperly, worrying, being argumentative, saying "no" before even hearing what is being said—dominate as responses. Instead of learning from an embarrassing, frustrating or hurtful life experience, those who have functional problems in this part of their brain are likely to dwell on the negative feelings. The cingulate is like the gear shift in your car. We can move it to the position we desire and proceed. Traumatized kids are often stuck in park. Many parents describe this stuck brain. "He sits and repeats, repeats and repeats! It just doesn't stop!" "She follows me around asking, "Why can't I have the new pants?" "Why?" "Why?" "Why?" "It goes on for hours! In the morning, she'll wake up—it starts all over again!" If you have this situation, go back to Chapter 4 and select a therapy or activity to help with this!

Chapter Summary

- Academic success starts with the parent–child relationship, the ability to self-regulate and a mantra of "I can" instead of "I can't." These three building blocks are the ABC's of a successful scholastic outcome for your adopted child.
- Trauma inhibits the timely development of abstract thought. The concrete thinker struggles with math, critical thinking, generalizing, mental rotation and manipulation, empathy and a future orientation. Parents are encouraged to work with school staff to select tools that can help the literal child expand in an abstract direction.
- Language skills and literacy go hand in hand. Talking, reading and writing are essential to a bright future. Maltreatment impedes language development. Receptive and expressive brain areas are immature and shut down when stressed. Tools and services exist to bolster speech and language, as well as the skills needed to become a fluent reader. Investing in your child's literacy pays off long-term.
- Executive functions consist of working memory, cognitive flexibility and inhibitory control. The traumatized brain is a brain stuck in a rut. It has one track when it comes to coping and problem-solving. It takes effort to help this brain learn that it's safe now. It's okay to jump the tracks to new avenues of learning and relating.
- The trauma-sensitive school movement is budding as studies, like

the ACE study, demonstrate the scope of trauma and the breadth of its potential negative impact. The advantage is a boom in information designed to help parents and school professionals best meet the scholastic needs of the traumatized child from preschool to graduation. Peruse and pass on this information. Adapt it to your youngster's, tween's or teen's academic plan for success.

Endnotes

1   Shelov, S.P., Altmann, T.R., Hannemann, R.E., & Trubo, R. (2014). *Caring for Your Baby and Young Child: Birth to Age 5*. New York: Bantam books, p.208.

2   Mendez, D. (2016, April 20). How patterns help children learn about life. https://wehavekids.com/parenting/How-Patterns-Help-Children-Learn-About-Life-predictions-math-balance

3   Shelov, S.P., Altmann, T.R., Hannemann, R.E., & Trubo, R. (2014). *Caring For Your Baby And Young Child: Birth To Age 5*. New York: Bantam Books, p.270.

4   Healy, J.M. (2004). *Your Child's Growing Mind: Brain Development and Learning from Birth to Adolescence*. New York: Random House.

5   McClelland, M.M., & Cameron, C.E. (2011). Self-regulation and academic achievement in elementary school children. *New Directions for Child and Adolescent Development, 133* (fall), p. 30.

6   *Ibid.*

7   McClelland, M.M., Acock, A.C., Piccinin, A., Rhea, S.A., & Stallings, M. (2013). Relations between preschool attention span-persistence and age 25 educational outcomes. *Early Childhood Research Quarterly, 28*, p.320.

8   Sheslow, D. & Lukens, C.T. (2005). Developing your child's self-esteem. https://myhealthylife.wordpress.com/2007/01/19/developing-your-childs-self-esteem/

9   MacLaughlin, S.S., & Parlakian, R. (2017, May 12). Read early and often. https://www.zerotothree.org/resources/1833-read-early-and-often

10 *Ibid.*

11 The ACE study is taken from the Centers for Disease Control and Prevention, National Center for Injury Prevention and Control, Division of Violence Prevention www.cdc.gov/violenceprevention/acestudy/index.htm

12 Craig, S.E. (2016). *Trauma-Sensitive Schools: Learning Communities Transforming Children's Lives, K-5*. New York: Teachers College Press, p.9.

13 National Scientific Council on the Developing Child. (2015). Supportive relationships and active skill-building strengthen the foundations of resilience: Working Paper 13. https://46y5eh11fhgw3ve3ytpwxt9r-wpengine.netdna-ssl.com/wp-content/uploads/2015/05/The-Science-of-Resilience2.pdf, p.1.

14 Healy, J.M. (2004). *Your Child's Growing Mind: Brain Development And Learning From Birth To Adolescence*. New York: Random House, p.16.

CHAPTER 12

Making Toast in the Toaster

Traumatized children have a hard time using coping and problem-solving skills. They tend to "make toast in the refrigerator." Most kids chuckle when we talk about all the stale cold bread that must be piled up in the family's fridge. Again, we do have to find playful ways to encourage children to heal. Images like this stick with kids. It is common that clients arrive for an appointment and say, "I've been using the fridge a lot lately." "I used the toaster this week." They are using a fun illustration to gauge their behavior. I am always quite excited when kids can begin to see their behavior for what it is. We can build on this.

Coping skill are ways to reduce stress. Problem-solving skills are the steps required to solve a problem. Calmness is needed to solve a problem. So, we'll talk about coping skills first. Then, we'll look a bit at problem-solving. In the end, we want adoptees to learn to "make toast in the toaster." We want children to learn to regulate themselves and then generate workable solutions to day-to-day situations that arise. Eventually kids will use the solutions before they lose it!

This will take time for the brain with one-track. I expect that a lot of repetition will be needed before there will be implementation of these skills. Therefore, I initially stay away from techniques like punching a pillow, hitting a tree with a stick, or walking away. I want to teach one set of skills that can be used in all situations throughout life. We can't always excuse ourselves from a meeting with a boss to go punch a pillow.

We certainly can't punch a pillow in the meeting with our boss. These techniques don't align well with life as we mature into adults. I certainly know folks who drive to a secluded wooded area, get out of their car, and yell at the trees. There is nothing wrong with this. But, we need coping and problem-solving skills—in the moment—that allow us to function peacefully in our classroom, at the grocery store, in a movie theater, at work, at church—everywhere. So, getting started with the techniques that can be utilized long-term is of benefit first.

Select one or two items from this menu of ten skills to implement with your adoptee.

Listing Workable Solutions

Working with parents and their child, we generate a list of the coping skills acceptable to the family. The more ways the youngster mirrors the family, the more we build attachment. We list them all on a flip-chart-size piece of paper. Home it goes so that it can hang in a well-trafficked area. Concrete thinkers need visual prompts.

> **Meg and Brad** parent four adopted children ranging in age from 11 to 15. Each of their daughters had deficits in terms of regulating their emotions. Small issues sent them into tailspins! Meg posted her list of coping strategies at the bottom of the staircase. The girls passed by it multiple time per day. For months and months, Meg and Brad kept directing their children to the list. It was torn down and crumpled up a couple of times. Meg had taken a picture of it, so she could easily re-create it. One day, their oldest daughter said, "I was having a bad time at school. Then, I counted my blessings." Meg and Brad high-fived each other and their daughter for this accomplishment!

It's good to celebrate these moments! They may not be achievements folks with typically-developing children acknowledge. Yet, when a new skill emerges in a child with a history of trauma, it is a triumph! It is the result of hard work!

Helpful Coping Skills

Counting Your Blessings

Among the skills moms and dads often list as helpful is counting your blessings. When life starts out negative, it tends to generate a belief that everything that happens is the end of the world. For example, if our basement floods, most of us are certainly frustrated at first. Then, we begin to turn this around. "Well, at least its just the basement." "Well, the washer and furnace still work." "Well, at least we don't have the problems of the Murphy family across the street. He lost his job." We start to list all the reasons why we are still fortunate. The traumatized adoptee almost tends to do the opposite. If she is having a hard time, she often copes by making her situation worse or by using the same techniques that have never worked.

> **Sharon**, age 9, is in a classroom that is part of an accelerated reading program. Sharon doesn't really like reading. So, each day, she pretends to read her book and respond to the computerized questions. She was surprised when her parents asked her about this at home. The teacher had informed them. Initially, Sharon was angry. She cried and ran off to her room. Once she settled, she was willing to sit with Mom and Dad. Eventually she shared a lack of confidence about her reading ability. Sharon's approach to any stressful situation is to avoid. She utilizes avoidance over and over, even though it always catches up with her. Sharon needs to develop the skills to calm her insecurities and to generate new solutions.

> **Brendan**, a teen, became aggravated when the coach wouldn't play him in games. As the season went on, Brendan became a behavior problem at practice. He wouldn't listen to the coach and eventually he swore at the coach. This resulted in being kicked off the team.

Brandan "had a flat tire. He got out of his car and smashed his windshield." He made his problem bigger. This is another analogy that works well with kids with poor beginnings. It helps kids to think about containing their reactions. Resulting consequences are then less harsh.

One way we can help kids is by providing opportunities to see that most situations are resolvable. Most things aren't as bad as they seem in life. Counting your blessings is a way many keep life in perspective. This tool allows us to calm down and move to solutions. We get buckets and mops and begin to sop up our basement.

Take a clear plastic container and some slips of paper and create a blessing jar with your sons and daughters. Get it out regularly and talk about the family blessings. Help your adoptee shift perspective to the positive side of life.

Community Service

Piggy-backing with the above, community service offers opportunities to see good fortune. Caring for others who are homeless, between jobs, experiencing food instability, or a host of other problems allows the chance to view life through a new lens. Kids see their difficulties as smaller. Volunteering teaches children how to be compassionate for others. They see themselves as helpful and kind. They learn the meaning of being a "quality kid."

There is a wonderful book, *How Full is Your Bucket? For Kids* by Tom Rath and Mary Reckmeyer. In this story, Felix learns that day-to-day inter-actions with others can put drops in your bucket or dry your bucket out. Felix also learns that when he does something kind, he gets a drop and so does the other person. Felix is learning reciprocity. Filling buckets results in mutually rewarding experiences for Felix and for those toward whom he shows positive actions. Every drop of kindness adds up to a bucket overflowing with good feelings about self and others.

Community service is a four-for-one skill builder. Children learn to view their life positively. They learn to feel good about themselves, to practice their qualities and that giving is filling.

Be More Like Spaghetti

Spaghetti is rigid out of the box and flexible once its been cooked.

Peter arrived at therapy stating loudly that all the other kids at school were "mean." He was certain they were talking about him when they were standing by their lockers. He hadn't heard the conversation, but he just knew it!

Peter's dad encouraged him to think "spaghetti." Dad meant, stop making assumptions. Think about other possibilities before being upset. He made Peter take a minute to think about what a group of kids could be talking about besides Peter. There had been an assembly late in the day about the upcoming talent show. His class had had a math test after that. This weekend was the start of football games. Peter realized that his classmates could be discussing lots of things. Dad's style of spaghetti thinking did the trick. Peter was able to move onto his therapy session.

Most days don't go as planned. Learning to be flexible and to re-prioritize are essential life skills. Spaghetti is a wonderful way to help kids get a taste for these skills.

1 to 5

Youngsters, tweens and teens can benefit from learning that there is a 2, 3 and 4 situated between 1 and 5. When you float around in life as an iceberg, you have an immense amount of pent-up emotions. Concrete thinking compounds this situation. Everything is rated a 1 or a 5. Taking out the trash is as big a deal as being abandoned. The parent who makes a simple, routine request is awash with a backlash of feelings well out of proportion for the situation.

On a piece of paper, draw a straight line and put the numbers 1 to 5 at regular intervals. Ones and twos are small things. These are day-to-day happenings that we need to let roll off our back. Threes are worth being irritated about. Fours and fives are big things. These would get anyone worked up. Yet, a socially acceptable response is still expected.

As situations arise, ask your child to write them on the 1 to 5 chart. In so doing we begin to help children develop a continuum. The concrete thinker can't picture things mentally in his mind. He needs visuals to help discern and learn gray areas. This coping skill contributes to the development of abstract thinking.

One to five has other applications as well. We use 1 to 5 to help kids and parents prioritize which behaviors must be ceased first, and which the family can live with temporarily. Together, moms and dads, brothers and sisters and the adoptee rate the undesired behaviors as a 1, 2, 3, 4 or 5. Hurting people, animals, property and stealing automatically are on the higher end. We ask kids to work on giving up the 4 and 5 conduct. We tell them, "You can keep your 1s, 2s, and 3s for a while." This helps each family member keep the priorities clear.

Parents can make 1 to 5 a daily part of life. Consistent use of 1 to 5—over time—will help traumatized adoptees internalize a coping continuum. Posting the 1–5 in a conspicuous place is suggested. Again, children who have experienced maltreatment need visual cues to make lasting changes.

Change the Channel

The one-track brain needs to learn to change the channel—to focus its attention on something happy. Kids decide what kind of images would help their mood improve, like a fun vacation spot, receiving an award, shooting the winning basket, or earning a good grade. They can draw one or more favorite memories. As they feel their temperature rising, they need to learn to use their remote-control powers to tell their brain to think of their happy and/or calming drawings. This shifts their focus in a positive direction. Most of us can easily shift from one topic to another internally in our brain. We can place our focus where we need it in the moment. We have this executive function. For children with early histories of trauma, this will be a challenging task that will require practice.

Using My Secure Base

School anxieties can be decreased by keeping parents present. A family portrait taped inside school notebooks, locker and/or desk or clipped to a backpack reminds children that all is well. The traumatized adoptee doesn't always use their parents as a secure base. This tip works to alter this situation. Kids who see their parents as a source of comfort will seek out and rely on their advice. This would solve so many problems!

Marylou, a creative mom, went to the local dollar store and picked out two inexpensive necklaces with fake jewels. Her girls break a lot of things. So, she wanted something that looked special, but wasn't costly. She told her daughters, ages 6 and 8, that these were heirlooms. She then described that an heirloom was a very special item passed from one family member to the next. She wanted her daughters to have the necklaces with them at school. If they felt nervous, they could hold onto the jewel and it would be like having their mom right there with them.

Marylou was setting the stage for her daughters to learn to rely on her. Coping and generating solutions go better when we have help. Who better to call when you need help than your mom or dad. Instilling this concept, in whatever ways we can, leads to learning that your family is your lifelong lifeline.

Light Bulbs

This idea comes from a mom as well. She traced a light bulb image she pulled from google onto a piece of white felt. Some silver glitter became the filaments and base. She attached the light bulb to a piece of poster board so that it became a pouch. Each time one of her four children generates a solution it gets written on a slip of paper. The solutions go in the pouch. When someone needs a bright idea—they go to the light bulb. Unbeknownst to her sons, she filled out a few slips of her own with items like, "I could have a fit." I could yell at Mom." "I could throw something." "I could hit my brother." "I could shout 'no' and stomp off to my room and slam my door." The first time one of these bright ideas was pulled, she texted me a photo of a child who was clearly surprised! He had apparently stated, "I can't use this idea. I'd get in trouble."

This is a mom who has moved out of the collective. She utilizes the "joining in" technique quite well! She's teaching her sons, in a fun way, to discern the skills that are effective and those that aren't.

Learning to be a Neurosculptor: Putting Control to a Good Use

Your Fantastic Elastic Brain by JoAnn Deak is a way to introduce the brain to boys and girls. This is a beautifully illustrated book. It describes various parts of the brain, including those related to the stress-response system. I most like that the book strongly sends the message that children can learn to stretch their brain. They can make it work the way it needs to. Youngsters, tweens and teens can be "neurosculptors." Plenty of examples are provided about how to shape the brain into working better.

As we teach parents about implicit memory, right and left hemispheres, and the Default Mode Network, we can provide children with these brain basics too. Lots of adoptees like the idea that they can learn to control their very own brain. They can tell their amygdala to stop overreacting or their corpus collosum to stretch itself to get that left side to turn on! We all know that early trauma creates a need for these youngsters to control, control and control! Educating the child with a history of maltreatment to become a neurosculptor is a great way to redirect that control to productive use!

Read this book with your kids today and let the sculpting begin!

Venting: Talking about My Feelings

Once upset, thoughts and feelings spin around in the child's brain like the *Wheel of Fortune* wheel. Boys and girls need to learn to vent. Adults do this everyday at the coffee maker or water cooler. Venting occurs with spouses, neighbors, friends, co-workers and relatives. Venting keeps the tank below the spillover level. It's a good way to keep releasing frustration so there is no explosion. Children can learn this art of venting. First, a definition of venting is provided. Then, venting can occur with Mom or Dad in the car after school or at snack time. Sometimes at dinner. Preferably, venting is a family affair at first. They pick an experience three or four times per week that was problematic. They talk with Mom and Dad about it. They cover:

- What happened?
- How did I feel?
- How did the other people feel?
- What could I do differently?

These are the basic factors in developing problem-solving skills. If these can be incorporated into the conversation—wonderful. To develop and use empathy youngsters need to be able to take other's feelings into account. Venting repetitively let's these steps sink in and become habit.

There are children who have a hard time making conversation. These children are often willing to write or draw out a problem in story board format. In any form, implanting the idea that each person in a situation has feelings and that each person's feelings need to be considered when making choices is what's important as a first step to becoming a moral person.

Solution Basket

Recently, I purchased a wicker basket and put all my solutions in it—remote control, paper and scented markers (smell can be very soothing), plastic numbers 1–5, fake spaghetti, three stress balls in the shapes of a heart, light bulb and brain for venting, thinking and generating solutions, and several children's books about feelings, deep breathing and relaxing. Now, as kids dysregulate, I direct them to the basket. They can see all their options and make a choice. This is what we all do every day.

Chapter Summary

- The one-track brain has a hard time learning to "make toast in the toaster." It keeps putting the bread in the refrigerator. It needs to practice coping skills designed to function in all environments every day. With repetition, the brain will learn to take a new path. It'll begin to put the bread where it belongs. New skills will be utilized.
- Teaching toast-making can encompass fostering pride, caring, reciprocity, attachment and conversation. The developmental gears are smoking when one skill fosters another.
- Linking coping skills and problem-solving skills to remote controls, spaghetti, light bulbs neurosculpting or blessings gives kids images they can easily relate to. It's easy to recall "light bulb" and then take then next step to "bright idea." Playful approaches are essential to help kids make the strides needed to "grow up."
- Whether you hang up a list or make a basket, its helpful when the adoptee can see all his options. He'll internalize the image or the contents. He'll have his tools with him wherever he goes.

CHAPTER 13

Think Inside the Box

This social domain of development includes how children interact with other people—individually and in groups. The development of relationships with parents, brothers and sisters, peers, etc. assuming social roles, learning the values and norms within groups, internalizing a moral system and eventually assuming a productive role in society are all social tasks.

Playing helps us learn to interact with others. I've described the value of peek-a-boo, hide-and-seek, nursery rhymes, collecting lightning bugs, exploring and making faces, examining patterns, reading books and dancing. I also put forth that there is worth in an environment rich with simple toys and household items, some we often think of as trash: empty power towel rolls, cardboard boxes, plastic bottles, old socks (hand puppets) and clothes, pot and pans, laundry baskets, measuring cups and spoons, shaving cream, plastic cups and empty food and laundry detergent containers (cleaned out). I think that lots of parents have exclaimed, on Christmas morning, how their kids enjoyed the boxes more than the new toys that came in the packages. Imagination and creativity thrive "inside the box." Kids get to be whatever and whoever they want to be.

Today, life is hectic. Work is demanding. The family's schedule is crowded. Moms and dads are driving from one extra-curricular to another, making phone calls along the way. Kids are completing homework in the car. Recently, one family couldn't schedule a therapy appointment for six weeks due to the after-school activities of their three children. The watches that text are becoming quite problematic. I'm literally talking about the child's sexual abuse or abandonment, while a mom or dad is dictating a text into their watch. It's hard to form an attachment under such circumstances. Devices have wreaked so much havoc in the waiting room that I've banned them for the most part.

> **Eve**, a teen, was waiting for her therapy appointment. She has an iPad and her own Jetpack. She has online access wherever she goes. A second teen, a boy, came for his appointment. He buddied up to Eve quickly. Eve, who has poor-self-concept, was flattered. She quickly opted to share her devices. The two were shortly viewing pornography.

> **Dominic** became enraged when a grade-school-age girl wouldn't share her Amazon Kindle. She was playing a video game and wanted to keep playing on her own. He grabbed the device and flung it down the hallway. Fortunately, it wasn't damaged.

> **Amelia** set her phone down on her chair while she went to the restroom. When she returned the phone was nowhere to be found. It was several days before another family located it in their home. Their son fessed up that he had stolen the phone. The dad drove the phone back to the office. Amelia's dad came and picked it up.

Incidents like these require new rules for the office. Many parents have inquired, "What will he do while we are talking?"

> A family arrived for the initial assessment with their 12-year-old son, **Brody**. The parents were deciding which of their cell phones to give him when I came out to greet them. I explained that I preferred that he not have either phone. The parents were clearly uncomfortable yet agreed. The young man sighed and rolled his eyes at me.
> Once inside my office, the dad said, "What do you expect him to do out there while we talk?" As a no brain sharing therapist, I said that I felt he could manage for the time we would be conversing. In a few minutes the dad again expressed concern about this matter. The bottom line was

he believed his son would be angry that they left him without a device. I said, "I'm fine with anger. But, I do think he'll be okay."

When we finished our discussion, the dad went to the waiting room with me to get Brody. He was surprised. His son and two other boys had laid wooden train track down the length of the hallway and looped it all the way back up. There are plastic hills that go with this train set. They inserted several of these. This was all completed within 30 minutes. They were happily watching their train cars go up and down the hills. When I interrupted, the boys were disappointed. They all agreed that they wanted to play with each other again. The dad was totally amazed! He told me several times that he had never seen his son play like that.

I provide these examples not as complaints, but as concerns. Busy lifestyles, jam-packed schedules, reliance on devices for entertainment and demanding academics need to be balanced with opportunity to play—especially for the child left immature by trauma's wrath.

These final chapters are about play. There's basic information, food for thought and there'll be tips. Given the option to play, a child with a history of maltreatment may not be able to decide what to play. He might not have the skills to engage the kids in the neighborhood. Or, he may not have the skills to get along with others. He might present safety issues like sexual behaviors or aggression. My first book, *Welcoming a Brother or Sister through Adoption*, includes a chapter on parenting sexual and aggressive children. There are articles about these issues on our website too.

The suggestions that go along with this chapter are ideas to help boys and girls advance their ability to "go out and play."

The ABCs: Bucking the Trend

The alphabet begins with the letters a, b and c. Think back to Chapter 11: cognitive, social, emotional, physical and brain development begin with attachment, self-regulation and self-concept.

Social competence is rooted in the relationships that infants and toddlers experience in the early years of their life. Everyday experiences in relationships with their parents are fundamental to children's developing social skills.[1]

Parental responsiveness and nurturance are key factors in the development of children's social competence.[2] Children who have close relationships with responsive parents early in life can develop healthy relationships with peers as they get older.[3]

Indeed, the single best childhood predictor of adult adaptation is *not* school grades and *not* classroom behavior, but rather the adequacy with which the child gets along with other children. Children who are generally disliked, who are aggressive and disruptive, who are unable to sustain close relationships with other children and who cannot establish a place for themselves in the peer culture are seriously at risk.[4] The risks of inadequate social skills are many; poor mental health, dropping out of school, low achievement, other school difficulties and poor employment history.[5] Parents are our first playmates, they cultivate our laughter and sense of fun. Let's not put the cart before the horse with our traumatized children. There is a common belief that the ability to play and improve social skills will happen if we place children in activities comprised of peers. Certainly, if the adoptee can play baseball, enjoy gymnastics and sing in the church choir, do continue their participation in these endeavors.

> **Katrina** arrived in her adoptive family at age 4. In second grade, her parents enrolled her in softball. Katrina was gifted athletically. The team welcomed her ability to hit home runs. Socially immature, she was loud, interrupted conversations, talked over kids and had poor boundaries. She always stood to close to the other girls.
>
> Mom and Katrina came to a therapy session. Mom had taken some pictures at Katrina's recent softball game. Katrina was sitting on a bench by herself. The rest of her teammates were sitting together on two other benches. Mom was heartbroken. Katrina herself said, "Yeah. They just don't like me." She cried.

There is a wide array of talents and skills among traumatized youngsters. Some have a superficial charm that is engaging to others. So, they appear to fare better socially, yet their friendships lack intimacy. Many are like

Katrina. Their immaturity renders making and keeping friends a struggle. It is heart-wrenching to moms and dads. Parents want their kids to have friendships. They want them to have fun times going to birthday parties, sleepovers, hanging out, playing ball, riding bikes, building a fort, painting nails, or jumping on the trampoline. Katrina did finish the season. Then, Mom and Dad opted to spend after-school time playing with Katrina themselves. Their three birth children continued with their extra-curriculars. When Katrina returned to a team sport, she not only hit a home run, she was invited out for the after-game pizza. Putting the horse before the cart paid off.

Societal pressure today trends in the direction of enrolling youngsters of all ages in organized activities. Adoption may mean bucking what's trending for the time being.

Initiative and industry: "I'm not lazy"

Once attachment, self-regulation and self-concept get going, children develop initiative—starting around age 3½. The child is learning to master and interact with the world around him. She's choosing her own behavior, and she feels more capable in her interactions. She wants to begin and complete her own actions for a purpose. Initiative includes:

- Experimenting for what it means to be an adult, "What kind of person could I become?
- Creating new games and stories, and imagining solutions to problems.
- Learning to cooperate with others, leading as well as following.
- Asking "Why?" about everything.
- Greater self-understanding and self-awareness—self is now described in terms of physical characteristics, material possessions and physical activities. "I am taller than Sally." "I am different from Sam because I have brown hair and he has black hair." "I have a bike and Peggy doesn't."
- Self-conscious emotions appear—embarrassment, guilt, shame, pride.
- Moral development broadens.

Initiative is a time of lots of activity and a surplus of energy! By its conclusion, children have a broader social world. The family is still the main relationship. If children have parents who give them the independence to think, to encourage them and to teach prosocial behavior, thoughts of "I am a good person" are reinforced.

Initiative leads to industry. Industry kicks off in grade school and lasts through junior high.[6] The grade-school youngster is learning reading, writing and arithmetic. Relationships with peers and teachers take on greater meaning. The child seeks praise for his achievements. There is pride in accomplishments. There is an eventual progression from free play to team sports, which are structured, competitive and have sophisticated rules. Self-discipline increases with demands like homework. There is a shift to carrying out responsibilities around the house and doing more things on their own.

Many adoptive parents lament the end of the school year, school breaks and weekends. They fear there will be oodles of cries of, "I'm bored." Many youngsters with a history of trauma haven't matured developmentally to the stage of initiative or industry. Helping these kids occupy their time can be an arduous task!

Reiterating, the motivation that accompanies initiative and industry is also thwarted by an overactive stress-response system.

Please realize that your child isn't "lazy" or "unmotivated." They are "young." Growth in all developmental domains is impaired without the idea that one has a purpose, and that one can step toward that purpose.

Red Flags

I've created a list of "red flags" that can help moms and dads recognize their child is off track in terms of being social and playful. The list includes items I've clinically observed that indicate delays in the ability to get along and be full of fun.

"My friends change frequently"
The traumatized adoptee changes friends constantly. Peer relationships are short-lived. "Billy" comes to play a few times, and then parents don't

hear about or see any more of Billy again. Billy is replaced by Sally, George, Mark, Matthew and so on! Friendships keep going around like a revolving door. A new playmate is always entering or exiting.

"I flit from toy to toy"

Children, with difficult beginnings in life, may handle a toy for a few seconds and then move on to the next toy. Sustained interest in one toy or activity is lacking. Pretty soon, every toy available has been looked at and tossed to the floor. Play equals making a mess.

> **Isaac** was 16 months old. He arrived for an assessment with his third foster family who intended to adopt him. Wow! Isaac was a handful. He darted all over the office throwing anything he could get his hands on. Dad grabbed him up and he wailed. He pushed and hit. The assessment was conducted standing up for the most part. Isaac ran around chronically.
>
> At home, the family had basically cleaned out the living room and installed baby gates to curtail Isaac and to keep him safe.

Isaac is not unique to our office. He was more extreme. Yet, we meet many children whose attention span is not increasing. They aren't developing a curiosity about their environment. They are chaotic instead.

"I prefer to be a couch potato"

Some adopted children prefer to sit—chronically! These children can sit among a room full of interesting toys and delightful arts and crafts supplies, and never make a move to sample any of this great stuff!

> **Rose** was adopted internationally at the age of 5½. Now age 11, she still hasn't mastered playing outdoors. If seated with a device, she can entertain herself for hours. Yet, ask her to go outside on a beautiful summer day and within minutes she'll be at the screen door begging to come inside. With a backyard full of amazing play equipment, in a neighborhood replete with potential playmates, Rose is totally out of her element.

"I play the same thing over and over and over"

> **Randy** is 11. He arrived on American soil at age 10 months. To date, his play continues to lag behind his actual age. In fact, Matchbox® cars are his only form of entertainment. Each day after school Randy smashes all the cars into each other—repetitively! This destructive play has been going on as long as Randy's parents can remember. The cars are never used to transport people around town, even though he has a lovely carpet imprinted with a Main Street full of shops, a park, a school and two neighborhoods.

"My play involves no people"

Play lacking people is particularly common among previously post-institutionalized children or domestically adopted youngsters who experienced neglect prior to their arrival in a healthy family. Animals often dominate the play (i.e. stuffed animals, animal figures, etc.). Animals are okay, for a while as they serve as transitional objects in a similar fashion, as does a favorite "blankie." However, children's play, especially from ages 2 and up should contain "people"—dolls or people figurines or props that the child designates as people. Imaginative play or pretend play in which kids work out feelings and act out all kinds of themes involving people—pretending to be their mom or dad, launching astronauts in a spaceship made from empty boxes, teaching dolls in a classroom, hiding from "bad" guys in a fort—should be a preferred type of play through age 7.

"My play is all electronic"

> **Brian** and **Bryce**, twins, adopted internationally arrived in their family at age 3½. They entered therapy when they were 13 years old. The parents presented a laundry list of behavioral issues and noted that these boys were totally absorbed with PlayStation®—about 25 hours per week! Board games, card games, arts and crafts, drawing, painting, playing an instrument—anything that required creativity—were snubbed in lieu of screen time. Interrupting them to help with dinner or get to their homework was difficult. They were totally engrossed with their video games.

The PlayStation® was packed up and given to nephews when services were initiated. Mom and Dad replaced the PlayStation® with an assortment of activities. The dining room table offered a puzzle, paint by number, board games, a deck of cards, a pile of LEGO®, a soccer ball, a kick ball, a baseball and bat, magna-tiles and crafting supplies. For three months, Brian and Bryce sat on the couch looking at the empty stand on which the PlayStation® used to sit. They were totally perplexed as to what to do. Mom and Dad held firm.

Finally, about four months into therapy, Mom left a voicemail for the therapist. The sound of laughter could be heard in the background of the message. Mom said, "You'll never believe it! Brian, Bryce and Marie (i.e. the family's birth daughter) are having a good time playing the board game, Trouble! I can't believe they are playing and enjoying themselves! This is the first time I remember the three kids doing anything like this together!"

Two years later the boys had each joined an ensemble at church. They had learned how to strum guitars. They both enjoyed a more active lifestyle of playing catch in the backyard and swimming at the local rec center.

Traumatized adoptees are perfectly content to let screens be their BFFs! Interacting with machines is far less complicated and hurtful than connecting with people!

"I break my toys"

Parents declare, "Every toy he has is broken." "Christmas morning, he'll receive great new toys. By Christmas evening, they'll all be broken or taken apart—the pieces will be scattered everywhere." "She just trashes all her possessions!" Certainly, children with a history of trauma view themselves as "broken." "Shattered" by being abused and abandoned, "destruction" becomes the metaphor for their experiences.

Older children who are "little" are hard on toys. Toys for toddlers are rugged. They're designed for kids still learning to be gentle. Toys for school-age youngsters are made for youngsters who have learned to take care of their things. They don't always hold up under the strength of "little" big kids.

"I re-enact my trauma in my play"

Brook came to live with her parents and two older sisters after spending her first 8 months of life in an orphanage. As she aged into the preschool years, she preferred to play orphanage. She'd line up all her dolls. Then, she'd feed each one and pretend to change their diapers. Brook spent hours each day attending to her dolls as the care givers had tended to her.

Blueprints Lead to Isolation

Brian, age 13, ran into his house, slamming the door behind him. "I'm going to kill myself." With that Brian ran to his room. Brian had a long history of failed friendships. This incident was set off by a fight with a boy down the street.

Brian had alienated most of his classmates. On Friday nights, Brian's family attended the high school football games. Brian's older sister was a cheerleader. Brian's mom noticed that none of Brian's classmates ever spoke to him. They walked by him like he wasn't even there.

Brian's mom was so sad for him. Brian could play. He loved to build with LEGO®. He made elaborate skyscrapers and animals. He enjoyed board games and puzzles. He was good at video games. He liked to play ball. He excelled at martial arts. He had a sharp sense of humor. All in all, Brian could be a fun kid.

Brian joined the family as a foster child at age two. His birth mom walked into the local social services office. The security desk is inside the door. She sat Brian on the desk and told the security guard that she couldn't handle Brian anymore. Brian never saw her again.

Brian harbored a deep emotional hurt that spilled over to his friendships. He said, "I want friends. I think they'll just leave me." So, it was easier to push kids away than to take a chance.

Brian was lonely. He talked of suicide frequently in the early days of therapy.

Corey, age 9, joined his family at age 5 after a history of physical and emotional abuse and multiple foster care placements. Corey was so excited when his dad announced he had signed him up for baseball. When they arrived at the field for the first practice, Corey leapt out of the car. His turn came for batting and he struck out. Corey threw his bat and ran to the car. He wanted to go home. This cycle happened in Karate, Boy Scouts, basketball and wrestling.

Corey's sense of shame was profound. The only time he got a moment's peace was when he felt he was the "best" at something.

The internal working model is a blueprint for *all* relationships. It can lead to isolation. Tweens and teens should become increasingly interested in spending more time with peers than parents. This is supposed to be the age when parents aren't "cool" and they suddenly "don't know anything." The traumatized teen may have a totally different experience in adolescence. Poor self-concept, fears of rejection, inability to trust lead to falling in with the "wrong crowd," risky sexual behaviors, using pornography or Internet relationships, substance abuse or, as in Brian's case, suicidal thoughts. All are used to fill the void of loneliness. Trauma and adoption are risk factors for increased suicidal behavior in adolescents.[7] High family connectedness decreases the likelihood of suicide attempts and represents a protective factor for all adolescents.[8]

I saw a Facebook post during National Suicide Prevention Month that encouraged parents to program the National Suicide Prevention Lifeline hotline number into their teen's cell phone or to secure it in their backpack, their wallet or purse—an item they typically carry with them. I thought this a very good idea. Please do this.

Recess, Social Skills, Cognitive Skills and Executive Functions

Advancing social skills, cognitive skills and executive functions can be accomplished through unstructured play. Recess time is shortening across America as schools feel the pressure of government-mandated testing. The after-school hours are packed with structured extra-curriculars.

The American Academy of Pediatrics (AAP) states:[9]

Recess is unique from, and a complement to, physical education—not a substitute for it. The American Academy of Pediatrics believes that recess is a crucial and necessary component of a child's development and, as such, it should not be withheld for punitive or academic reasons.

AAP goes on to state that:

Recess offers its own, unique benefits. Recess represents an essential, planned respite from rigorous cognitive tasks. It affords a time to rest, play, imagine, think, move, and socialize. After recess, for children or after a corresponding break time for adolescents, students are more attentive and better able to perform cognitively. In addition, recess helps young children to develop social skills that are otherwise not acquired in the more structured classroom environment.

Free play differs from games. In free play, rules governing play are negotiated by the players, are flexible and are re-negotiated as need be. So, unstructured play builds skills like negotiation, cooperation, sharing, problem-solving and coping skills.[10] These are skills for cognitive and social success.

Advocate for recess at your school if need be. Find ways to balance structured activities with time inside the box.

The Teen Brain: Remodeling in Process

Brainstorm: The Power and Purpose of the Teenage Brain, by Daniel Siegel, is a wonderful read. I highly recommend it if you are parenting a child nearing or in adolescence, or if you are a professional working with teens. The pages remind us of the struggles of navigating the teen years—puberty and sexual development, the emergence of acne, the loss of our first love, fitting in, finding a group of friends to hang with and talk to for hours, trying to individuate and decide who we are, what we want to do, what the world is all about and what our feelings mean!

The book also takes us beyond the "it's the hormones" mentality. By

11 and 12 years old, the brain starts an amazing process dubbed "remodeling." Siegel makes this process come alive and he encourages us to view adolescence as an opportunity to shape the lives of kids, rather than just a stage to get through. I really like this approach. Our office is recognized for our work with adolescents. They usually arrive in turmoil. Underneath all the storming, they are truly remarkable kids!

Below I'm giving a synopsis of *Brainstorm*'s[11] most salient points about remodeling for adoptive families.

Dopamine

Dopamine, a neurotransmitter, increases in the teen years. The brain circuitry that utilizes dopamine is responsible for creating our drive for reward—for pleasure and happiness. This enhanced dopamine causes adolescents to gravitate to thrilling experiences and exhilarating sensations. While the baseline of dopamine is lower, its release response is higher. So, teens may be bored until they engage in a stimulating activity, then they get a powerful sense of being alive.

Dopamine is the same neurotransmitter in action in addiction. Our brains are wired to repeat pleasurable activities. Whenever the reward circuit is activated by a pleasurable experience—a drug for example, a burst of dopamine signals that something important is happening that needs to be remembered.[12] The dopamine signal causes changes in neural connectivity that make it easier to repeat the activity again and again—leading to habits.[13] These large rushes of dopamine teach the brain to seek drugs.

There is a strong correlation between substance abuse and trauma in adolescents.[14] Though one in five teens between the ages of 12 and 17 engages in abusive/dependent or problematic use of illicit drugs and alcohol each year, the rate is three times higher among those teens with histories of sexual abuse, sexual assault or physical abuse.[15] Up to 59 percent of adolescents diagnosed with Posttraumatic Stress Disorder subsequently develop substance abuse problems.[16] Visit the National Institute on Drug Abuse and learn the facts about drugs.

I would also like to mention that fast food and sugar are other dopamine rushes for the brain. Many of you parent children, tweens and teens who want to consume vast amounts of sugar and carbohydrates—candy, sweets, pop, bread, potatoes, chips and pasta. Dopamine is the culprit behind these food issues!

Remodeling

The adolescent brain undergoes "pruning." The brain reduces the number of neurons and their connections. Throughout childhood, there is an over-abundance of neurons produced. In adolescence, we keep what we've been using and discard what we haven't been using. The process of myelination (see Chapter 3) brings the brain up to speed. This moves the brain toward enhanced integration. We have a brain that is specialized and faster and more efficient in how it processes information. We can now think abstractly and conceptually. We shed impulsivity and hyperrationality—putting more weight on the potential benefits of our actions than the risks. Teens are often aware of the risks of the actions. They choose what seems the exciting, stimulating path. Via the remodeling process, teens move into what Siegel calls "gist" thinking—relying more on intuition to see the larger picture of a situation and therefore make wiser decisions.

Unfortunately, if there are any vulnerabilities in the brain—like trauma, they become more apparent through the remodeling process. What's left after pruning may not be enough to sustain mood or appropriate thought processes. Bipolar Disorder or depression may appear for the first time.

We receive the most calls for services for kids at ages 13 and up right as the brain is remodeling. Teens with histories of complex trauma plummet behaviorally, emotionally and socially. The brain is struggling to complete its final stages of integration. Many had issues prior to remodeling. The commencement and process of remodeling or new emerging mental health issues led to decline instead. The adoptive moms and dads calling our office are at their wits end! Conflict is prevalent! The home is a battleground.

Remodeling is compounded by identity development. Adolescence is prime time for figuring out, "Who am I?" The teen adoptee often "tries on" the behavior of the birth family. Trauma narrative work, earlier than the teen years, can help adolescents navigate this life stage with less strife. It is easier to decide who you are when you know where you have come from. You can integrate your past and present experiences and come to define yourself. Identity formation is like putting a puzzle together. You need all the pieces. While we don't have the entire background history for many clients, we can give them the pieces we do have. This helps fill in the picture to the degree possible. Trauma narrative is one key to helping a turbulent teen get back on the right track.

The good news is that teens are very workable in therapy. Most know that life isn't going well for them. They want it to be different—better!

Armed with this cutting-edge information about teen brain remodeling and the identity development process, we can parent, nurture, empathize and "play" with adolescents in ways that reduce the brainstorm's backlash!

Table 13.1 contains a chart highlighting the developmental milestones that lead to social and play skills. Notice that the development of language and motor skills accompanies the advancement of these skills.

Again, ask yourself, "has my son or daughter accomplished these early developmental milestones?" Remember, we want to get an idea how "young" your adoptee is. This helps us select the best tools to get the gears turning!

Table 13.1: The development of social and play skills from birth to age 3

By age 1	By age 2	By age 3
1 month	• The toddler begins to engage in parallel play by 14 months.[29]	• The child aged 3–4 years shares toys.[39]
• Smiles and giggles.[17]	• Young toddlers are "ego-centric." He is the center of the world and most concerned with where things are in relation to self.[30]	• The child takes turns with assistance.[40]
• Parents can begin to predict when the baby will smile, look at parent, make sounds and pause for a time-out from play.[18]	• Young toddlers can be physical in their responses to the children around them.[31]	• The child will initiate play with other children.[41]
• Parents and infant recognize each other's patterns of responsiveness so that play becomes a dance.[19]	• The toddler begins to imitate the world around him by 18 months.[32]	• The child engages in fantasy play or sociodramatic play or make-believe.[42]
2 months	• The toddler begins symbolic play.[33]	• The child shows affection for friends without prompting.[43]
• "Social smile"—the infant is now smiling in response to social cues like Mom's voice.[20]	• The toddler is more likely to initiate interactions with other people.[34]	• Children take on gender-related character-istics even if both parents work and share household responsibilities. They see role models on TV, in magazines, books or via family friends.[44]
• Cooing.	• The toddler recognizes himself in a mirror or pictures. He makes faces at himself.[35]	• The child can work toys with buttons, levers and moving parts.[45]
• Baby spends much of each day watching and listening to people around him.[21]	• The toddler begins to be helpful.[36]	• The child can put together puzzles with 3 or 4 pieces.[46]
3 months	• The toddler points to things or pictures as they are named.[37]	• The child can build towers with more than 6 blocks.[47]
• Playing now with parents and others familiar.[22]	• The toddler begins to sort shapes and colors.[38]	• The child can run and climb well.[48]
• Reaching, tracking objects, manipulating/playing with hands.		• The child can carry on a conversation of 2 to 3 sentences.
4–6 months		
• Peek-a-boo and pat-a-cake.[23] Infant matches parents' facial expressions (leads to turn-taking).[24]		
• As parents talk, infant will move arms, legs and open mouth in a rhythm with the parents' speech. This maps the brain for conversation.[25]		
• Expands to a variety of toys—mirror, musical toys, old magazines, baby books for example.[26]		
• Can distinguish shades of red, blue and yellow.[27]		
• Object permanency emerges.[28]		

6–12 months

- At 7 months eye sight matures. Infant can now follow the path of moving objects and can grab objects.[49]
- Infant can sit up now.
- Infant notices individual sounds a parent makes. The infant is babbling and begins to imitate sound of speech. The infant will recognize many words although he isn't speaking yet.[50]
- Gains ability to grasp.
- Moves things smoothly from one hand to another.[51]
- Wants to reach out and touch everything.[52]
- Explores things in different ways like shaking, banging or throwing.[53]

Examples:

- Baby grins back at parent while alert.
- Infant often seems happy/joyful.[54]
- Infant likes to play with others especially parents.[55]
- Infant likes to look at himself in mirror.[56]
- Baby holds gaze for longer and longer periods of time.[57]
- The infant has a favorite toy.[58]
- Infant can roll a ball back and forth.
- Interested in toys with moving parts.
- Interested in blocks.
- Puts objects in a container and takes them back out.[59]
- Infant hands parent a book when he wants to hear a story.[60]

Examples:

- The toddler feeds a teddy bear with a bottle (symbolic play). The toddler brushes the doll's hair.
- The toddler realizes that a doll stands for a person. This is a precursor to language—to be able to use words to stand for other things.[61]
- The toddler begins to help clean up his toys. He wants to sweep the floor with you or help make dinner. Helping is a social skill.
- The toddler can say his own name by 18 months.[62]
- The toddler gets excited when in the company of other children.[63]
- Builds towers of 4 or more blocks.[64]
- Kicks a ball and throws ball overhand.[65]

Examples:

- The child starts to recognize certain children as friends.[66]
- The child can work out disputes with friends over a toy by trading for another toy or taking turns with the toy in dispute.[67]
- Playing house, superheroes—make believe play expands, becomes more inventive and takes on importance in exploring social ideas.[68]

By age 4

- Make believe play includes playing their mom and dad.[69]
- The child would rather play with other children than play by himself.[70]
- The child cooperates with other children.[71]
- The child talks about what he likes and is interested in.[72]

Chapter Summary

- The value of unstructured play can't be stressed enough. Inside the box are unlimited possibilities for fun adventures and rich development of life skills for success: cooperating, negotiating, problem-solving, turn-taking, sharing, creativity, imagination, attention, planning and strategizing—just to name a few. Busy lifestyles and reduced recess stifle free play. Parents who find ways to increase time in the box help themselves and their sons and daughters reap priceless rewards.

- Play skills start with our developmental ABCs—attachment, emotional regulation and self-concept. Initiative and industry follow. These should be busy years. Preschoolers are digging, lugging, pushing, pulling, running, jumping, peddling and hopping. The grade-school-age child is learning to read, write, add, subtract, multiply, divide and navigate the playground. Perceptions that the adoptee is "lazy" or "unmotivated" must shift. Emphasis remains laser-focused on growing up the adopted youngster.

- Various red flags, the internal working model and identity development can be barriers to enjoying playing and making friends. Kids can become lonely and isolated. Substance abuse, falling in with the "wrong" crowd, sexual promiscuity and suicidal ideation or attempts threaten the well-being of the child. Parents are advised to get the facts about drug use, Internet safeguards and suicide. Recognize the warning signs. Seek help quickly. Teens are very workable in therapy. Its never too late to get on the path to recovery.

- Remodeling is a process that prepares the brain to think in gist, to see the bigger picture, to weigh options and to make wise choices. The brain needed to thrive in adulthood emerges. Adverse life experiences make remodeling turbulent. Many teens with a history of trauma can take steps backward, rather than forward. Armed with this information parents can constuct a game plan, smoothing the brainstorming phase. Knowledge is always a key companion when helping the traumatized adoptee heal. Never stop reading, talking to other parents and seeking help.

Endnotes

1   Peth-Pierce, R. (2001). A good beginning: Sending America's children to school with the social and emotional competence they need to succeed. The Child Mental Health Foundations and Agencies Network (FAN). https://files.eric.ed.gov/fulltext/ED445810.pdf, p.vii.

2   Casas, P. (2001). Toward the ABCs: Building a healthy social and emotional foundation for learning and living. Chicago: Ounce of Prevention. p.9. https://eric. ed.gov/?id=ED468498. Updated version https://www.theounce.org/wp-content/ uploads/2017/03/TowardtheABCsfinalPDF.pdf

3   Peth-Pierce, R. (2001). A good beginning: Sending America's children to school with the social and emotional competence they need to succeed. The Child Mental Health Foundations and Agencies Network (FAN). https://files.eric.ed.gov/fulltext/ED445810.pdf, p.vii.

4   Hartup, W. (1992). Having friends, making friends, and keeping friends: Relationships as educational contexts. ERIC Digest ED345854 https://www.ericdigests.org/1992-3/friends. htm, p.2.

5   Peth-Pierce, R. (2001). A good beginning: Sending America's children to school with the social and emotional competence they need to succeed. The Child Mental Health Foundations and Agencies Network (FAN). https://files.eric.ed.gov/fulltext/ED445810. pdf, p.vii; Katz, L., & McClellan, D. (1991). The teacher's role in the social development of young children. ERIC Digest ED331642 https://eric.ed.gov/?id=ED331642, p.1.

6   Child Development Institute. (n.d.). Erik Erikson's stages of social-emotional development. https://childdevelopmentinfo.com/child-development/erickson/#. W4nKa_ZFyUl

7   Craig, S.E. (2017). *Trauma-Sensitive Schools for the Adolescent Years: Promoting Resiliency and Healing, Grades 6–12*. New York: Teachers College Press, p.43; Slap, G., Goodman, E., & Huang, B. (2001.) Adoption as a risk factor for attempted suicide during adolescence. *Pediatrics*, 108(2). http://pediatrics.aappublications.org/content/108/2/e30.short

8   *Ibid*.

9   Murray, R., & Ramstetter, C. (2013.) The crucial role of recess in school. *Pediatrics*, 131(1). http://pediatrics.aappublications.org/content/131/1/183

10   *Ibid*.

11   Siegel, D.J. (2013). *Brainstorm: The Power and Purpose of the Teenage Brain*. New York: Jeremy P. Tarcher/Penguin Group

12   National Institute on Drug Abuse. (2018, July). Drugs, brain, and behavior: Science of addiction. https://www.drugabuse.gov/publications/drugs-brains-behavior-science-addiction/drugs-brain

13   *Ibid*.

14   Craig, S.E. (2017). *Trauma-Sensitive Schools for the Adolescent Years: Promoting Resiliency and Healing, Grades 6–12*. New York: Teachers College Press, p.52.

15   The National Child Traumatic Stress Network. (2008, June). Understanding the links between adolescent trauma and substance abuse. https://www.nctsn.org/sites/default/ files/resources//understanding_the_links_between_adolescent_trauma_and_substance_ abuse.pdf, p.5.

16   *Ibid*.

17   The Urban Child Institute. (n.d). What do we know about social and emotional development in early childhood?: The first years last a lifetime. http://www.urbanchildinstitute.org/resources/publications/good-start/ social-and-emotional-development

18   Shelov, S. P., Altmann, T. R., Hannemann, R. E., & Trubo, R. (2014). Caring for your baby and young child: Birth to age 5. New York: Bantam books. p.169.

19   Ibid.
20   Eliot, L. (1999). What's going on in there: How the brain and mind develop in the first five years of life. New York: Bantam Books. p.301.
21   Shelov, S. P., Altmann, T. R., Hannemann, R. E., & Trubo, R. (2014). Caring for your baby and young child: Birth to age 5. New York: Bantam books. p.215.
22   Centers for Disease Control and Prevention. (2018, June 6). Important milestones: Your baby by six months. https://www.cdc.gov/ncbddd/actearly/milestones/milestones-6mo.html
23   Brazelton, T.B. (2006). Touchpoints, birth to 3: Your child's emotional and behavioral development. Cambridge, MA: Perseus Books Group. p.340.
24   Eliot, L. (1999). What's going on in there: How the brain and mind develop in the first five years of life. New York: Bantam Books. p.302-303.
25   Klaus, M., Klaus, P., Keefe, M., & Fox, N. (Producers). (2011). Amazing Talents of the Newborn [Motion picture on DVD]. United States: Johnson & Johnson Pediatric Institute LLC
26   Shelov, S. P., Altmann, T. R., Hannemann, R. E., & Trubo, R. (2014). Caring for your baby and young child: Birth to age 5. New York: Bantam books. p.232.
27   Ibid., 233.
28   Ibid., 237.
29   Brazelton, T.B. (2006). Touchpoints, birth to 3: Your child's emotional and behavioral development. Cambridge, MA: Perseus Books Group. p.342.
30   Shelov, S. P., Altmann, T. R., Hannemann, R. E., & Trubo, R. (2014). Caring for your baby and young child: Birth to age 5. New York: Bantam books. p.304.
31   Ibid., 306.
32   Brazelton, T.B. (2006). Touchpoints, birth to 3: Your child's emotional and behavioral development. Cambridge, MA: Perseus Books Group. p.342. Public Broadcasting Service. (n.d.).The ABC's of child development: Developmental milestones for your child's first five years. http://www.pbs.org/wholechild/abc/index.html
33   Brazelton, T.B. (2006). Touchpoints, birth to 3: Your child's emotional and behavioral development. Cambridge, MA: Perseus Books Group. p.342.
34   Public Broadcasting Service. (n.d.).The ABC's of child development: Developmental milestones for your child's first five years. http://www.pbs.org/wholechild/abc/index.html
35   Ibid.
36   Ibid.
37   Centers for Disease Control and Prevention. (2018, June 19). Important milestones: Your child by two years. https://www.cdc.gov/ncbddd/actearly/milestones/milestones-2yr.html
38   Ibid.
39   The Urban Child Institute. (n.d). What do we know about social and emotional development in early childhood?: The first years last a lifetime. http://www.urbanchildinstitute.org/resources/publications/good-start/social-and-emotional-development
40   Public Broadcasting Service. (n.d.).The ABC's of child development: Developmental milestones for your child's first five years. http://www.pbs.org/wholechild/abc/index.html
41   Ibid.
42   Ibid.
43   Centers for Disease Control and Prevention. (2018, June 19). Important milestones: Your child by three years. https://www.cdc.gov/ncbddd/actearly/milestones/milestones-3yr.html
44   Shelov, S. P., Altmann, T. R., Hannemann, R. E., & Trubo, R. (2014). Caring for your baby and young child: Birth to age 5. New York: Bantam books. p.385.
45   Centers for Disease Control and Prevention. (2018, June 19). Important milestones: Your child by three years. https://www.cdc.gov/ncbddd/actearly/milestones/milestones-3yr.html
46   Ibid.

47 Ibid.
48 Ibid.
49 Ibid., 234.
50 Ibid., 235.
51 Centers for Disease Control and Prevention. (2018, June 6). Important milestones: Your baby by nine months. https://www.cdc.gov/ncbddd/actearly/milestones/milestones-9mo.html
52 Shelov, S. P., Altmann, T. R., Hannemann, R. E., & Trubo, R. (2014). Caring for your baby and young child: Birth to age 5. New York: Bantam books. p.238.
53 Centers for Disease Control and Prevention. (2018, June 6). Important milestones: Your baby by one year. https://www.cdc.gov/ncbddd/actearly/milestones/milestones-1yr.html
54 Centers for Disease Control and Prevention. (2018, June 6). Important milestones: Your baby by six months. https://www.cdc.gov/ncbddd/actearly/milestones/milestones-6mo.html
55 Ibid.
56 Ibid.
57 Brazelton, T.B. (2006). Touchpoints, birth to 3: Your child's emotional and behavioral development. Cambridge, MA: Perseus Books Group. p.70.
58 Centers for Disease Control and Prevention. (2018, June 6). Important milestones: Your baby by one year. https://www.cdc.gov/ncbddd/actearly/milestones/milestones-1yr.html
59 Ibid.
60 Ibid.
61 Brazelton, T.B. (2006). Touchpoints, birth to 3: Your child's emotional and behavioral development. Cambridge, MA: Perseus Books Group. p.150.
62 Shelov, S. P., Altmann, T. R., Hannemann, R. E., & Trubo, R. (2014). Caring for your baby and young child: Birth to age 5. New York: Bantam books. p.306.
63 Centers for Disease Control and Prevention. (2018, June 19). Important milestones: Your child by eighteen months. https://www.cdc.gov/ncbddd/actearly/milestones/milestones-18mo.html
64 Centers for Disease Control and Prevention. (2018, June 19). Important milestones: Your child by two years. https://www.cdc.gov/ncbddd/actearly/milestones/milestones-2yr.html
65 Ibid.
66 Shelov, S. P., Altmann, T. R., Hannemann, R. E., & Trubo, R. (2014). Caring for your baby and young child: Birth to age 5. New York: Bantam books. p.384.
67 Ibid.
68 Ibid., 385.
69 Centers for Disease Control and Prevention. (2018, June 19). Important milestones: Your child by four years. https://www.cdc.gov/ncbddd/actearly/milestones/milestones-4yr.html
70 Ibid.
71 Ibid.
72 Ibid.

CHAPTER 14

Let's Get Inside the Box

We'll need to get down to the level of kids if we want to improve their ability to play, and to reap the rich skills that grow from free play. This may mean getting down on the floor or in the box. The tips in this chapter offer a variety of ways to improve your adoptee's ability to play, be social and let loose some giggles.

The child with a history of trauma missed days, weeks, months or years of plain old fun! Teaching them to be joyful won't always be easy. Yet, the family who can laugh and frolic together is a happier family. The child who can play has stronger executive functions, can learn better and can make friends. His future is brighter.

There are tips for kids age infant through adolescent. Pick those that encourage the "growing up" that best matches your child's unique needs.

The Skills that Help Kids Succeed Socially

Just so that we are all on the same page, the social skills that help youngsters succeed socially are:

- Taking turns.
- Making conversation.
- Formulating and communicating opinions.
- Greeting.
- Maintaining appropriate personal space.
- Being able to read faces and tone of voice.

- Giving and receiving compliments.
- Really listening to what others are saying.
- Developing a sense of humor.
- Sharing.
- Making eye contact.
- Negotiating and compromising.
- Being able to enter a group to join a discussion or an activity.
- Demonstrating problem-solving skills.

Is your child at an age where she should be exhibiting these skills? Are there skills listed she needs to develop? The suggestions below will help advance these skills. These abilities fall out of play.

Get Down, On the Floor

Shortly after babies are born, we put them on a blanket on the floor. We sit and play with them. Once they get up and moving, we often contain them to a portion of the house or yard. Or, we have them in a stroller or play pen. If you have young children who aren't developing an attention span, spread a blanket on the floor. Select an item or two that could hold your child's attention—a kaleidoscope, top, jack in the box, sock puppet, cups and water, pots and a spoon, a toy that makes noise or music. See if you can engage their interest in the toy. Gently pull them back to the blanket as need be. Here are some guidelines for attention span:

- 8–15 months: 1 minute or a little longer.
- 16–19 months: 2–3 minutes.
- 20–24 months: 3–6 minutes.
- 25–36 months: 5–8 minutes. (At this age, the child has learned to shift attention to an adult and back to what they were doing.)
- 3–4 years: 8–10 minutes.

You can help increase attention span by saying, "Let's make Jack pop up one more time." "Let's find one more blue item in the story." You can use this technique with all age children. Increasing attention span does often happen by stretching activities out one more moment. One mom found that her 3-year-old son liked to get a hot chocolate at the grocery store café. She could point out all kinds of things about the store and shoppers from this vantage point. He'd sit with her for ten minutes or more. She made this a habit. If carried out a few times per day, kids will learn to be calmer overall. They'll become engaged with what their environment has to offer.

Getting on the floor is effective with boys and girls whose play is repetitive. You can introduce them to novel toys and activities. You can build or draw or paint with them. You can expand their interest.

Remember, the overall purpose of the tips in this chapter is to help improve play. Sitting on the floor is giving your child your time—strengthening attachment. Lengthening the attention span and generating curiosity in new activities—builds creativity, self-confidence, self-regulation and executive function. The play doesn't need to include the latest toy designed to facilitate cognitive learning. The cognitive skills will fall out of spending time on the floor, in the yard or in the box.

Younger Toys, Simple Crafts

If we go back to the Vinelands we saw in Chapter 1, we can see that traumatized children's development is scattered. Different domains are evolving at different ages. Sprinkling mixed-age play things meets this developmental pattern. This is another way to parent children at their "younger" age as we learned about in Chapter 2. Put out some items for little ones and some for older ones. Kids will find their way to what suits their development in the moment. Over time, they'll grow out of play-things just like any child.

One mom recently sent me a video of her 12-year-old totally enjoying a shape sorter. He was giggling as he fit the shapes into the correct slots. The video was captioned, "This is so weird." Yes. This isn't what other 12-year-olds are doing. This tween didn't get these experiences as a toddler. Giving him the opportunity to repair these missing cogs now, gets the gears turning. He'll flourish socially, emotionally, cognitively and physically.

Yard sales and thrift shops are great places to find inexpensive used toys. Pick some up. Put them amidst your child's other toys. The play things in our waiting room are all for youngsters under 5 years old. I white out or remove the age labels. This way kids—of all ages—don't experience any shame or avoid using them because they think they're "baby" toys. Frequently, they dump the contents of the plastic tubs on the floor and drum on the containers, just as toddlers explore all the fascinating items in the kitchen cupboards. Each day, there is fun and enjoyment. This is what matters.

Crafts go better when they can be completed in a few minutes. A craft kit with three or four steps is enough. Remember the simple arts and crafts projects you made as a child? A few Fall leaves were placed between wax paper. Mom would run the iron over the wax paper. A place mat was ready to use. Pipe cleaners, an egg carton and felt became a bouquet of flowers. Crafting stimulates creativity. Kids bask with good feelings of self when complimented on their finished product. Between Pinterest and Amazon, there's no shortage of simple craft ideas.

Shifting Trauma Patterns

Children use various types of play to learn the world around them. Here are some examples. Infant play is sensory and motor. This leads to muscle strength, muscle control, fine motor skills, visual control and learning that there are aromas to smell, textures to feel, sounds to hear and sights to see. Solitary play—the child plays by herself. She learns to occupy her time. Onlooker play—a child observes other children playing. Parallel play is two children playing side-by-side, not talking. Associative play is two or more children talking while playing, but not necessarily working together on a common goal. Two children are building with blocks, each building something separate. They may share blocks back and forth. This is the start of a friendship. Cooperative play—preschool age—is where children start playing together like putting a puzzle together, engaging in a board game, building a city or singing a song. Once there is cooperative play, fantasy play emerges. A broom becomes a horse. Stuffed animals are invited to a tea party. Kids play dress up, restaurant, doctor, cops and robbers, astronauts in a spaceship, house, school—the possibilities are endless.

Traumatized children tend to replay traumatic experiences over and over. Previously, we met Brook who lined up all her orphanage dolls. She repeated this scenario every day. There are also children who play house. Yet, the people are beating each other up or using drugs. The police may come.

The repetition of these themes certainly gives us insight into what happened to these youngsters. We can clearly see that these experiences remain on their mind. They are using their play to make some meaning of their pre-adoptive life. Therapy can provide the means to resolve these traumas. We can work to expand imagination at home. In Brook's case, her three older siblings were happy to act out all kinds of scenes with Brook. Each style of play builds skills. Fantasy play leads to vital skills emerging: turn-taking, sharing, problem-solving and language. There is planning, learning symbols—a plastic bowl becomes a hat. It includes trying on all kinds of roles. Kids get to sample the world and prepare to be a part of the world.

If you notice that your child is stuck in a play "rut," get down on the floor and cause a shift (get some therapy as well.) If you're child isn't moving through different types of play, grab some props or a play cash register and see what you—or other children in your family—can help your adoptee envision. The benefit of richer development is worth the time and effort.

Create Opportunities to Play with Younger Children

Colleen didn't arrive in her adoptive family until she was 10 years old. Her delays were significant. Colleen's family belongs to a church with a large congregation and so there are many Sunday school classes. Her parents arranged for Colleen to be a "helper" in the classes with children ranging in age from toddler through Kindergarten. Mom and Dad simply presented the idea to Colleen in terms of the teachers needing her assistance.

Garrett, age 15, lives in a neighborhood with lots of younger boys. Summers and weekends, he plays ball with these kids at the park. Garrett looks forward to this time when he can be with his "friends." He prefers the younger age group.

Garrett's parents have come to accept and support his immaturity. They've stopped telling him "to grow up" and "act your age." Gradually Garrett is progressing. He's been joining his parents for UNO® and other card games. He cares about his appearance, and he picks up his room.

Colleen mastered playing the piano, and she has become a talented artist. She now teaches a Sunday school class and is in community college. The trajectory was different than that of her peers. Yet, today, she can complete college-level work and mingle in the student lounge. Garrett and Colleen needed to do "little" things to grow up. What opportunities can you create for your adoptee?

Set the Timer

Recently, I asked a family about playing with their son. I wondered if he could play or what he liked to play. Right away, the dad said, well mostly he watches TV or plays video games. We tried to have family game night but, he gets enraged when he doesn't win, he cheats, he changes the rules—it was horrible!

Board games offer a wealth of skills: turn-taking, waiting for your turn, planning, strategizing, persistence and critical thinking.

Setting a timer can make board games more feasible. If you have 10 or 15 minutes free , say, "I have 15 minutes; let's play cards." When time's up, you conclude, "Wow! That was fun! I have to go do the laundry." This offsets having a winner and a loser. Your adoptee got to practice playing.

Ruth, the older sister to three younger adopted siblings, practiced Old Maid and Crazy Eights with her brother and sisters for a long time. One evening, their mom texted me a video of all of them laughing while playing Old Maid. The caption was, "success." Ruth's tenacity paid off.

Homework or Monopoly?

Homework is another issue for help from the timer. Reading, writing, arithmetic and science-fair projects can consume an inordinate amount of after-school time. Parental tempers flare as the child with a history of maltreatment lacks the motivation, compliance, attention, self-confidence, emotional regulation or skills to finish calculations, projects and work-sheets in a timely manner. Evenings become a battleground. Parents are exhausted. Little fun occurs. The typical kids flee to friends' homes or lock themselves in their rooms—they won't be seen until breakfast!

Homework battles require some re-thinking. Remember, the best child-hood predictor of adult adaptation is not school grades. It's the ability with which children can get along with other children—brothers, sisters and friends.

Mothers and fathers may want to consider setting the timer when it comes to homework. Give the child an adequate period to complete his assignments. Then, calmly pack up the homework and move on. My expe-rience has been that most kids will begin to comply with the set timeframe.

Moms and dads are encouraged to talk with teachers about ways to reduce the work coming home and/or to make sure you're getting the best accommodations from your child's special learning needs. Take advan-tage of after-school math or reading lab. Consider if a tutor is financially feasible.

Striking a better balance between academics, extra-curriculars and family fun is critical. Giggling, joking, teasing and playing are as essential as the three Rs to your children's futures.

Fun Is the Parents' Choice

Frequently, the adoptee winds up in charge of the family fun. It goes like this. The mom or dad says, "If you're 'good' all week, Saturday we'll go to Sky Zone." Faithfully, by Friday evening some rule violation occurs, and the trip is taken away. Or, because natural and logical consequences have piled up, the family decides to stay home so Billy can wash the kitchen floor, rake the leaves, vacuum and carry out all kinds of other chores. The troubled child has determined the family's weekend plans.

Who does this benefit? A now angry family is stuck at home together. Or, typical children take to their bedrooms or the neighbor's house. The family is separated. If you want to go to Sky Zone on Saturday, then go.

Chores can wait. "Good" isn't likely going to happen for a long time. "Good" won't happen if parents and brothers and sisters are always angry at their sibling. Fun is necessary for attachment and for "growing up." So, go!

There needs to be a balance of fun, nurture and discipline to form close family connections with the child who arrives after complex trauma.

Going back to the adolescent brain, the impact of dopamine can be offset by engaging in outings that offer the brain a thrill. Recommendations include skiing, bicycling or running. The idea is to respect the dopamine-driven need for risky activities, but then channel this drive in helpful ways.[1] We are fortunate in Cleveland to live close to Cedar Point, home of some of the world's largest roller-coasters. We're on a Great Lake and we can jet-ski, water-ski and go boating. We also have a wonderful park system. One of our parks has a zip-line course. Winter brings with it snowboarding, tubing and sled riding.

What does your community offer?

Learning to be Social Using Resources

The children's books *Don't Behave Like You Live in a Cave* and *Dude, That's Rude: Get Some Manners* offer advice for grade-school-age children and tweens on just about every social situation you can imagine. The text is short and to the point, and the illustrations are colorful and funny.

> **Brianna** was in second grade. She had been adopted as an infant. She was very loud. She lacked many social graces. She read *Don't Behave Like You Live in a Cave* with her mom. Mom suggested that Brianna could learn to give compliments. Mom and Brianna role-played telling a classmate that she liked a new sweater, backpack or shoes. Mom also suggested that when Brianna approaches a group of children talking, she remains silent. "Just listen to the types of things the girls are talking about. This will help you decide what you could talk about."
>
> It took Brianna some time to take Mom's advice. One day, she came home from school and said that her friend's family had just come home from a cruise. She was able to relay some of the details of the trip. Brianna was learning to listen to what the kids were talking about. Soon, she'd be able to participate in conversation.

Helping youngsters identify skills that will help them engage effectively with peers and practicing how the skills are utilized focuses them on the specifics of what they need to do if they want friendships. It's up to them to take the advice.

It's always nice when you and your child can read and talk together. However, there are adoptees who don't want to take help from the family. These are kids who think they need to be self-reliant, "I can't trust adults to take care of me." Offering them resources, is a way to build their skills.

I encourage moms and dads to offer their kids printed materials. For example, if you see an article in the paper about Internet dangers, clip it and leave it out in a conspicuous place where your teen is sure to see it. If you see advice about dating while you're surfing the Internet, pass the link along.

Many schools and community agencies offer social skills classes. Take advantage of these programs. Teaching traumatized children to get along in this world requires multiple approaches. Utilize all options available.

Speaking of Resources...

The Center on the Developing Child at Harvard University is a leading organization in the study of trauma. They have parent-friendly videos and articles about all aspects of trauma and brain development. One paper is, *Enhancing and Practicing Executive Function Skills with Children from Infancy to Adolescence.* After an overview of what executive functioning is, they provide suggestions for play activities that build executive functions. The activities are listed by age. They're all fun! I suggest reading this article (see Resources). Pick a few fun items to try out!

Start Sexual Education Conversations Early

Don't put off talking with your children about sex until they're "older." Kids know about sex early nowadays. I see 9-year-olds who are quite versed in what boys and girls can do together.

Traumatized adoptees have victim mentalities and, as we've established, poor self-concept. They can't always be relied on to say "no." Or, they're seeking sex to fill a void.

Some adoptees have a history of sexual abuse. They have confusion about love and sex.

> **Lilly**, age 15, was sexually abuse by her birth father and birth uncle until she was age 7. She came into foster care and was adopted by her foster family. She was flirtatious as a young child. As she aged, she was preoccupied with her outward appearance. Her hair and make-up had to be just right. Clothing was an issue. She preferred more revealing clothing than her parents. She'd trade her jeans and blouses with other girls. So, she obtained short skirts and skimpy tops. Once she got to school, she'd change outfits. She used her cell phone to offer "blow jobs" and send revealing selfies. Lilly's sexual abuse left a lasting impression that her value was how she looked and what she had to offer sexually.

When you talk with your children about sex, stress the relationship in which sex should occur. Talk with them about the order in life that best leads to success—finish high school, go to college, get a job, save money, get married, buy a house and then have children. Repeat, repeat and repeat. Don't be afraid to remove devices as need be—for extended periods of time if necessary.

Be nosey. You can't monitor everything, but you can use the safety tools possible to manage devices. You can also check up on your kids.

> **Mary**, a mom to four adoptees, carried out random checks on her children frequently. They lived in a medium-size town which had a rec center. Kids regularly hung out there. She'd stop in periodically. She'd also follow-up if her children were supposed to be at a friend's house or the movies. Other kids comment to Mary's sons and daughter that none of them even try to get away with anything because they never know when Mary might be checking! This is in jest. Yet, Mary's random pop-ins give kids pause. Mary is quite popular among her children's friends.

Today, Mary's oldest daughter is a young adult. Her sons are still in high school. Mary's daughter is doing well. She is living life in order!

Mary's strong parenting style helps her children spend time with friends, yet under a watchful eye. "Little" teenagers can benefit from a parent who can balance giving them freedoms, while providing supervision.

It's Prom Time

Special school events do sometimes cause stress for parents. We are often asked, "Should I let him go to the prom?" "She wants to go to a school dance. I told her that Dad and I would think about it." "The class is going to Washington, DC for four days. What do you think about this?"

The teen's immaturity is concerning. This morning she was making mud pies. This evening she's asking if she can accept an invitation to a formal dance! Behaviors may not always seem to warrant these privileges. Yet, if the occasion is workable, consider letting your child go. Adopted teens need to have "normal" experiences in order to be "normal."

Exclusion leads to isolation. The Monday after the prom, they'll be out of the loop. Isolation, as we learned in the previous chapter, has its repercussions. Parenting a traumatized child does become a balancing act in the adolescent years. Investigate the supervision of the event, trip or sleepover. Based on how you feel about the safeguards, give them as many opportunities to be involved as is possible.

Unplugging

The suggestions in this chapter don't need batteries or chargers. Try turning off your devices for a couple of evenings each month. Go out in the yard and play flashlight tag or do some stargazing. Unplug in the car occasionally too. Play the billboard game. Go through the alphabet using words on signs. Remember? Have some good old-fashioned fun! The child with a history of trauma has a hard time being joyful. She needs your presence—your undivided attention. Be silly. Be playful. Help her see the delight that comes from close family connections.

Chapter Summary

- Teaching children to be social and playful means that we must get in the box and down on the floor. Parents are a child's first playmates. It may be arduous at first. Persist! You'll cultivate a social growth spurt that, in turn, spins the cognitive and emotional gears too! The biggest payoff is a family that can have lots of giggles and chortles. The adoptee is fun to be around!

- A menu of options exists to produce playful results. Key to all the choices is to start at the youngster's "little" age. Even when it feels "weird" watching your child craft, color, build or play in other "young" ways, know you've selected the right tools. The interventions are stabilizing your adoptee's developmental underpinnings. She can "grow up."

- Helping the adopted teen play becomes a balancing act. Dances, class trips, dating and hanging out with friends require riding the teeter totter of letting go, while simultaneously keeping tabs. Traumatized adolescents do need "normal" experiences to prevent isolation. Parents are encouraged to offer as many opportunities to mingle with peers as possible. Popping in randomly doesn't hurt!

- Create time to unplug. Have a water balloon fight. Make banana splits for dinner. Take a moment to think about your own childhood—what are your fond memories? Go do these things with your children. Instill joy!

Endnote

1   Siegel, D.J. (2013). *Brainstorm: The Power And Purpose Of The Teenage Brain*. New York: Jeremy P. Tarcher/Penguin Group, p.78.

Resources

Books and Websites for Parents

Adoption

20 Things Adoptive Parents Need to Succeed: Discover the Unique Needs of Your Adopted Child and Become the Best Parent You Can, by Sherrie Eldridge. New York: Delta Trade Paperbacks, 2009.

Adopting the Hurt Child: Hope for Families with Special-Needs Kids: A Guide for Parents and Professionals, by Gregory C. Keck and Regina M. Kupecky. Colorado Springs: NavPress, 2009.

In On It: What Adoptive Parents would like you to know about Adoption, A Guide for Friends and Relatives, by Elisabeth O'Toole. St. Paul, Minnesota: FIG Press, 2011.

No Biking in the House Without a Helmet: 9 Kids, 3 Continents, 2 Parents, 1 Family, by Melissa Fay Greene. New York: Sarah Crichton Books, 2012.

Our Own: Adopting and Parenting the Older Child, by Trish Maskew. Morton Grove, Illinois: Snowcap Press, 2003.

Toddler Adoption: The Weaver's Craft, by Mary Hopkins-Best. London: Jessica Kingsley Publishers, 2012.

Twenty Things Adopted Kids Wish Their Adoptive Parents Knew, by Sherrie Eldridge. New York: Delta Trade Paperbacks, 1999.

Adoption Learning Partners (ALP)—www.adoptionlearningpartners.org
ALP seeks to improve adoption outcomes for all members of the adoption circle. ALP offers valuable, timely, web-based educational

resources for adoptive parents, adopted individuals, birth parents and the families that love them.

Adoptive Families—www.adoptivefamilies.com

This online magazine features articles of substance about all aspects of pre- and post-adoption. There are wonderful resources for parents and teachers about adoption-related school projects and understanding the unique classroom needs of children who joined their families via adoption.

Child Welfare Information Gateway—www.childwelfare.gov

The Child Welfare Information Gateway is sated with reader-friendly articles on all aspects of adoption and trauma.

Attachment

Attaching in Adoption, by Deborah D. Gray. London: Jessica Kingsley Publishers, 2012.

Attaching Through Love, Hugs and Play: Simple Strategies to Help Build Connections with Your Child, by Deborah D. Gray. London: Jessica Kingsley Publishers, 2014.

Brain-Based Parenting: The Neuroscience of Caregiving for Healthy Attachment, by Daniel A. Hughes and Jonathan Baylin. New York: W.W. Norton & Company, 2012.

The Connected Child: Bring Hope and Healing to Your Adoptive Family, by Karyn Purvis, David Cross and Wendy Sunshine. New York: McGraw-Hill, 2007.

Creating Loving Attachments: Parenting with PACE to Nurture Confidence and Security in the Troubled Child, by Kim S. Golding and Daniel A. Hughes. London: Jessica Kingsley Publishers, 2012.

Parenting with Theraplay: Understanding Attachment and How to Nurture a Closer Relationship with Your Child, by Helen Rodwell and Vivien Norris. London: Jessica Kingsley Publishers, 2017.

Parenting Your Internationally Adopted Child: From Your First Hours Together to the Teen Years, by Patty Cogen. Boston: Harvard Common Press, 2008.

Adoption & Attachment Therapy Partners—www.adoptattachtherapy.com

This is the website of Arleta James. The website offers over 100 articles on parenting the adopted child with a history of trauma. There are also assorted videos. The adoption-attachment-trauma informed services available are described.

Lunchbox Love—www.sayplease.com
  Lunchbox Love specializes in unique love notes for children.
The Theraplay Institute®—www.theraplay.org
  Theraplay has as its goals enhancing attachment, self-esteem, trust in others and joyful engagement. Because of its focus on attachment and relationship development, Theraplay has been used successfully for many years with foster and adoptive families. Theraplay games are fun!

Parenting

Adoption Parenting: Creating a Toolbox, Building Connections, by Jean MacLeod and Sheena Macrae (editors). Warren: EMK Press, 2006-7.

Brainstorm: The Power and Purpose of the Teenage Brain, by Daniel J. Siegel. London: Penguin Publishing Group, 2013.

Building Self-Esteem in Children and Teens who are Adopted or Fostered, by Sue Cornbluth. London: Jessica Kingsley Publishers, 2014.

How You Feel is Up to You: The Power of Emotional Choice, by Gary McKay and Don Dinkmeyer. Atascadero: Impact Publishers, 2002.

Parenting from the Inside Out: How a Deeper Self-Understanding Can Help You Raise Children Who Thrive, by Daniel J. Siegel and Mary Hartzell. New York: Jeremy P. Tarcher/Penguin, 2003.

Parenting the Hurt Child: Helping Adoptive Families Heal and Grow, by Gregory C. Keck and Regina M. Kupecky. Colorado Springs: NavPress, 2009.

Siblings Without Rivalry: How to Help Your Children Live Together So You Can Live Too, by John W Gardner and Elaine Mazlish. New York: W. W. Norton & Company, 2012.

The Whole-Brain Child: 12 Revolutionary Strategies to Nurture Your Child's Developing Mind, by Daniel J. Siegel and Tina Payne Bryson. New York: Delacorte Press, 2011.

The Whole-Brain Child Workbook: Practical Exercises, Worksheets and Activities to Nurture Developing Minds, by Daniel J. Siegel and Tina Payne Bryson. Eau Claire, Wisconsin: PESI Publishing & Media, 2015.

The Yes Brain: How to Cultivate Courage, Curiosity, and Resilience in Your Child, by Daniel J. Siegel, Tina Payne Bryson. New York: Random House Publishing Group, 2018.

KidsHealth—www.kidshealth.org

KidsHealth provides families with accurate, up-to-date, jargon-free medical and mental health information. There are separate areas for kids, teens, and parents—each with its own design, age-appropriate content, and tone. There are literally thousands of in-depth features about medical illnesses, mental health issues, school issues, child development and more!

Love and Logic—www.loveandlogic.com

The Love and Logic Institute is dedicated to making parenting and teaching fun and rewarding, instead of stressful and chaotic. They provide practical tools and techniques that help adults achieve respectful, healthy relationships with their children.

Culture

Cross Cultural Adoption: How to Answer Questions from Family, Friends, and Community, by Amy Coughlin and Caryn Abramowitz. Washington, D.C.: Lifeline Press, 2004.

Dim Sum, Bagels, and Grits: A Sourcebook for Multicultural Families, by Myra Alperson. New York: Farrar, Strauss, Giroux, 2001.

Does Anybody Else Look Like Me?: A Parent's Guide to Raising Multiracial Children, by Donna Jackson Nakazawa. Cambridge: Da Capo Lifelong, 2003.

I'm Chocolate, You're Vanilla: Raising Healthy Black and Biracial Children in a Race-Conscious World, by Marguerite Wright. New York: Jossey-Bass, 1998.

Inside Transracial Adoption: Strength Based, Culture-Sensitizing Parenting Strategies for Inter-Country or Domestic Adoptive Families that Don't Match. Gail Steinberg and Beth Hall. London: Jessica Kingsley Publishers, 2012.

The Lost Daughters of China: Adopted Girls, Their Journey to America, and the Search for a Missing Past, by Karin Evans. New York: Jeremy P. Tarcher, 2008.

North American Council on Adoptable Children (NACAC)—www.nacac.org

NACAC promotes and supports permanent families for children and youth in the U.S. and Canada who have been in care. The NACAC website contains articles covering all aspects of transcultural adoption as well as all other facets of adoption. They offer an annual cutting-edge conference for parents and professionals.

Pact—An Adoption Alliance—www.pactadopt.org

Pact has a primary mission to serve children of color in need of adoption or who are growing up in adoptive families. If you are looking for information related to any transcultural or transracial adoption issue, you are sure to find it on the Pact website!

Child Development

Ages and Stages: A Parent's Guide to Normal Childhood Development, by Charles E. Schaefer and Theresa Foy DiGeronimo. New York: John Wiley and Sons, 2000.

Building Healthy Minds: The Six Experiences that Create Intelligence and Emotional Growth in Babies and Young Children, by Stanley I. Greenspan and Nancy Breslau Lewis. New York: Perseus Publishing, 2000.

Building Moral Intelligence: The Seven Essential Virtues that Teach Kids to do the Right Thing, by Michele Borba. Hoboken, New Jersey: Jossey-Bass, 2002.

Caring for Your Baby and Young Child, 6th Edition: Birth to Age 5, by American Academy of Pediatrics. New York: Bantam Books, 2014.

Thinking Developmentally: Nurturing Wellness in Childhood to Promote Lifelong Health, by Andrew Garner and Robert A. Saul. Itasca, Illinois: American Academy of Pediatrics, 2018.

What's Going on in There?: How the Brain and Mind Develop in the First Five Years of Life, by Lise Eliot. New York: Bantam Books, 1999.

Whole Child Parenting: Infant (Birth to 12 months)—Parents, Teachers and Babysitters Will Learn How Best to Encourage Growth and Skill-Building in All Six Developmental Areas, by Whole Child Parenting. Whittier, California: Whole Child Parenting, 2016.

Whole Child Parenting: Toddler (12 to 24 months)—Parents, Teachers and Babysitters Will Learn How Best to Encourage Growth and Skill-Building in All Six Developmental Areas, by Whole Child Parenting. Whittier, California: Whole Child Parenting, 2016.

Whole Child Parenting: Infant (Age Two)—Parents, Teachers and Babysitters Will Learn How Best to Encourage Growth and Skill-Building in All Six

Developmental Areas, by Whole Child Parenting. Whittier, California: Whole Child Parenting, 2016.

Whole Child Parenting: Toddler (Age Three)—Parents, Teachers and Babysitters Will Learn How Best to Encourage Growth and Skill-Building in All Six Developmental Areas, by Whole Child Parenting. Whittier, California: Whole Child Parenting, 2016.

Whole Child Parenting: (Age Four)–Parents, Teachers and Babysitters Will Learn How Best to Encourage Growth and Skill-Building in All Six Developmental Areas, by Whole Child Parenting. Whittier, California: Whole Child Parenting, 2016.

Your Child's Growing Mind: Brain Development and Learning from Birth to Adolescence, by Jane M. Healy. New York: Harmony Books, 1987.

Child Development Institute (CDI)—www.childdevelopmentinfo.com Founded by Robert Myers, Ph.D., a psychologist with 25 years of experience working with children, adolescents, families and parents, this website is packed with information about child development and play.

Zero to Three—www.zerotothree.org Zero to Three's mission is to support the healthy development of infants, toddlers and their families. This organization advances this mission by informing, educating and supporting adults who influence the lives of infants and toddlers. This website is packed with articles about all aspects of child development for infants and toddlers.

Mindfulness and Yoga

10 Mindful Minutes: Giving Our Children–and Ourselves–the Social and Emotional Skills to Reduce Stress and Anxiety for Healthier, Happy Lives, by Goldie Hawn, Wendy Holden, and Daniel J. Siegel. London: Penguin Publishing Group, 2012.

Aware: The Science and Practice of Presence: The Groundbreaking Meditation Practice, by Daniel J. Siegel. London: Penguin Publishing Group, 2018.

Mindful Kids: 50 Activities for Calm, Focus and Peace, by Whitney Stewart. Cambridge, Massachusetts: Barefoot Books, 2017.

Mindfulness for Beginners: Reclaiming the Present Moment–and Your Life, by Jon Kabat-Zinn. Louisville, Colorado: Sounds True, 2012.

Planting Seeds: Practicing Mindfulness with Children, by Thich Nhat Hanh.
Berkeley, California: Parallax Press, 2011.

Sitting Still Like a Frog: Mindfulness Exercises for Kids (and Their Parents), by
Eline Snel. Boulder, Colorado: Shambhala Publications, 2013.

The Center for Mindfulness—https://umassmed.edu/cfm
If you are stressed or depressed, check out the calendar for upcoming
mindfulness classes. Professionals interested in adding mindfulness to
their practice, will find a variety of training programs.

Mindful Schools—www.mindfulschools.org
Mindful Schools is one of the key players in the movement to integrate
mindfulness into the everyday learning environment of K-12 classrooms.
Training and curriculum are provided to educators in K-12 settings.

Social Media

*The Boogeyman Exists; And He's In Your Child's Back Pocket (2nd Edition):
Internet Safety Tips & Technology Tips For Keeping Your Children Safe
Online, Smartphone Safety, Social Media Safety, and Gaming Safety,* by Jesse
Weinberger. Scotts Valley, California: CreateSpace Publishing, 2017.

Digital Kids: How to Balance Screen Time and Why it Matters, by Martin
Kutscher. London: Jessica Kingsley Publishers, 2017.

Screenwise: Helping Kids Thrive (and Survive) in Their Digital World, by
Devorah Heitner. Florence, Kentucky: Routledge, 2016.

Common Sense Media—www.commonsensemedia.org
Dedicated to helping kids thrive in the realm of social media, Common
Sense Media provides current information and ratings for all forms of
media content. They have programs for schools, and blogs for parents to
address and get to answers to concerns.

Ditch the Label—www.ditchthelabel.org
Ditch the Label is an international anti-bullying charity. Their mission
is to combat bullying by tackling the root issues and to support young
people aged 12–25 who are impacted. The website contains startling
statistics about the impact of bullying. Articles, guides and mentors are
available to help with all aspects of bullying. Lost of help is available at
this website.

OvernightGeek University—www.overnightgeekuniversity.com

This is the website of Jessie Weinberger, author of, *The Boogeyman Exists; And He's In Your Child's Back Pocket*. Check out her speaking schedule and her writings.

Talking with Kids about Adoption and Trauma

Connecting with Kids through Stories: Using Narratives to Facilitate Attachment in Adopted Children, by Denise Lacher, Todd Nicholas and Joanne May. London: Jessica Kingsley Publishers, 2012.

Lifebooks: Creating a Treasure for the Adopted Child Updated and Revised, by Beth O'Malley. Winthrop, Massachusettes: Adoption Works Press, 2011.

Telling the Truth to Your Adopted or Foster Child: Making Sense of the Past, by Jayne E. Schooler and Betsy E. Keefer. Santa Barbara: Praeger Publishers, 2000.

ReMoved—https://youtu.be/lOeQUwdAjEo

This is a poignant 12-minute video featuring a young girl who is removed from her birth family due to their substance abuse. We follow her through foster homes as she attempts to make meaning of her experiences. This film is realistic. It is very well made.

Wo Ai Ni Mommy—www.pbs.org/pov/woainimommy

What is it like to be torn from your Chinese foster family, put on a plane with strangers and wake up in a new country, family and culture? This is the story of Fang Sui Yong, an 8-year-old orphan, and the Sadowskys, the Long Island Jewish family that travels to China to adopt her. Sui Yong is one of 70,000 Chinese children now being raised in the United States. Through her eyes, we witness her struggle with a new identity as she transforms from a timid child into someone that no one—neither her new family nor she—could have imagined

Trauma Sensitive Schools

The Invisible Classroom: Relationships, Neuroscience & Mindfulness in School, by Kirke Olson. New York: W.W. Norton & Co., 2014.

Lost at School: Why Our Kids with Behavioral Challenges are Falling Through the Cracks and How We Can Help Them, by Ross Greene. New York: Scribner, 2014.

Trauma–Sensitive Schools: Learning Communities Transforming Children's Lives, K-5, by Susan Craig. New York: Teachers College Press, 2016.

Trauma-Sensitive Schools for the Adolescent Years: Promoting Resiliency and Healing, Grades 6–12, by Susan Craig. Teachers College Press, 2017.

American Speech-Language-Hearing Association (ASHA)—www.asha.org/public/speech/disorders

ASHA is the national professional associations for audiologists; speech-language pathologists; speech, language, and hearing scientists. Use this website to find a speech-language pathologist near you.

Centers for Disease Control and Prevention (CDC)—www.cdc.gov

The CDC houses the Adverse Childhood Experiences Study (ACE Study) www.cdc.gov/violenceprevention/acestudy/index.html; The CDC is also a wealth of information about child development.

Helping Traumatized Children Learn—https://traumasensitiveschools.org

This website is offering comprehensive information to advocate for or to create trauma-sensitive schools. Read their bulletins. Helping Traumatized Children Learn 1 and 2—pass them on. Visit their YouTube channel too!

Reading Rockets—www.readingrockets.org

Reading Rockets is a national multimedia literacy initiative offering information and resources on how young kids learn to read, why so many struggle and how caring adults can help. It is an amazing source of information about helping children advance their speech, language and reading skills.

Speech and Language Kids—www.speechandlanguagekids.com

This is the website of Carrie Clark, Speech-Language Pathologist. Visit the parent resource page to learn how to identify and find help for all aspects of speech-language problems.

Trauma and Trauma-Related Issues

104 Activities that Build: Self-Esteem, Teamwork, Communication, Anger Management, Self-Discovery, Coping Skills, by Alanna Jones. Richland: Rec Room Publishing, 1998.

Creative Ways to Help Children Manage BIG Feelings: A Therapist's Guide

to Working with Preschool and Primary Children, by Fiona Zandt and
Suzanne Barrett. London: Jessica Kingsley Publishers, 2017.

*Helping Children with Sexual Behavior Problems: A Guidebook for Professionals
and Caregivers*, by Toni Johnson Cavanagh. San Diego: Institute on
Violence, Abuse and Trauma, 2007.

Interoception: How I Feel: Sensing My World from the Inside Out, by Cara N.
Koscinski. South Carolina: Pocketbooks for Special Needs, 2018.

Mirroring People: The Science of Empathy and How We Connect to Others, by
Marco Iacoboni. New York: Picador, 2009.

Sensational Kids: Hope and Help for Children with Sensory Processing Disorder,
by Lucy Jane Miller. New York: Penguin Books, 2006.

The Simple Guide to Child Trauma: What It Is and How to Help, by Betsy de
Thierry. London: Jessica Kingsley Publishers, 2016.

Understanding Children's Sexual Behaviors: What's Natural and Healthy, by
Toni Cavanagh Johnson. San Diego: Institute on Violence, Abuse and
Trauma, 2007.

*When the Brain Can't Hear: Unraveling the Mystery of Auditory Processing
Disorder*, by Teri James Bell. New York: Atria, 2003.

Center for the Developing Child—https://developingchild.harvard.edu/
This is the most cutting-edge website for information about the impact
of trauma on children and adolescents. The website has great videos and
parent and professional friendly articles. If you are seeking information
about trauma, this is a must read.

National Child Traumatic Stress Network (NCTSN)—www.nctsn.org
NCTSN is a unique collaboration of academic and community-based
service centers whose mission is to raise the standard of care and
increase access to services for traumatized children and their families
across the United States. Via articles and videos, there is coverage the
impact of all types of trauma on children's development.

The National Organization on Fetal Alcohol Syndrome (NOFAS)—www.
nofas.org
NOFAS is the leading voice and resource of Alcohol-Related Neurodevelopmental Disorders community. This website provides articles and
additional resources for those parenting or working with children with
ARND.

National Institute on Drug Abuse (NIDA)—www.drugabuse.gov
   NIDA provides information on prenatal drug-alcohol exposure and
   drug addictions. Go here to find the facts about all kinds of drugs in use
   today, as well as the signs and symptoms that could indicate your child
   is involved in drug use.
National Suicide Prevention Lifeline—https://suicidepreventionlifeline.org/
   This organization staffs a 24-hour hotline to prevent suicide. Go here
   to find the warning signs of potential suicidal behaviors. They also offer
   free literature to spread the word about suicide prevention.

Adoption Music CDs (available at Amazon.com)
Adoption...the Songs You Love, by Various Artists. 2002.
Do You Have a Little Love to Share? by Janice Kapp Perry & Joy Saunders
   Lundberg. Gilbert: Adoption Media, 2005.
Same/Same: Songs for Adoptive Families, by Chuck Kent. CD Baby, 2003.
The Spirit of Adoption, by Adoptive Music. Shabach Music, 2006.

Books and Workbooks for Children and Adolescents

Adoption
At Home in this World: A China Adoption Story, Jean MacLeod. Warren, New
   Jersey: EMK Press, 2003.
*The Confusing World of Brothers, Sisters and Adoption: The Adoption Club
   Therapeutic Workbook on Siblings*, by Regina Kupecky. London: Jessica
   Kingsley Publishers, 2014.
The Day We Met You, Phoebe Koehler. New York: Aladdin Paperbacks, 1990.
*Friends, Bullies and Staying Safe: The Adoption Club Therapeutic Workbook on
   Friendship*, by Regina Kupecky. London: Jessica Kingsley Publishers, 2014.
Help!: I've Been Adopted, by Brenda McCreight. Mount Herman: Adoption
   Press, 2010.
*How Do We Feel About Adoption?: The Adoption Club Therapeutic Workbook
   on Feelings and Behavior*, by Regina Kupecky. London: Jessica Kingsley
   Publishers, 2014.
*Let's Learn About Adoption: The Adoption Club Therapeutic Workbook on
   Adoption and Its Many Different Forms*, by Regina Kupecky. London:
   Jessica Kingsley Publishers, 2014.

Mommy Far, Mommy Near: An Adoption Story, by Carol Antoinette Peacock. Morton Grove, Indiana: Albert Whitman and Co., 2000.

A Mother for Choco, by Keiko Kasza. New York: Puffin Books, 1992.

The Mulberry Bird: An Adoption Story, Anne Braff Brodzinsky. London: Jessica Kingsley Publishers, 2012.

A Place in My Heart, by Mary Grossnickle. London: Jessica Kingsley Publishers, 2014.

We Belong Together: A Book about Adoption and Families, by Todd Parr. New York: Little, Brown Books for Young Readers, 2007.

Welcome Home Forever Child: A Celebration of Children Adopted as Toddlers and Preschoolers and Beyond, by Christine Mitchell. Bloomington, Indiana: Author House, 2006.

Who We Are and Why We Are Special: The Adoption Club Therapeutic Workbook on Identity, by Regina Kupecky. London: Jessica Kingsley Publishers, 2014.

Zachary's New Home: A Story for Foster and Adopted Children, by Geraldine Blomquist and Paul Blomquist, Washington: Magination Press, 1990.

Attachment

The Boy Who Built a Wall Around Himself, by Ali Redford. London: Jessica Kingsley Publishers, 2015.

Caleb's Healing Story: An Interactive Story with Activities to Help Children to Overcome Challenges Arising from Trauma, Attachment Issues, Adoption or Fostering, by Kathleen A. Chara and Tasha Lehner. London: Jessica Kingsley Publishers, 2016.

How Full is Your Bucket: For Kids, by Tom Rath and Mary Reckmeyer. Washington: Gallup Press, 2009.

The Kissing Hand, by Audrey Penn. Logan: Perfection Learning, 2010.

Love You Forever, Robert Munsch. Richmond Hill, Ontario: Firefly Books, 1986.

Pinocchio: A Classic Illustrated Edition, by Carlo Collodi. San Francisco: Chronical Books, 2001.

The Runaway Bunny, by Margaret Brown Wise. New York: Harper Trophy, 1977.

A Safe Place for Caleb: An Interactive Book for Kids, Teens and Adults with Issues of Attachment, Grief, Loss or Early Trauma, by Kathleen A. Chara and Paul J. Chara, Jr. London: Jessica Kingsley Publishers, 2005.

Culture

The Colors of Us, by Karen Katz. New York: Henry Holt and Company/BYR Paperbacks, 2007.

If the World Were Blind: A Book About Judgment and Prejudice, by Karen Burnett. Felton, California: GR Publishing, 2001.

Pieces of Me: Who Do I Want to Be?, by Robert Ballard. Warren: EMK Press, 2009.

We Can Get Along, by Lauren Murphy Payne. Minneapolis: Free Spirit Publishing, 1997.

Coping

Being Me: A Kids' Guide to Boosting Confidence and Self-Esteem, by Wendy Moss. Washington: Magination Press, 2010.

Emotions: Making Sense of Your Feelings, by Mary Lamia. Washington: Magination Press, 2012.

How to Take the Grrr Out of Anger, by Elizabeth Verdick and Marjorie Lisovskis. Minneapolis: Free Spirit Publishing 2002.

Understanding Myself: A Kids' Guide to Intense and Strong Feelings, by Mary C. Lamia. Magination Press, 2010.

What to Do When Your Temper Flares: A Kids' Guide to Overcoming Problems with Anger, by Dawn Huebner. Washington: Magination Press, 2007.

When I Feel Angry, by Cornelia Maude Spelman. Morton Grove: Albert Whitman and Co., 2000.

When I Feel Jealous, by Cornelia Maude Spelman. Morton Grove: Albert Whitman and Co., 2003.

When I Feel Sad, by Cornelia Maude Spelman. Morton Grove: Albert Whitman and Co., 2002.

When I Feel Scared, by Cornelia Maude Spelman. Morton Grove: Albert Whitman and Co., 2002.

Mindfulness and Yoga

I Am Yoga, by Susan Verde. New York: Abrams Books, 2015.

Listening to My Body: A Guide to Helping Kids Understand the Connection Between Their Sensations (What the Heck Are Those?) and Feelings So That They Can Get Better at

Figuring Out What They Need, by Gabi Garcia. Austin, TX: Take Heart Press, 2016.

Mindful Movements: Ten Exercises for Well-Being, by Thich Nhat Hanh. Berkeley, California: Parallax Press, 2008.

Self-Regulation and Mindfulness: Over 82 Exercises & Worksheets for Sensory Processing Disorder, ADHD & Autism Spectrum Disorder, by Varleisha Gibbs. Eau Claire, Wisconsin: PESI Publishing & Media, 2017.

Trauma and Trauma-Related Issues

A Family that Fights, by Sharon Chesler Bernstein. Morton Grove, Illinois: Albert Whitman and Company, 1991.

The Bad Seed, by Jory John. New York: HarperCollins Publishers, 2017.

Borya and the Burps: An Eastern European Adoption Story, by Joan McNamara. Indianapolis: Perspectives Press/St.Paul: Koryo Press, 2005.

Don't Behave Like You Live in a Cave, by Elizabeth Verdick. Minneapolis, Minnesota: Free Spirit Publishing, 2010.

Don't Let Your Emotions Run Your Life for Kids: A DBT-Based Skills Workbook to Help Children Manage Mood Swings, Control Angry Outbursts, and Get Along with Others, by Jennifer J. Solin and Christina L. Kress. Oakland, California: New Harbinger Publications, 2017.

Don't Let Your Emotions Run Your Life for Teens: Dialectical Behavior Therapy Skills for Helping You Manage Mood Swings, Control Angry Outbursts, and Get Along with Others, by Sheri Van Dijk. Oakland, California: New Harbinger Publications, 2011.

Dude, That's Rude!: (Get Some Manners), by Pamela Espeland, Elizabeth Verdick. Minneapolis, Minnesota: Free Spirit Publishing, 2007.

Feeling Better: A Kid's Book about Therapy, by Rachel Rashkin. Washington: Magination Press, 2005.

Finding Fish: A Memoir, by Antwone Fisher and Mim E. Rivas. New York: Harper Torch, 2002.

Forgetful Frankie, The World's Greatest Rock Skipper, Fetal Alcohol Spectrum Disorder, by Jill Bobula and Katherine Bobula. Ottawa: Wildberry Productions, 2009.

The House that Crack Built, by Taylor Clark. San Francisco: Chronicle Books, 1992.

It's Not Your Fault: A Guide for Children to Tell if They're Abused, by Judith
Lance. Indianapolis: Kidsrights, 1997.

Jabari Jumps, by Gaia Cornwall. Somerville, Massachusetts: Candlewick
Press, 2017.

*Kids with Behavior Challenges: How to Make Good Choices and Stay Out of
Trouble*, by Tom McIntryre. Minneapolis: Free Spirit Publishing, 2013.

Like Family: Growing up in Other People's Houses, a Memoir, by Paula McLain.
New York: Back Bay Books, 2004.

Sad, Sad Seth, The World's Greatest Writer, Depression, by Jill Bobula and
Kathleen Bobula. Ottawa: Wildberry Productions, 2011.

Sorry!, by Trudy Ludwig. New York: Tricycle Press, 2006.

What Do You Stand For? For Teens, by Barbara A. Lewis. Minneapolis: Free
Spirit Publishing, 2005.

The Words Hurt: Helping Children Cope with Verbal Abuse, by Chris Loftis. Far
Hills, New Jersey: New Horizon Press, 2006.

Your Body Belongs to You, by Cornelia Maude Spelman. Morton Grove: Albert
Whitman and Co., 1997.

Your Fantastic Elastic Brain: Stretch It, Shape It, by JoAnn Deak. Naperville,
Illinois: Little Pickle Press, 2010.

Subject Index

Author Index